CHURCH EMBATTLED

Library of Politics and Society: Editor Michael Hurst

CHURCH EMBATTLED:
Religious Controversy in Mid-Victorian England

M. A. Crowther

DAVID & CHARLES
ARCHON BOOKS 1970

This edition first published in 1970 in Great Britain by
David & Charles (Publishers) Limited, Newton Abbot, Devon,
and in the United States by Archon Books, Hamden, Connecticut

ISBN 0 7153 4929 5 (*Great Britain*)
ISBN 0 208 01091 2 (*United States*)

Set in eleven on twelve point Imprint
and printed in Great Britain
by Latimer Trend & Company Limited Plymouth

Contents

Preface

THE AIM of this book is to show how the Church of England, at a crucial stage in its history, found practical action blocked by internal controversies. By 1860 the Church had realised the extent of the problem which faced it in winning over the majority of the working class to religion, but it was also confronted by another crisis: the threatened secession of educated people from the Church as a result of new methods of criticising traditional teaching. Developments in such criticism also came at a time when others were attacking the Bible, especially the Old Testament, for presenting an erroneous or old-fashioned system of morality. The Church decided to spend much of its energy on the problem of educated doubt, but, because churchmen responded to it in many different ways, the Church split into factions which tended to pursue their own ends regardless of the general good. The basis of most controversy was theological, so I have dealt with theological questions to some extent, but I have been more concerned with their significance than their details. I have also tried to show how they distracted the Church from practical reorganisation.

Fears and dissensions within the Church had been growing since the time of the Oxford Movement, and in the middle of the century they reached a climax, especially with the publication of *Essays and Reviews* in 1860. Religious inquirers within the Church, who were given the name of Broad Churchmen, believed that, unless a reformation in the Church's teaching brought it to discard many of its outworn ideas, Christianity in England would be overcome by the two extremes of superstition and rationalism. The challenges to orthodox belief in the Bible which the Broad Church presented caused a period of introspection amongst orthodox clergy. They looked into their Church to find out what constituted its authority and the inquiry disturbed them. There was no pope to represent the church militant, and the bishops were men whose power was weakened by the State's influence over the established Church. The very origins of the Anglican Church were tainted with secular politics, and it did not have the right to choose its own leaders or the final authority in ecclesiastical law. The Prayer Book and the Thirty-Nine Articles were difficult to interpret, and the Bible even more so.

I have centred my discussion around the Broad Church rather than Darwin, although the *Origin of Species* appeared a year before *Essays and Reviews*. Darwin's work has obviously made a greater impact on history than the now unread and almost unreadable *Essays and Reviews*; but, as almost any Church periodical of the time would show, the Church considered the second book a greater danger to orthodox religion and responded to it accordingly. Nor did the Church consider Darwin's work startlingly original, although the idea of 'men descended from monkeys' caused much commotion. Darwin was not the first to question the accuracy of the Book of Genesis as a historical account, for the German scholars had begun a powerful tradition of Biblical criticism based on historical and linguistic grounds—a tradition which the Broad Church accepted. Not surprisingly, the Church turned on those men whom it believed to be traitors to their own side, and even Carlyle denounced the Broad Church as sentries who had deserted from their post.

The resulting attempt to find the source of authority in the Church was a long one, not abandoned until after the end of the nineteenth century, when most churchmen at last conceded that the Church could comprehend many different ideas. In the mid-nineteenth century the search for authority was undertaken by clergymen at all levels, from the bishops in Parliament and Convocation, through a number of new societies for Church organisation and defence, down to the humblest cleric who could wield a pen against the Broad Church. Perhaps, too, the theological subtleties of the Broad Church presented a more tempting target for many clergymen to whom Darwin's scientific approach was foreign.

The first part of this book deals with the challenge which the

Broad Church presented to long-held ideas, with particular reference to the clerical authors of *Essays and Reviews*. The essayists were not all men of eminent abilities. Benjamin Jowett and Mark Pattison built reputations as scholars and heads of colleges; Jowett, in particular, branded his personality on a whole generation of Balliol scholars who later formed a distinctive network in the civil service both in Britain and the Empire. Pattison, the misanthrope, was perhaps the better scholar and a critic of much penetration. Frederick Temple achieved the greatest distinction in the Church of England as an archbishop of unusual practical abilities; Baden Powell founded a distinguished family and was a well-known academic. Rowland Williams and Henry Bristow Wilson are now almost forgotten. In their day they were men of solid yet modest achievement; their intellects were not much superior to those of many English clergy of good background and capacity for application. Yet they were captured by the inquisitive spirit of the Broad Church, with its fundamental moral anxieties, and therefore their ideas will be discussed in some detail, not because they were leaders, but because they were led. The minds of undistinguished men may reflect more accurately than the greater intellects the everyday problems of their time. I have concluded the study of the Broad Church and its background with a short description of the career of Charles Voysey, who tried to push Broad Church ideas to their logical conclusion and was forced out of the Church as a result. He is a good example of the controversial spirit of a time when men were determined to put forward their own ideas whatever the cost to themselves.

The second part of the book discusses the orthodox section of the Church and its reaction to the problem of educated doubt and the attempted compromise of the Broad Church. This reaction showed itself in the search for authority through re-examination of the bishops' functions, societies for Church defence, and movements towards central organisation. These efforts were not, of course, only a response to heterodox ideas within the Church, but can be seen as the result of pressures which had been accumulating since the beginning of the century, in particular the threat of organised dissent. It was also becoming obvious that the Church's machinery was too antiquated to cope with the difficulties of industrial society. I have paid some attention to these other pressures, but have been more interested in discussing the part which liberal ideas played in provoking an authoritarian reaction. Yet in all these efforts the party divisions of the Church dissipated its aims; the division also affected the reorganisation of clerical education, which was vital to the life of the Church.

The spirit of party hostility, often expressed in an unhealthy zeal for lawsuits, lingered on during the seventies and was further inflamed by the Public Worship Regulation Act of 1874. Gradually, however, Broad Church ideas which had been in question since the time of Thomas Arnold were being accepted by more clergymen, and the views of the essayists were not as shocking in 1880 as they had been in 1860. Unfortunately, by the time that most of the hostility had died down most of the social forcefulness of the Church had died too. The great theological battles of the mid-century had taken up much public attention, but by the end of the century they were of less interest, for they seemed of little importance in comparison with the overriding social problems. As Britain's economic position declined, society seemed to be hardening into much less flexible divisions, with the prospect of imminent conflict before them. Imperial policies might overshadow social problems for a time, but not indefinitely. The churches had failed to solve these problems, and had even opposed solutions which detracted from their own authority, such as national control over education. A study of the crucial years in the mid-century might lead one to think that the Anglicans in particular wasted precious time over internal controversies and over battles with dissent. The Church's ablest leaders were thwarted at every turn by sectional interests, and in an age when every department of government was learning the value of central organisation, the Church had to depend on the scattered efforts of well-meaning individuals.

I believe that one of the chief causes of the Church's weakness was its growing fear of rationalist attacks on the authority of the Bible and its intolerance towards any compromises within its own ranks. Even Tractarianism had arisen partly from the fear that the Church would be left without any kind of authoritative doctrine, and Newman and others went to Rome as the only Church which claimed the power to overcome their own inner conflicts. The arguments of the period now seem drier than the dust on the volumes which provoked them, yet, unless we can understand why so many intelligent men were roused to passionate indignation over these debates, we shall not know why the Church lacked force and leadership in its attitude towards the social evils which we now think were the chief problem of the nineteenth century.

Chapter 1 CHURCH PROBLEMS AND CHURCH PARTIES

IN DECEMBER 1862, Archibald Campbell Tait, Bishop of London and one of the most intelligent churchmen of his age, said in his episcopal charge to his clergy in St Paul's Cathedral:

> Our Church, has, committed to it by God, in the middle of the nineteenth century, in an inquisitive and restless age, the difficult task of gathering together, fostering, developing, restraining, and guiding the Christian feelings and thoughts, and energetic life of many millions of intelligent Englishmen, impatient both of political and still more of ecclesiastical control.[1]

Tait told them that the Church had three main problems: first, the spirit of free inquiry and criticism which was gradually alienating many educated people from the Church; secondly, the difficulties of an established Church in an age of freedom of worship, and in a State which was no longer wholly Anglican; and thirdly, the ever-growing population of England, in which a generation of the working class was now growing up without any knowledge of the Church or indeed of Christianity itself.

Although the order in which Tait listed these problems was perhaps accidental, it is nevertheless indicative of the Church's sense of priorities in the mid-nineteenth century. A modern reader would probably count Tait's third point, the alienation or indifference of the working class, as the Church's most difficult and important problem of that time. The Church was certainly aware of it. The investigation into the state of religious worship which had formed part of the census of 1851, however inaccurate, did show clearly that a very large proportion of the people, possibly as much as 38 per cent, attended no church, and that nearly half of the remainder were Dissenters.[2] The Church made efforts to grapple with this; from early in the century there were associations which hoped to win back the poor through education, evangelisation or charity. The National Society for Promoting the Education of the Poor in the Principles of the Established Church (founded 1811) had in its hands a great deal of responsibility for national education, and for a long time it successfully opposed any attempt to set up a centralised, secular educational system.

Churchmen rallied to provide more clergy and more churches so that the Church might expand with the population. In nearly every diocese church building was proceeding rapidly by the middle of the century, though not as rapidly as the growth of the population. Between 1801 and 1831, 500 new churches were built; between 1831 and 1851 the number was 2,029.[3] Many others were restored. In London, Bishop Blomfield was a tireless church-builder, and other bishops pledged themselves to the cause of church extension. Yet these efforts were not only failing to keep up with the population, but the new churches were often half-empty. In spite of the dedication of individuals and of organisations who undertook evangelical crusades and social work in the slums there was no cohesion in the Church.

Many churchmen of the 1860s would not have agreed that their chief problem was the indifferent masses. They believed that the Church's greatest danger lay in the increasing alienation of many educated men, stimulated by a new spirit of free inquiry into many fields of learning, including science, history and theology. No ancient belief was sacred in the eyes of the new critics, many of whom abandoned their faith or built up systems unacceptable to the Church. Science in particular was developing along new lines, but it is easy to exaggerate the effect of evolutionary theories. The publication of Darwin's *Origin of Species* in 1859 was not such a thunderbolt to the Church as might be imagined, nor did it suddenly undermine the faith of a generation. In the scientific world it certainly produced a convulsion, and a new group of scientists emerged, led by Huxley, no longer believing in the comfortable idea that the duty of science was to praise the harmony and order of God's creation.[4] The course of science had been diverted, but the Church, although startled, remained unshaken.

In the first place, it was possible for the Church to point to the arguments of an older generation of scientists, men like Adam Sedgwick, who thought that Darwin's hypotheses were unsound; hence the Church periodicals devoted some space to refuting Darwin but had their attention more fully occupied in the following year by more stirring internal controversies. Secondly, Darwin was not the root cause of contemporary unbelief, though some young men like Leslie Stephen were upset by him. Darwin added scientific weight to doubts which were already felt by many.

Darwin's ideas were already in the air before he published the *Origin*; not merely the scientific air, but the entire intellectual climate of England. The theory of evolution was not incompatible with the great ideas about progress and the march of mind. Thoughtful Victorians believed that the human race was insensibly improving, with education as its great instrument. They thought that the progress of the race was shown, not only in its material welfare, but in its moral development. Britain, over a period of sixty years, seemed to have achieved standards of humanity and justice which were unequalled in the world, and which were now being conferred on the backward peoples of the Empire. Under British law there was no discrimination of persons (except for women); political reform was approaching once again; and only atheists were debarred from sitting in the House of Commons, after the emancipation of the Jews in 1858. Charity and compassion were accepted as the two essential principles of social and private virtue. Yet a section of educated Victorians, holding strongly to the moral standards of their day, found that, according to these moral standards, the Scriptures had become unacceptable.

This educated group was in a minority, but it was vocal and included many gifted people. Their arguments turned on the accuracy of the Scriptures and their sufficiency as a moral guide in the nineteenth century. Scientists, even before Darwin, were casting doubts on the literal truth of the Old Testament, and their conclusions were being reinforced, mainly by German scholars, in the fields of history and philology. These sophisticated ideas were not likely to go far beyond an educated élite in England, but the arguments of the moralists were more pervasive.

J. A. Froude, F. W. Newman, A. H. Clough, George Eliot and others rejected orthodox Christianity because they found in the Scriptures ideas which were not compatible with an advanced nineteenth-century view of moral justice.[5] The God of the Old Testament was often arbitrary and unjust; He condoned slaughter and sacrifice; the Church taught that He condemned sinners to everlasting torments and that only the blood of the innocent Christ had mollified His wrath at the fall of man. Once these moral doubts had been experienced, it was easy to accept continental writings which taught that the Bible was a profane compilation like the sacred books of any other religion. George Eliot adopted the view that a stern sense of moral duty was higher than a mere unthinking acceptance of orthodox dogma. The philosophical school of Mill was also opposed to the Church. Froude and Clough, in particular, seemed to speak for a generation of young men who had experienced agonising religious doubts while at the university. Their numbers could not be estimated, but they were vocal enough to give the impression of being numerous and so aroused great fears within the Church. Frederic Harrison, the positivist, said with some satisfaction in 1861 that the universities were 'honeycombed with disbelief, running through every phase from mystical interpretation to utter atheism'.[6] Clough was not a popular poet, but his work expressed the uncertainty of some of his contemporaries.

> Eat, drink and die, for we are souls bereaved,
> Of all the creatures under this broad sky
> We are most hopeless, that had hoped most high,
> And most beliefless, that had most believed.
> (*Easter Day* 1849)

Parallel to the religious doubts expressed in intellectual circles was the militant unbelief of the secularist groups, who attributed social injustice to Christianity and tried to spread this belief among the working classes. Some of the former Chartists, especially Henry Hetherington, expressed social discontent in terms of atheism and maintained that the churches fostered class distinctions. G. J. Holyoake (1817–1906), also a former Chartist, began the London Secular Society in the early 1850s, and the secularists became even more notorious later in the century under the leadership of Charles Bradlaugh (1833–91). He organised the National Secular Society in 1866, and the secularists also ran a number of small and violent periodicals, notably Bradlaugh's *National Reformer*.[7]

Many churchmen came to believe that their first task was to defend the doctrines of their Church from the attacks of rationalists, and they began to look for an authority which should be strong enough to repulse all assaults. By the 1860s this search for authority in the Church had become a major preoccupation, and it was intensified because of fear, not only of rationalism, but of dissent. While the rationalists tried to undermine the Church's doctrine, the dissenters aimed at its temporal privileges. After gaining a voice in the administration of the country, the dissenters, especially the Congregationalists, became increasingly militant. They demanded that education should not be left entirely to the Church, they wanted university degrees, the right to perform legal marriage ceremonies, the use of churchyards for burials, and, in particular, exemption from paying rates in support of the established Church. The most active agitation began in 1844, when Edward Miall (1809–81), a Congregationalist minister and editor of the influential journal the *Nonconformist*, started the British Anti-State Church Association, which changed its name in 1853 to the Society for the Liberation of Religion from State Patronage and Control, more commonly known as the Liberation Society. Miall himself became MP for Rochdale in 1851, and the Liberation Society, through publications, lecture tours, and petitions to Parliament, became the nucleus of discontent among dissenters.

Educated doubt and militant dissent were more vociferous than the indifferent masses, and the Church turned to face them. Orthodox churchmen looked for more authority within the Church; less orthodox churchmen denied that such authority was necessary and adopted a policy of compromise towards those who attacked the Church. These incompatible aims split the Church into warring parties, in an atmosphere of bitter and personal controversy. Militant dissent was partly a State problem and was resolved in spite of the Church, but doubt was the Church's responsibility.

Recent authors have seen this period as one of religious uncertainty, in which those who had abandoned orthodox religion were more confident of their position than those who tried to save it.[8] Yet it seems that the tragedy of the Church at this time was not its doubts but its certainties. Each group was utterly convinced of the truth of its position and was not prepared to admit differing viewpoints. Perhaps men like John Henry Newman had turned to the Church of Rome in an attempt to stifle all uncertainty, but those who remained were unshaken in their beliefs. The leaders of the three great divisions of High, Low and Broad Church showed no chinks in their armour; and whatever their differences of opinion, all rested on a dogmatic sense of certainty. Few showed tolerance. Tait reflected to himself: 'The great evil is—that the liberals are deficient in religion and the religious are deficient in liberality.'[9] Nor was Tait himself free from intolerance.

Church divisions were accentuated because they were always carried on under the public eye. The newspapers were willing to give plenty of attention to ecclesiastical rifts and doctrinal problems, and helped to awaken the interest of the reading public in difficult points of theology, not always intelligently. As an article in the *Spectator* stated:

> Of all tastes common among the middle class, the taste for discussing half-understood theology is perhaps the most pronounced. Every word of the arguments in the Gorham case, every quotation cited, every explanation offered, were perused by men usually content with police reports and the Debate. . . .[10]

Even the remotest country clergyman was unable to remain unaware of controversies in Oxford or London; the newspapers and popular periodicals brought him into contact with the thoughts of others, and he too was prompted to indulge in controversy. The privately-printed pamphlet was a recognised way for a clergyman to express his opinions, as may be seen by the innumerable examples of this type of literature which survive.

Church parties had always existed of course, but during the eighteenth century their hostility had been more political than doctrinal. The Church was stirred from its apathy towards the condition of the industrial towns by the advent of Methodism, and in the early years of the nineteenth century its spiritual life awakened and it involved itself more wholeheartedly in social action. This was the period of anti-slavery campaigns, societies for popular education and evangelisation, Sunday schools and missionary effort overseas. High and Low Churches had their differences, but these were not really in dispute until a great wedge was driven between them by the Oxford Movement and the publication of *Tract XC*. The Oxford Movement itself may be seen as a search for authority by men who feared the encroachments of rationalism, and who looked back to the days of a powerful and authoritarian medieval church, with final power to pronounce on all matters of doctrine. The Tractarian view of Church authority and the power of the priestly hierarchy gave comfort and hope to many, but to a large section of the Church it was 'popish' and untenable. Rifts appeared in the Church societies. The National Society split between High Churchmen and Evangelicals, and the latter left in 1851 to form a separate Church Education Society. The Church Pastoral Aid Society, begun in 1836 to provide more curates and lay workers, also split, and High Churchmen formed another group, the Additional Curates Society. Party differences were thus allowed to interfere with the essential work of the Church.

Yet both High and Low Churchmen were seeking for authority: the High Church within the Church itself, the Low Church in the sole authority of the Scriptures. The Broad Church brought further disruption by claiming that the only authority lay in private judgment and in the individual conscience, which could alone interpret the Scriptures. They hoped to bring peace by encouraging latitude of opinion, but succeeded only in stirring up more strife, for the orthodox of all parties could not conceive of a faith without complete certainty. In the course of the debate some Broad Churchmen became embittered and as dogmatic as their opponents, as will be seen in the case of Rowland Williams. The ecclesiastical courts were used as battlegrounds for party conflicts. The teaching of the Church of England, as set forth in the Articles and Prayer-Book, was difficult to interpret, but in the mid-nineteenth century the final power of interpretation was left to a court which many churchmen could not accept. In 1832 the power to judge ecclesiastical appeals was handed over from the unwieldy, slow and expensive Court of Delegates to the Judicial

Committee of the Privy Council. Although this court included any bishops who happened to be members of the Privy Council, it also included laymen, and there was no provision that any member should be learned in ecclesiastical law.[11] Many churchmen were not satisfied with such a court, and believed that the Church itself should have sole right to judge matters of doctrine.

Between 1845 and 1865 the ecclesiastical courts were busy with doctrinal cases, and their decisions kept the Church in a continual state of anger and anxiety. During the 1870s the litigation continued with prosecution of ritualists. The two greatest commotions before 1860 were caused by State action in Church affairs. The first was Lord John Russell's appointment of Renn Dickson Hampden to the see of Hereford in 1847 in the teeth of opposition from many churchmen, for Hampden was suspected of unorthodox opinions. This was followed by a further shock in 1850 when the Judicial Committee accepted that the Calvinistic ideas of baptism taught by the Rev George Cornelius Gorham were not contrary to the doctrines of the Church, although Henry Phillpotts, Bishop of Exeter, and a majority of High Churchmen thought they were.[12] Both cases were attended by much publicity.

Apart from these there were several other scandals: ritualists were prosecuted, Pusey was suspended from preaching for two years, and anti-ritual riots occurred in London at St Barnabas's in Pimlico and St George's-in-the-East. In 1860 Lord Ebury (1801–93), a Liberal peer who was most interested in Church reform, informed the House of Lords indignantly that there had been at least sixteen expensive ecclesiastical cases in the previous eighteen years. 'It has been conjectured,' he said, 'that the total amount of money spent in these unseemly contentions would be sufficient, as far as money can do so, to provide the means of coping with all the spiritual destitution of the Metropolis.[13]

In the 1860s matters reached a climax. In 1860 six clergymen and a layman published *Essays and Reviews*, which was an open statement of Broad Church opinions. The only two beneficed clergy of the group, Rowland Williams (1817–70) and Henry Bristow Wilson (1803–88), were tried for heresy, suspended from their livings for a year by the Court of Arches, and then had the sentence reversed on appeal to the Judicial Committee in

1864. The notoriety which this long case attracted was increased by the similar case of John William Colenso (1814–83), Bishop of Natal, who had questioned the literal accuracy of the Old Testament. Colenso was tried and deprived by the Bishop of Capetown in 1863, only to be acquitted by the Judicial Committee in 1865. As Colenso's 'heresies' and the results of his trial almost duplicated those of the essayists, they will not be discussed here except for occasional comparison, because there were other most complicated factors involving the legal relationship between the Church in England and in the colonies.[14] It must be remembered, however, that the closeness of these two trials helped to keep Church tempers inflamed for most of the decade. During the 1860s it was difficult for any clergyman to keep clear of party disputes, and a slight detail in his dress or his services might stamp him as a party man in the eyes of partisans, however mild his personal ideas. Even a bishop as moderate as Lonsdale of Lichfield could not escape calumny; when he attempted to found a theological college and to encourage the training of nurses for purely practical reasons, he was accused of supporting Jesuit seminaries and popish sisterhoods. Churchmen tended to see their differences in black and white; only the Broad Church maintained that shades of grey existed.

Although clergymen might lean towards one party or another, there were, of course, infinite gradations of opinion, while the extremists tended to be the most clamorous. As party groupings were so important to the Church at this time it will be necessary to consider them in some detail, and to mention the men who led them.

The Evangelicals, as the Low Churchmen were now called, had undergone great changes since the end of the eighteenth century. Traditionally they were men who put the teaching of the Scriptures before the organisation of the Church, and who insisted on the Protestant value of personal devotion rather than priestly mediation. In the eighteenth century a general reaction against 'enthusiasm' and fanaticism of any kind caused them to decline into a somewhat soporific state, and towards the end of the century the term Low Church denoted little more than a connection with political Whiggery against the combination of High Churchmanship and the power of the Crown. During this period, however, there was a revival of religious fervour among some Evangelicals which ran concurrent with, but independent of the Wesleyan movement.[15] The Evangelicals were accused of putting a somewhat narrow piety before learning, but allied themselves with many worthy social causes, notably the abolition of slavery, and worked to bring religion to the industrial cities and the mission fields.

By 1860 the Evangelicals were at the height of their influence in government and society, and were on the whole contented with the existing relationship between Church and State. The Judicial Committee supported the evangelical Gorham, so before 1860 the Church's legal machinery did not disturb them as much as it did the High Church. They were no longer considered vulgar enthusiasts, were favoured by the Queen and Prince Albert, and received aristocratic support from Lord Shaftesbury, who had considerable influence with Palmerston in Church appointments. They preferred pastoral work to politics and were generally apathetic towards any Church organisation which was not for spreading the Gospel and aiding its ministers. Hence they were active in the mission societies but were not particularly interested in the revival of Convocation, diocesan synods or gatherings of bishops; indeed, as these things were favoured by the High Church, they usually distrusted them. Only in the 1860s, when their ideas seemed threatened by both ritualism and rationalism, did they start forming party organisations.

The political quietism of the Evangelicals appealed to ministers like Palmerston, who did not want any alteration in the relations between Church and State, so by 1860 there were sixteen bishops out of the twenty-seven who had fairly evangelical inclinations,[16] and this position was not altered much until Gladstone came to power. In spite of their old reputation for lack of learning, the Evangelicals had several weighty scholars amongst them, though none on the bench except Ellicott of Gloucester, who helped to produce a revised version of the Bible. His main defence against unbelief of any kind was that many passages of the Bible had been mistranslated in the Authorised Version, which had led to misconceptions. There were also William Goode, Dean of Ripon, who refuted ritualism with solid erudition, and Alexander M'Caul, Professor of Hebrew and Divinity at King's College,

London, who defended Genesis from Darwin and *Essays and Reviews*. Of a lesser order, but still of some weight, was Edward Garbett (1817–87), who was at various times editor of the two major Evangelical newspapers, the *Record* and the *Christian Advocate*. He delivered the Boyle lectures in 1861, devoted to refuting *Essays and Reviews*. But on the whole the Evangelicals could produce few men who could pretend to deal with educated critics on their own ground.

Evangelical publications, especially the *Record*, were often mere uninformed vituperation, and none were as erudite as the High Church *Christian Remembrancer*. The Evangelical ideal was found less in learning than in the piety of families like the Bickersteths, who in two generations produced a famous Evangelical leader, two bishops and an archdeacon, all men of exemplary life but not writers or scholars. As individuals the Evangelicals undoubtedly did much good work, but as a party they were frequently narrow-minded and short-sighted. Because they depended on the Scriptures they tended to class all Bible critics together, whatever their motives, as enemies of religion and, as will be seen later in the cases of diocesan synods and theological colleges, they opposed a great deal of much-needed organisation in the Church through suspicion of the ritualists.

The High Church was equally insistent on the authority of Bible and Prayer Book, but relied on the authority of the Church to interpret them. The High Church had also undergone a revival of religious life earlier in the century, and escaped from the indignity of the term 'high and dry'. A group of High Churchmen, nicknamed the 'Clapton Sect', had set an example of charity and personal piety to the High Church, but a much greater revolution had come in the 1830s with the Oxford Movement. Newman attracted not only members of the High Church, but erstwhile Evangelicals who, like the future Bishop of Salisbury, Walter Hamilton, did not find Newman's insistence on personal devotion and austerity incompatible with their own beliefs, and accepted with this his ideas on Church authority. Both the old High Church and the Tractarians emphasised the authority of the Church, but whereas the old High Church tended to look no further back than the English Reformation, the Tractarians revived interest in the medieval Church. Both were more interested in Church organisation than the Evangelicals, who were more concerned with societies for practical social ends.

After some of the original Tractarians had left the Church of England for Rome, their ideas continued among a generation of young men whom they had influenced, and these were more easily identified as a 'ritualist' party because of their concern for more elaborate services and church ornaments. Such practices were of doubtful legality at the time. Old-fashioned High Churchmen did not suffer these innovations gladly, and both Archbishop Longley and Bishop Gilbert of Chester, who were High Churchmen of the old school, engaged in prosecutions against them. On the other hand there were peaceable High Church bishops like Jacobson of Chester who would not countenance ritual prosecutions though he disapproved strongly of ritualism. Perhaps the most famous of these old High Church bishops was Phillpotts of Exeter, a relic of a period which had not considered political and ambitious bishops unusual, though by 1860 his days of controversy were ended by the feebleness of age. The High Church had in the past produced many learned bishops, such as William Warburton of Gloucester, but by the 1860s, when learned bishops were less esteemed than practical ones, the bench had no great reputation for scholarship. High Church bishops like Jacobson and Browne of Ely tended to be more scholarly than the Evangelicals on the bench, but their duties gave them little time for study, as Browne's biographer remarked regretfully: 'the pen ever drops into the second place when the crosier comes into use'.[17]

In the universities also the old High Church still had its adherents. At Oxford there was Edward Hawkins (1789–1882), Provost of Oriel for forty-six years until his retirement in 1874. It was Hawkins's misfortune to have supremacy in the college over those who later became more famous than himself, and as he opposed all university reform he appears as a stiff, dry reactionary. He was a churchman on the eighteenth-century model, who disliked religious enthusiasm of any kind and therefore he quarrelled with Newman, Hurrell Froude and R. I. Wilberforce, who were the Fellows of Oriel. Hawkins was equally suspicious of ritualism and rationalism, but the long sermon and pamphlet warfare he waged against theological opponents did not lead him into personal rancour. With Newman and Keble he was on respectful terms, and he treated the doubts of the young Clough gently. Newman himself admitted that he owed a debt to Hawkins's meticulous criticism of details.[18] In personal life, too, Hawkins was representative of the old High Churchmen of his day; in his youth he and his friends at Oriel had occasioned some surprise by breaking with the eighteenth-century boisterousness of college life. For him the Church was no longer a place for drinking and hunting parsons. This attitude, however, did not lead to rigid puritanism, and he was later reported to find the severe asceticism of the younger Oriel Fellows rather dull.

One of Hawkins's best-known pupils and admirers, who carried on his theological battles, was J. W. Burgon (1813–88), who became vicar of the university church of St Mary the Virgin in 1863. Burgon was as reactionary as Hawkins, though with more humour, and died as Dean of Chichester after publishing two volumes of laudatory biographies of men with similar views to his own; the tombstones, as it were, of the old High Church party.

In the eighteenth century the High Church had been the foremost 'Church and State' party, but their attitude gradually changed during the nineteenth century. After the Hampden affair and the Gorham case they grew steadily more suspicious of State interference in ecclesiastical affairs and realised that the State no longer reflected the interests of the Church now that other religious groups were represented in Parliament. Yet the High Churchmen did not want disestablishment, though some of them began to see it in the distance as the only hope of preserving the Church from secular interference. Instead, they tried to find a compromise in Convocation, diocesan synods and episcopal authority, because these things might give the Church an independent voice to preserve the balance of power with the State. While they tried to develop these independent groups, they also defended the Church's temporal privileges to the last, and tried to save Church rates and the Irish Church for as long as possible. Their views were represented mainly in the *Guardian*.

The ritualists, attacked by High and Low parties, had little love for the Church as an establishment. They were in constant fear of specific legislation against their practices; a fear which was realised in the Public Worship Regulation Act of 1874. They looked back to a Church unhampered by State interference, and wished ecclesiastical law to be free of State control. The Judicial Committee was their special aversion, and its decisions on Gorham, *Essays and Reviews* and Colenso brought home to them forcefully that separation from the State might be necessary, even if it meant disendowment. Gladstone sympathised with their views, and he and his friend Hamilton, the first bishop with Tractarian tendencies, thought that disestablishment might become inevitable if the Church's integrity were to be preserved.[19] The great hostility which they aroused caused many ritualists to regard themselves as persecuted upholders of the unadulterated faith of the Church against Erastianism, and they did not believe that ideals should be compromised in order to conciliate public opinion, as an article in one of their periodicals, the *Literary Churchman*, reveals:

> What if an impetuous Member of Parliament lay the axe to the root of our continuance as a national establishment? That does not affect our vitality as a Church. What if our revenues are assailed? Nothing can deprive us of the Apostolic Succession, which is the key-stone of our ecclesiastical system, and worth more to us than the favour of princes, the suffrages of Parliament, and the impertinent patronage of the daily Press.[20]

The ritualists encouraged works of learning, especially with a view to proving the historical validity of their own ideas; Lathbury's *History of Convocation* (1842) is a fundamental example. By 1860, in spite of popular hostility after the revival of Roman Catholic sees in England, the ritualists were gaining ground. Their ideas were expressed in the *Christian Remembrancer*, a quarterly review which had begun in 1819 during the days of the Clapton Sect, and had later come under Tractarian influence. Many of its articles were of a high scholarly standard and appealed to many thoughtful churchmen, though it came to an end in 1868. Its passing was a victory, Mark Pattison thought, for the more unenlightened section of ritualist opinion, which preferred the less erudite *Literary Churchman*.[21] There was also the monthly *Ecclesiastic* which ran from 1846 to 1868; a much less intelligent review of Church affairs and current literature which poured unreasoning contempt on both the 'puritan' (Evangelical) and 'rationalist' (Broad Church) sections of the clergy.

The ritualist party was more truly a 'party' in that a sense of persecution and self-justification gave it more solidarity than most other churchmen felt. It also had its honoured leaders. In 1860 Pusey and Keble were the venerated remnants of the original Tractarians: the former still an active controversialist though sixty years of age; the latter in seclusion at Hursley, but emerging occasionally to lend the prestige of his name to gatherings of the ritualists. Also in Oxford was Henry Parry Liddon, Pusey's admirer and later his biographer, who was Vice-Principal of St Edmund Hall from 1859 to 1864 after having been forced to resign his post at Cuddesdon College because of his views. He later received promotion through the offices of Hamilton and Gladstone, and was finally appointed to a canonry in St Paul's. Like Newman, he had a great influence over young men at Oxford.

Of widespread controversial fame was George Anthony Denison (1805–96), Archdeacon of Taunton, who was the most outspoken of the ritualists and their leader in the Lower House of the Convocation of Canterbury. Denison became something of a hero to ritualists after a long series of legal actions between 1854 and 1858, in which he defended the ritualist view of the Eucharist.* Though Denison had brought the suit on himself by his inflexible attitude and determination to vindicate his ideas legally, the series of trials from the Archbishop of Canterbury's diocesan court to the Court of Arches to the Judicial Committee, from which he at last escaped through a legal loophole, made him very popular among fellow-ritualists. He championed their views as often and as loudly as possible, in his charges, in pamphlets and in Convocation. He thought that the ritualists were the only true defenders of religion in England, and prophesied doom for Christianity if education ever fell into secular hands.[22] He directed a great deal of energy against the Broad Church, and he continually asserted the Church's right to judge and excommunicate those who did not preach the literal accuracy of the

* Chadwick, *Victorian Church*, p 491 ff. The ritualists asserted that the Eucharist contained an inward reality (real presence) which was received by all who partook of it, whatever their state of mind. To the orthodox, this sounded the same as the Romish doctrine of transubstantiation.

Bible. It is easy to see him as his opponents among the liberal clergy did, as an inquisitor or witch-hunter, but he was always consistent and courageous in his views, a capable organiser, an emphatic and witty speaker, who commanded the attention of Convocation.

The stresses of the mid-century tended to throw party differences into sharper relief as men tried to define the boundaries of their beliefs. But within the Church parties there were many variations of opinion, and three of the most influential clergymen of the time fitted into no group, though they might receive support from a particular section of the clergy. The first, Connop Thirlwall, was Bishop of St David's from 1840 to 1875, and was an isolated figure, the only bishop of that period to conform to the eighteenth-century idea of a scholarly bishop. He did not care to parade his theological opinions, but politically he was a Liberal, and commanded the respect of liberal clergy. Of him much will be said later.*

The second, Samuel Wilberforce, Bishop of Oxford from 1845 to 1869 and then Bishop of Winchester, was Thirwall's antithesis in that his life was devoted to diocesan organisation and Church leadership. Posterity has acclaimed the first object above the second, but in the 1860s he was the best known of all the defenders of orthodoxy. He began life in a famous Evangelical family, but his views changed later, and his contemporaries thought of him as a High Churchman or even a ritualist. In reality he belonged to no one group, although his sympathy with and refusal to prosecute ritualists caused him to be suspected by Evangelicals. But he had many of the qualities of the Evangelicals in his love of popular speeches and extempore preaching.[23] The High Church bishops followed him willingly. Nor did he really accept ritualist ideas, except in a very mild way, but because he was less a thinker than a man of action it is impossible to sift a coherent system of theology from his writings, except a conservative love for the Bible and Prayer Book and an intense feeling of personal devotion.

The third bishop, Archibald Campbell Tait, who was Bishop of London from 1856 to 1868 and then Archbishop of Canterbury, had been a Fellow of Balliol and a great headmaster of

* See Chapter 4.

Rugby. His life, like that of Wilberforce, was devoted to practical rather than intellectual works. He and Wilberforce were the two most active parliamentary bishops, though they usually voted on opposite sides in Church affairs, and also in Convocation. Tait might have been classed with the Evangelicals because of his nonconformist Scottish background and his hatred of ritualism, but it was not so much the ornate services of the ritualists he disliked as the tendency many of them showed to try and set up a Church system with rigid doctrines, with all critics excluded.[24] Tait's ideal was comprehensiveness, and the narrow Biblical beliefs of the Evangelicals were as alien to him as the exclusive church practices of the ritualists. He wished the Church to remain the established Church so that it might be saved from narrowness of life and dogma, and he thought this could be achieved only by tolerance, compromise and greater administrative efficiency. For this reason he was not hostile, as Wilberforce was, to any clerics who ventured to criticise the Church's teachings; indeed he knew many of the critics personally, and in the 1860s he was under considerable strain as the claims of friendship conflicted with the pressure put upon him to condemn *Essays and Reviews*, which he himself thought had gone too far. His main weakness was his intolerance towards ritualism, and he was instrumental in the passing of the Public Worship Regulation Act. He was also one of the few bishops to approve of the Judicial Committee of the Privy Council as an ecclesiastical court, because he thought it saved the law of the Church from falling into the hands of any one Church faction, whereas Wilberforce desired a purely clerical court which would have the power to judge all matters of doctrine.

The group which aroused the fear and wrath of all orthodox clergy of many shades of opinion was commonly known as the Broad Church. This term is misleading, because it suggests an organised party, and because it also implies a group falling somewhere between High and Low. The Broad Church was not a party, but a set of individuals, many of whom disagreed with each other except in the idea that the authority of the Bible and the Church might be subjected to historical and scientific criticism. They also considered that certain parts of the Scriptures were not useful as a moral guide, but that the spirit of Christianity, and of the Church of England, was strong enough to withstand any such criticism, for only false or antiquated ideas would be in danger. The Broad Church was not a faction but a restless and critical attitude of mind, and Broad Churchmen were drawn together more by the hostility they provoked than by their common ideas. They became the focal point of heated arguments about how much liberty of opinion should be allowed to clergymen who had affirmed at their ordination that they believed wholeheartedly in all the doctrines contained in the Articles and Prayer Book. Lay critics who sympathised with the Broad Church, like Goldwin Smith, the Regius Professor of Modern History at Oxford, had no such pressure on them, and did not arouse quite the same fury as the clerical Broad Churchmen.

'Liberal Anglicanism' has also been used as a synonym for Broad Church,[25] and describes more adequately their attitudes towards theology, but it does not mean that these men were necessarily political Liberals, or even particularly advanced in their views of society, for this was not always the case. As 'Broad Church' was the term which was used at the time,[26] it will be used here. Even though the Broad Churchmen did not think of themselves as members of a party, their contemporaries did, especially after the publication of *Essays and Reviews*, which seemed to show that the Broad Churchmen were gathering to overthrow orthodox religion.

The Broad Churchmen can be seen to fall roughly into two generations, of intellectual activity rather than of age, and the first had finished its work by 1855 when the work of the second was just beginning. The clerical members of the first generation included Thomas Arnold (1795–1842), Julius Charles Hare, Archdeacon of Lewes (1798–1855), and his brother Augustus William; Connop Thirlwall (1797–1875), Frederick Denison Maurice (1805–72), Richard Whately, Archbishop of Dublin (1787–1863), and Baden Powell (1796–1860). Charles Kingsley also had affinities with this group, though he was famous chiefly as a novelist and practical worker. Hampden was classed as a Broad Churchman because his Bampton Lectures of 1834 had expressed the opinion that many Scriptural ideas had been obscured by centuries of dogma, but he had little connection with the mainstream of Broad Church thought. His ideas were derived more from eighteenth-century English traditions than from the new philosophy of Germany, which was the major influence on the Broad Church. Hampden contributed nothing to the theology of his time and specifically rejected the Broad Church in the 1860s.[27] It should be noted, however, that several of the Broad Churchmen of the older generation who survived into the 1860s reacted like Hampden and disowned their successors. Whately and Thirlwall, who had also reached episcopal dignity, strongly rejected *Essays and Reviews*.

The second generation, whose work might be said to reach fruition in 1855 with the publication of Benjamin Jowett's commentaries on St Paul and Rowland Williams's *Rational Godliness*, reached the peak of its notoriety in the 1860s. It included the clerical authors of *Essays and Reviews*, who were Jowett (1817–93), Williams (1817–70), Frederick Temple (1821–1902), Mark Pattison (1813–84), and Henry Bristow Wilson (1803–88). (The two remaining essayists were Baden Powell, who died in the year the book was published, and a layman, C. W. Goodwin.) *Essays and Reviews* stirred up much controversy, less because of the originality of its ideas than because six of its authors were clergymen, some well-known. It sold 15,000 copies in three months and 22,250 in a decade.[28]

Other Broad Churchmen of repute included Arthur Penrhyn Stanley (1815–81), the most devoted of Thomas Arnold's pupils, who became Dean of Westminster in 1863. Henry Hart Milman (1791–1868), Dean of St Paul's, was also generally considered a Broad Churchman, though his views were not as advanced as Stanley's. Stanley, who possessed rather more personal charm than most of the Broad Churchmen, achieved notoriety mainly through his claim that subscription to the Articles and Prayer Book was damaging to the intellectual level of the clergy because it repelled thoughtful men from the ministry. Milman and Stanley both published histories of the Jews which treated the Old Testament as the history of Bedouin tribes and minimised the miraculous elements. Milman also shared Stanley's views on subscription, but took little part in active controversy.

Several of the leading Broad Churchmen formed a tightly-knit circle, strengthened by some common ideas and by affinities of friendship and relationship. This encouraged the impression that they were a 'party'. Julius Hare and his brother had been friends with Thirlwall when they were all at Cambridge. Julius Hare became the tutor of F. D. Maurice at Cambridge, and he and Maurice subsequently married each others' sisters. Augustus Hare was connected by marriage with the Stanleys. A. P. Stanley was taught at school by Arnold and at Balliol by Tait; he was a close friend of Julius Hare, and also of Jowett and Temple, who had been Tait's pupils as well. These links tended to soften differences of opinion; Stanley, for instance, made himself unpopular in orthodox circles by a discussion of *Essays and Reviews* in the *Edinburgh Review*, which defended the essayists' right to their opinions, even though he did not agree with all of them.[29] He was also more complimentary to the essays of Temple and Jowett than to those of the others, who were not his personal friends.

The essayists were aware that educated men were turning away from the Church, and wished to prevent this, even if in the process some of the Church's traditional teachings had to be discarded in order to preserve its most important truths. Nor did they believe that doubt could be confined to the educated only; they maintained that all churchmen had the right to interpret Scripture for themselves, nor need they accept everything which they found in it. The essayists thought that if educated people were forced to conform to a literalist belief in the Bible they would abandon religion altogether. This would have repercussions at all levels of society, as Jowett wrote:

> I cannot help anticipating that increased freedom of opinion may lead to a real amendment of life. Hitherto, religion seems to have become more and more powerless among the educated classes. Do we not want a Gospel for the educated . . . not because it is more blessed to preach to the educated than to the poor, but because the faith of the educated is permanent, and ultimately affects the faith of the poor?[30]

The Broad Churchmen all loved and venerated the Scriptures, but most of them were prepared to accept Jowett's maxim that they should be read and criticised 'like any other book'. They were supremely confident, however, that the value of the Bible, especially the New Testament, as a moral guide and spiritual revelation would arise unspotted from all objections that could be fairly levelled at it. Conservative clergymen frequently believed that every word in the Bible had been divinely inspired and that it therefore could contain no error, whereas the Broad Church accepted that the writers of the Bible, although their moral message was from God, were liable to human errors in matters of fact.

Orthodox churchmen, on the other hand, although they sometimes sympathised with doubters, were uncompromisingly hostile towards doubt. They considered that doubt was a kind of disease —'a moral sickness', Wilberforce called it—which was self-induced because man, in the pride of his intellect, attempted to judge the revelation which God had given him. Wilberforce was particularly aware of doubt among young men because of his connection with Oxford University, and in 1861, while the *Essays and Reviews* controversy was gaining momentum, he preached two sermons on the subject in the university pulpit. These two sermons show him at the height of his oratorical powers; in long, rolling sentences he declared that no Christian ethic could stand without the strength of divine revelation behind it. He described vividly the process of doubt in the mind, arising from the belief that unaided human intellect could judge the truth of certain portions of the Scriptures, and finally resulting in a rejection of the whole. He attacked the intellectual pretensions of Biblical critics:

> It is but the smallest part of the mysteries of the eternal world which can be grasped by our feeble faculties. . . . Once let the mind, instead of receiving humbly, begin to doubt, and doubt will be everywhere. The struggles of such a soul in the uncertainty around it are like the plunging of the maddened herd into the boundless morass. Every effort engulfs in the quagmire more of the surrounding sward, and sinks the powerless victims in ruin.[31]

The climax of the second sermon was a highly-coloured description of the death of a doubter in agonies of despair at his own uncertainty, followed by a solemn warning to teachers who had been responsible for planting the seeds of criticism in a young man's mind. His advice to his hearers was to fling away doubt 'as if it were a loaded shell shot into the fortress of the soul'. The sermon drew forth a strong protest from Goldwin Smith, who objected that the suppression of doubt resulted in superstition and hypocrisy, 'The inevitable effect of your language', he wrote to Wilberforce, 'as it appears to me, will be to taint with the deepest suspicion every article of our belief, into which you would scare us from enquiry.'[32]

Edward Garbett also inveighed against doubt, and recognised that it sprang from historical, philosophical and scientific roots, all of which he denounced as shallow and conceited, but said that the clergy should try and understand these things in order to combat them.[33] Neither Garbett nor Wilberforce maintained that all critical inquiry into the Scriptures ought to be stopped, but they thought it should be undertaken only in a reverent frame of mind which would predispose men to make the right judgments. Tait also took up the question in his episcopal charge of 1862. He realised that many young men had difficulty in accepting the Bible as literal truth, and recommended that ministers deal gently with them, but he could find no better solution than Wilberforce; if all critical inquiry were undertaken reverently, then the inquirer would not stray far from the paths of orthodoxy. He did not think, however, that prosecutions for heresy would have any effect in deterring such inquiry. Tait's old pupils were disappointed at his attitude, especially after he joined the other bishops in condemning *Essays and Reviews*. He received an angry letter from Temple, who considered that Tait had led his pupils into the inquiries he now condemned.

> To tell a man to study, and yet bind him under heavy penalties come to the same conclusion with those who have not studied it is to mock him. If the conclusions are prescribed, the study is precluded.[34]

The Broad Churchmen were not, of course, the first clergymen to doubt the Biblical revelation. In the previous century there had been many latitudinarians within the Church who had considered that it was not always consistent with reason, and had looked for a revelation instead in the orderly workings of the universe and the inherent sense of propriety in the mind of man. In its extreme form, latitudinarianism led to deism, which bypassed the Scriptures altogether, and accepted the universe as a sufficient revelation in itself. Yet the deists, except perhaps

Hume, did not doubt the existence of God or the necessity of religion. Deists tried to make religion conform to their idea of reason, but they had no way of attacking the Scriptures except to show up internal inconsistencies, or to maintain that miracles had no part in an ordered Newtonian universe. This led them to seek for natural explanations for miraculous events in the Bible, especially by discrediting the authority of the Evangelists or maintaining that the Apostles had manufactured 'miracles' for their own ends. One of the most notorious works of this kind was Conyers Middleton's *A Free Enquiry into the Miraculous Powers* (1747), which tried to show that the witnesses of the miracles in the primitive Church could not be trusted.[35]

By the mid-nineteenth century, however, the whole basis of Biblical criticism had altered, and the Broad Church based their criticism, not on 'reason', which tried to discredit the Evangelists, but on new historical and scientific evidence which threw doubt on the date and authorship of many of the Scriptures. It is noteworthy that this type of criticism was in full swing long before the *Origin of Species* added the testimony of natural science against the literal accuracy of the Old Testament. Nor do the Broad Churchmen seem to have been particularly influenced by Darwin; there is only one mention of his work in *Essays and Reviews*, where Powell, himself a scientist, used it to buttress one of his own points.[36] Orthodox clergy, however, misunderstood the basis of Broad Church criticism and considered that they were merely refurbishing the ideas of the deists. Wilberforce and Garbett thought they saw deism reincarnate in *Essays and Reviews*, and Bishop Jackson of Lincoln maintained: 'the defunct deism of the eighteenth century has lent its blunted arms to be furbished up anew by the rationalistic scepticism of the nineteenth'.[37] This was a too-convenient dismissal of Broad Church theories. It was generally accepted in the Church that eighteenth-century deism had been routed by the works of divines like William Butler and William Paley, and Butler's stately prose and Paley's ingenious explanations were still extremely popular. The orthodox therefore relied on these champions to save them once again, without realising that the whole argument had changed.

By 1860 Broad Churchmen believed with some justification that they were suffering from ecclesiastical persecution. The men of the older school had incurred hostility for views which were not even directly expressed. Thirlwall never wrote his own manifesto, but was suspected because he and Julius Hare had translated some German works. He was fortunate to receive a bishopric, which was presented to him mainly because Melbourne had some difficulty in finding Whigs who were of the right calibre for the bench. Thomas Arnold, later acclaimed by all parties as one of the foremost churchmen of the nineteenth century, and probably the most famous of English headmasters, never received a bishopric because of his enthusiastic ideas for a comprehensive Church which would include Dissenters. Arnold was much more notorious than Thirlwall, and so Melbourne cautiously refused to promote him, though he finally gave him the Regius chair of modern history at Oxford in 1841. Julius Hare remained an archdeacon, engaged in vindicating himself and his friends from orthodox attacks. In 1853 Maurice was forced to resign his divinity chair at King's College, London, because he doubted whether the torments of the wicked would be everlasting. He, like Arnold, won fame through his practical works and was respected for these in spite of his theological opinions.

The younger generation of Broad Churchmen believed themselves especially aggrieved by the weight of orthodox authority. Stanley had no chance of a bishopric because of his views, although he was an eminent candidate. Jowett's commentary on St Paul's Epistles included a passage which denied that God was a wrathful figure who was only appeased by the sufferings of the innocent Christ, and for this the Vice-Chancellor of Oxford requested him to sign the Thirty-Nine Articles once again; a great humiliation. Pusey and his followers blocked all proposals to annex a Christ Church canonry to the Regius chair of Greek, which had a miserable salary, because they did not wish to endow a chair whose holder might not be an orthodox churchman. Nor did Jowett realise his ambition to become Master of Balliol until 1870. Mark Pattison suffered similar setbacks, and became an embittered man after he lost the election to the Rectorship of Lincoln College in 1851. This was mainly due to intrigue and divided loyalties among the Fellows, but Pattison was always aware of religious hostility.[38] Williams and Wilson were arraigned in the Church courts, and Williams especially suffered from a sense of persecution. Temple managed to rise above earlier attacks when Gladstone made him Bishop of Exeter in 1869, but his consecration aroused anger in many High Church clergy. Edward Hamilton rejoiced that his brother, the late Bishop of Salisbury, had not lived to see the day, and Burgon, who had been an old friend of Temple, wrote to Wilberforce:

> To forgive personal iniquities, is, I hope, easy; but just as an Ambassador *could* not condone an offence offered to his Sovereign, so I feel that I have no alternative but to remain in an attitude of suspended hostility. Never shall Temple preach in my pulpit—nor will I ever call him my friend again—nor cease to regard him as a dishonorable man. That he is a dangerous one, I know full well—and you will all know, to your cost, ere long! (We were *very* intimate once.)[39]

Although it might seem from this description that Broad Church ideas were confined to the more intellectual members of the clergy, some cases which found their way into the ecclesiastical courts show that humble men adopted them as well. German theology and the intellectual equipment needed for personal research into the Scriptures were not available to all, but a sense of the moral issues at stake was more common. Broad Church ideas could prove costly to the careers of ordinary clergy without influence, as the example of three parish clergy will show.

A case in point was the Rev John MacNaught, vicar of St Chrysostom's in Liverpool. MacNaught was inspired by Coleridge and had some knowledge of German ideas. At meetings of the Liverpool Clerical Society, which was a society of local clergymen formed for the purpose of studying the Scriptures, MacNaught voiced his opinion that not all parts of the Bible were divinely inspired. In 1856 his shocked fellow-members expelled him from the society, and he offended the orthodox even further by publishing a short book explaining his ideas. These were not very different from those found in *Essays and Reviews*, though MacNaught was more sceptical of the truth of miracles than most of the essayists. He experienced further hostility from his fellow-clergy and his doubts increased. In 1860 he resigned his living and went to London, where he thought of becoming a lawyer or a Dissenting minister, though he longed to return to the Church of England. He wrote another work to explain that miracles were not the most important evidences of Christianity, which rested on the truth of its moral system. Finally, in 1867, he set up a proprietory chapel in Bath; a place of worship on the fringes of the Anglican communion, which catered for the spiritual needs of a shifting holiday population.[40]

In February 1860 the Court of Arches sat to try Dunbar Isidore Heath, vicar of Brading on the Isle of Wight, who had been arraigned by his bishop, Sumner of Winchester, for unorthodox ideas. His opinions were largely based on Maurice's, and were concerned with various moral aspects of Christian teaching, In particular he urged that 'justification' meant that God would do justice to the whole human race, and he rejected the idea that Christ's death had 'propitiated' God's wrath against man. Heath had convinced himself, by ingenious verbal manoeuvring, that he was not contravening the Thirty-Nine Articles, but after several hearings in both the Court of Arches and the Judicial Committee he was deprived of his living. Heath was perhaps not a normal example, being certainly an eccentric man, who had also constructed a fantastic theory of the future life, but his eccentricity was no greater than that of numerous respectable Evangelical clergy who uttered equally incredible prophecies on the basis of the Book of Revelation.

Another humble Broad Churchman who became notorious was Charles Voysey (1828–1912), a parish priest who was influenced by *Essays and Reviews* but who had worked out his opinions before the book appeared. He was convicted of heresy in the Chancery Court of York in 1869, appealed to the Judicial Committee, but lost, and was deprived of his living. His case appeared to point out the dangers of the Broad Church position, and will be discussed in more detail in Chapter 6.

The publication of *Essays and Reviews* itself was in some measure an attack on what its authors believed to be a system of ecclesiastical terrorism. Jowett, whose experience over his commentaries still rankled, wrote to Stanley urging him to contribute to the volume: 'We do not wish to do anything rash or irritating to the public or the University, but we are determined not to submit to this abominable system of terrorism, which prevents the statement of the plainest facts, and makes true theology or theological opinions impossible'.[41] Stanley did not wish to disturb the ecclesiastical peace at the time, but Mark Pattison reflected moodily on the atmosphere of hostility surrounding any clergyman with unorthodox ideas. 'Every clergyman,' he wrote in 1863, 'is compelled, on pain of professional ruin, to maintain a fair repute as "orthodox". His orthodoxy is his point of honour, and like a woman, to be suspected is to be lost.'[42]

This atmosphere caused the Broad Churchmen to look back into history for their vindication. While the ritualists deplored the Reformation as the rent in the Church's seamless coat, the Broad Churchmen hailed it as the triumph of private judgment and individual inquiry over organised ecclesiastical tyranny. Pattison, with his usual acuteness, realised that current debates about the nature of the Reformation had special relevance to his own time.[43] By 1860 many Broad Churchmen thought that a second Reformation was in the air, and they its harbingers. Williams, during his trial, wished to be a martyr like Latimer and Ridley. Stanley, who was more modest, wrote to a friend in 1865:

> I agree with you that the prophet of the second Reformation has not yet appeared. Perhaps he never will. But that a second Reformation is in store for us, and that the various tendencies of the age are preparing the way for it, I cannot doubt, unless Christianity is doomed to suffer a portentous eclipse.[44]

Perhaps Stanley was more of a prophet than he thought.

Notes to this chapter are on pages 246–8

Chapter 2 THE THREAT FROM GERMANY

In Germany, too, moderate churchmen hoped for a second Reformation. Religious life there over the past century had foreshadowed events in Britain. The Scriptures had been subjected to scholarly attacks which became increasingly sophisticated, and this had led to a strong reaction among orthodox Lutherans in favour of church authority, in the manner of the Tractarians. This in turn provoked an evangelical revival against the presumptions of the clergy, and also a moderate movement akin to the Broad Church, which urged a certain amount of compromise with the findings of critical scholarship. An English churchman's attitude towards Germany was largely conditioned by his own religious beliefs, and nothing divided the Broad Churchmen more sharply from their orthodox opponents than their knowledge and partial acceptance of the German discoveries of the past eighty years. This had been a period of great development in German thought, undertaken with an intensity and professionalism which was not often found amongst the Fellows of Oxford and Cambridge colleges. It would be impossible here to describe this renaissance in any detail, for it embraced almost every kind of creative effort, but certain aspects had a profound influence on the religious life of Europe.

By 1850 the German system of education was one of the finest in the world. There were six universities in Prussia alone, including recent foundations at Berlin (1810), and Bonn (1818), and fifteen in the other German states. This was at a time when England had only the two ancient universities, together with Durham and the University of London, which could grant degrees. There were also four universities in Scotland and Trinity College in Dublin. Teaching methods varied greatly between the two countries; the German universities favoured lectures from professors, supplemented if possible by individual instruction by junior teachers. Oxford and Cambridge (and to some extent Durham, though not London) concentrated on private tutoring in the colleges. German professors lectured in their special subjects, and because secondary education was on the whole better than in England, they were not burdened with elementary instruction. In the English universities lectures were not so highly regarded, though the new universities depended on them more than the old. In Oxford and Cambridge there were comparatively few professorships, and it sometimes depended on the goodwill of the professor whether he ever delivered lectures at all.[1] Unless the lectures were compulsory for examinations students did not pay them much attention, whereas the German students responded to the professors' attempts to attract a large audience. Tait, Jowett and Stanley all hoped in vain that the professorial system would be introduced into Oxford as a result of the Royal Commission's report on the University in 1852.

Because the German Protestant Churches did not demand a statement of belief from a clergyman apart from a promise to teach the Scriptures, a German professor, even if he were a pastor, had great liberty of religious opinion. In England a clerical teacher was bound by his subscription to the Thirty-Nine Articles and Prayer Book. Since the early nineteenth century German university teachers had enjoyed a freedom of speculation in philosophic and religious studies which was the envy of Broad Churchmen in England. In theology, certain eighteenth-century German writers had been influenced by the English deists, and maintained that a supernatural revelation was both irrelevant to faith and incompatible with reason. Of these, Christian Wolf (1679–1754) was one of the first and most famous, and was expelled from his position in the University of Halle in 1723 for promulgating these views, but the German climate of opinion rapidly became more tolerant. Similar doubts were expressed by K. F. Bahrdt (1741–92), who wrote a life of Jesus in 1782 which followed English deists like Toland in trying to find natural explanations for miraculous happenings in the New Testament by challenging the integrity of the Apostles.

Eighteenth-century criticism was summarised by the dramatist Lessing, who in 1774 and 1777 published some parts of a work by the scholar H. S. Reimarus, under the title of *Fragment eines Ungenannten*, and then defended them against orthodox criticism in a series of tracts, notably the *Axiomata* of 1778. Reimarus had attempted to cast doubts on the Resurrection by finding discrepancies in the Gospel narratives; Lessing himself in the *Axiomata* summarised his own views in a series of propositions which he considered self-evident to common sense. He stated that the Bible contained much that was unnecsssary to religion, and that this additional matter was not divinely inspired or free from errors. Christianity depended for its reception on its intrinsic moral value, not upon Biblical revelation; its spirit existed before the Evangelists wrote, and would exist if the whole Bible were lost. However valuable the Bible was as an explanation of spiritual truth, it was not in itself an object of devotion, and criticism directed at it was not necessarily criticism of religion.[2] Lessing set out most clearly the themes upon which the nineteenth-century debate was also to revolve, but the basis of argument was to alter completely after his death in 1781, which was the year in which Kant published his *Critik der reinen Vernunft*.

Kant founded a system of philosophy which affected religious studies profoundly by postulating a division of reason into 'pure' and 'practical'. Pure reason was the power to draw logical conclusions from sense experience; practical reason was the mind's ability to deduce abstract concepts like God, freedom and immortality from *a priori* knowledge. This basic principle was to influence both the new theological studies in Germany and the Broad Church in England. From Kant arose a subjective or 'idealistic' school of philosophy, which was developed by Fichte and Schleiermacher.[3] At almost the same time there arose a new 'realistic' school of history, which believed in testing historical documents in every possible way to determine their authenticity, and which would accept no traditional account of events unless it could be confirmed from impartial sources. This method was first applied to classical studies and then to Scriptural ones. Barthold Georg Niebuhr (1776–1831) was the greatest exponent of the new historical method. His history of Rome, which appeared in two volumes in 1812 and in a revised three-volume edition between 1827 and 1832, was notable for its criticism of traditionally hallowed sources like Livy, and its use of previously unknown documents. These new historical techniques were soon applied to Biblical studies and were reinforced by a greater knowledge of philology. Germany outdistanced the rest of Europe in the study of classical and oriental languages, led by erudite scholars like J. D. Michaelis (1717–91).

During the first half of the nineteenth century there was a ferment of religious opinion among German scholars. J. G. Eichhorn (1752–1827) and W. M. L. de Wette (1780–1849) produced immensely long, learned and essentially devout commentaries on the Scriptures, yet treated them with the same philological care that might be applied to any ancient documents. Eichhorn tried to find the relationship between the Old Testament and the times at which it was written, and postulated that Genesis had been written by at least two authors. De Wette showed from historical and philological evidence that the first five books of the Bible were not written by Moses, but at a period long after his death.[4] Eichhorn taught oriental languages and Old Testament literature at the new university at Berlin, and his ideas were developed by his pupil G. H. A. Ewald (1803–75). By the middle of the century the most intensive theological work was being carried out by F. C. Baur (1792–1860) and his colleagues at the University of Tübingen.

As philological and historical criticism continued to shake confidence in the literal accuracy of the Scriptures and to challenge their traditional authorship, an idealistic movement led by F. E. D. Schleiermacher (1768–1834) tried to find a securer basis for Christianity. Schleiermacher looked inward for the sources of religion, and found them in man's sense of dependence on something greater than himself. Here the Kantian division of the reason was useful, and Schleiermacher adopted the idea that certain concepts, such as religion, were not derived from external sources but from the nature of the human mind. Schleiermacher, who was a minister of the Prussian Evangelical Church, preached undogmatic Christianity from his pulpit in Berlin, and his works were extremely popular among students in the first decades of the nineteenth century. He set an example, which was copied in England as well as Germany, of casting away much of the Old Testament but insisting on the New because Christ represented the ideal of the human spirit.[5] Schleiermacher was attractive because he taught a fervent and devout Christianity, but in his theology many traditional dogmas, such as those of the Fall and the Atonement, were discarded.

Schleiermacher's greatest rival in Berlin was Hegel, whose philosophy moved far beyond the Biblical revelation and explained men's moral sense not as being in an external God, but in the gradually unfolding spirit of the human race, which was moving through history towards full self-awareness and was an aspect of the Divine. Hegel's system of dialectic logic profoundly influenced theologians, including Baur, but his most notorious disciple was David Friedrich Strauss (1808–74), whose *Leben Jesu*, first published in 1835, removed the New Testament from the sphere of historical reality and treated it as a myth, in which the spirit of the Jewish race sought to express itself in an ideal man, who was Christ. Strauss was a pastor of the Evangelical Church; his book won him international notoriety and went into four editions by 1840. Though he adopted Hegelian terms, his philological and historical methods were closer to those of Baur, whose pupil he had been. Whereas critics like Ewald tried to dissect truth from fiction in the Scriptures, or to attribute miracles to mistaken interpretations of natural events, Strauss did not attempt to judge the relative authenticity of the Gospels, but was satisfied that none of them had been written by eyewitnesses, and that all were literary expressions of a religious ideal. Yet, unlike Hegel, Strauss emphasised the importance of Christianity; he maintained that although the New Testament was not historical truth it was spiritual truth, and that the person of Jesus was the ideal to be emulated by all men.[6] He could therefore still claim that he was a Christian and remain within the Church; this attitude caused a stir among orthodox Germans and also disturbed the Church of England, whose orthodox members clung more closely to clerical subscription as a defence against heretical priests.

The German clergy were not of the ruling class in any of the German States, and served the function of an educational civil service, more dependent than the English clergy on the State, which in most cases paid them. As contemporary English observers liked to reflect, Germany seemed to allow freedom of speculation in religious matters as a substitute for political activity.[7] Yet there were orthodox forces within the German Protestant Churches which strongly opposed the new criticism and hoped to unite the Churches against rationalism. The foundation of unity was laid by Frederick William III of Prussia, who evolved a plan to unite the Lutheran and Reformed (Calvinist) Churches by using a common litany and central synod, though the old forms of worship were not to be stopped. The union was effected in 1817, and the United Evangelical Church spread through Prussia in spite of fears that it was a covert plan for the State to gain complete control over the Church.

Yet the success of the union, although helped by a surge of nationalist feeling after the Napoleonic wars, was far from complete. Its founders had wanted communal worship and sacraments without sacrificing the Confessions, which were the cornerstones of the Protestant Churches of Germany; but there were many extremists, especially among the Lutheran pastors and nobility of the northern states, who feared the loss of the Confessions and a decline of their own authority. Some Lutheran congregations therefore remained outside the union, but others accepted it with motives which foreshadowed those of the Tractarians. They opposed a loose union of congregations without definite principles of faith, and feared the encroachments of rationalism; this led them to demand a strong Church hierarchy with more power in the hands of the clergy. This attitude favoured the Erastian tendencies of the Prussian monarchy. At Berlin the most influential leader of this 'confessionalist' party was E. W. Hengstenberg (1802–69), who became professor of theology at the University of Berlin in 1826. He edited the chief periodical of the orthodox Lutheran party, the *Evangelische Kirchenzeitung*, which began in 1827. Hengstenberg had some influence at court through various ministers, and was suspected of having a network of spies in the provinces to report on rationalist ideas amongst the clergy.[8]

Frederick William IV, a deeply pious man, continued his father's interest in the state of religion in Germany, and opposed the appointment of rationalists to important posts. He continued to work for a closer union of the churches, but this was prevented by the mutual hostility of the confessionalist and evangelical parties. In Germany, as in England, the evangelical spirit was aroused by suspicion of both the 'clerical' and 'rationalist' forces in the Churches. The Evangelicals, who included Baron von Bunsen, hoped to focus religious life on the congregation, not the priest. By 1857 they had won some concessions from Frederick William, but in spite of his declarations in favour of church autonomy, he did not relinquish his hold on church affairs.

In England the effect of German ideas was felt very slowly. The German language was not yet a polite accomplishment like French or Italian, nor was it taught in the schools or universities as a rule; therefore those who studied it usually had a special reason or encouragement. The literary works of German masters were familiar in translation to educated Englishmen almost from the beginning of the century, but philosophy and theology were comparatively neglected. Nevertheless there were tentative links.

In 1813 Mme de Staël published her *De l'Allemagne* in both French and English. She expressed great admiration for German literary and philosophical works (without knowing much about them), and influenced the English Romantic school, including Byron, Southey and Shelley. Her book stimulated translations of the foremost German authors, especially Lessing, Goethe, Schiller and the Schlegel brothers.[9] Henry Crabb Robinson, who had spent several years studying in Germany, also helped to spread an interest in German works among literary circles in England. German imaginative literature was therefore well served by the translators, but philosophical and religious works were not. Kant, one of the most difficult of philosophers, was almost unknown in England, except to a select few, forty years after the publication of the *Critik der reinen Vernunft*. Two admirers published unsatisfactory descriptions of his work at the end of the eighteenth century,[10] but a full-scale translation was not undertaken until F. Haywood made an indifferent attempt at the *Critik* in 1838. There was a certain vogue for Kant among students at the University of Edinburgh early in the century, and the Scottish philosopher Dugald Stewart became interest in him, but Niebuhr noticed on a visit there that he was only imperfectly understood.[11] Scottish theology was somewhat less insular than English, however; as young Scottish Dissenters were debarred from taking a degree at the English universities, it was not uncommon for them to spend some time abroad for study, often in a German university.

A similar obscurity attended the writings of Schleiermacher. Connop Thirlwall translated his essay on St Luke's Gospel in 1825, but the *Reden über die Religion* (1799) and other works, which had been most influential in Germany, were unknown in England. The *Reden* were not translated until 1893, though an interesting biography of Schleiermacher, containing translations of his letters, was produced by Frederica Rowan in 1860. Hegel received only slightly better treatment. A truncated version of the *Logik* (1812–16) appeared in 1855, in the same year that T. C. Sandars produced an abstract of Hegel's ideas on law and right in *Oxford Essays*. In 1857 J. Sibree published a distinguished translation of the *Philosophy of History*, which had been produced by Hegel's pupils from lecture notes after his death in 1831. Sibree's translation went into a second edition in 1861. Lessing's plays were translated abundantly, but not his philosophical works, and when a selection from his tracts in defence of Reimarus appeared, they were under the auspices of an obscure freethinker, who used the occasion to attack the Church of England in a poor imitation of Carlyle. The selections were published in 1862, to add an extra sting to *Essays and Reviews*.[12]

By the middle of the century, the time-lapse between the appearance of an important work in Germany and its translation into English had shortened a little. This happened mainly because there was now a group of scholars outside the Church who were willing to undertake translations in order to win others from orthodoxy. Strauss's *Leben Jesu* first appeared in English in 1842, seven years after its first publication, and, as its anonymous translator stated, this gap was because English publishers feared to contravene the blasphemy laws by taking it up.[13] This first translation, in four cheap and shoddy volumes, was published in Birmingham between 1842 and 1845, and its preface proclaimed the freethinking beliefs and intentions of its translator. Strauss was also available to the working classes at the same time, when Henry Hetherington, the Chartist and publisher of cheap illegal papers for the poor, published it in penny numbers.[14] Hetherington was also a renowned freethinker, and had already fallen foul of the blasphemy laws in 1840. His translation was apparently from a French version.

The leaders of the secularist movement, however, were not usually educated men, and the chief effort to introduce German theology into England came from the freethinking circle which surrounded George Eliot. She herself translated the *Leben Jesu* in 1846, and followed it eight years later with a translation of Feuerbach's *Wesen des Christenthums* (1841), both of which were admirably executed. G. H. Lewes was also deeply interested in German thought, and his *Biographical History of Philosophy* (1846) contained short sketches of Kant, Fichte, Schelling and Hegel. The philosopher R. W. Mackay was particularly interested in the theology of the Tübingen school, and explained the ideas of Baur, of whom no work was translated until 1873. Three of Mackay's major works, *The Progress of the Intellect* (1850), *A Sketch of the Rise and Progress of Christianity* (1854) and *The Tübingen School and its Antecedents* (1863), all showed the pervasive influence of German thought, with which Mackay was well acquainted. He thought the English clergy unlearned and bound by superstitious dogmas, in comparison with the religious freedom allowed to the clergy of Germany. 'We have emancipated the negro', he wrote, 'the Catholic, the trader, the university undergraduate; the clergyman, it is to be feared, must wait for emancipation.'[15]

It should be remembered, however, that a reading of German literature had not been the prime cause of religious doubts among these writers. George Eliot, F. W. Newman and J. A. Froude had all felt strong doubts from an early age about the morality of certain orthodox doctrines, especially those of the eternal punishment of the wicked and the vicarious sacrifice of Christ. A knowledge of German authors had mainly served to confirm their belief that the Scriptures were not an adequate basis for religion. They accepted German speculations because these supported the ideas they had already formulated.[16] Yet because the most famous freethinkers in England encouraged the spread of German literature, the Anglican Church became increasingly suspicious of it, especially as its translators seemed to have ulterior motives.

Certain Dissenters were also interested in German literature, and the Unitarian leaders James Martineau (1805–1900) and J. R. Beard (1800–76) both read German. Beard translated (from the French) A. Saintes's *Critical History of Rationalism in Germany* (1841) in 1849, which, although critical of most German theology, did give an intelligent summary of the chief arguments and maintained that reason was an essential part of religion. Beard also edited a group of anti-Strauss essays by French and German theologians, including the distinguished writers J. A. W. Neander and F. A. G. Tholuck.

Valuable work was also undertaken by two sisters who became well known: Susanna (1820–84) and Catherine Winkworth (1827–78). Although they originally belonged to the Church of England, the two sisters were hardly orthodox. Catherine experienced religious doubts after reading Goethe, but remained within the Anglican communion and was much influenced by the Christian Socialists. Both sisters became friends and protégées of Baron von Bunsen after Catherine met him in 1850, and Catherine's chief work was a translation of his collection of German hymns, some of which became very popular. Susanna was influenced by the Martineaus and moved into Unitarian circles, although James Martineau himself disliked the 'impersonal' idea of God which he thought the Germans inculcated. The sisters were daughters of a silk merchant and lived in Manchester, where there was an intellectual circle gathered around the Unitarian congregation of William Gaskell and J. J. Tayler. This included several German merchants. German works were discussed among them, and through the famous novelist Mrs Gaskell Susanna met many of the foremost literary figures of the time. She said in 1865 that she knew all the famous 'heretics' in England except Jowett. In 1852 she published a translation of the *Life of Niebuhr* by D. Hensler, and in 1856 of Bunsen's *Signs of the Times* (1855–6). Susanna was liberal-minded in religious matters, and was not perturbed by *Essays and Reviews* because she believed that outspoken doubts were better than 'passive latent unbelief'.[17] But she had certain reservations about the kind of work she ought to translate, for she shared the general view that a translator must be identified with the works he chooses. When Bunsen tried to persuade her to translate Kuno Fischer's writings on Bacon's philosophy, she refused firmly.

> I wish, and believe it to be my calling, to work for religion, not by writing myself, but by translating books which I believe to be calculated to promote true religion. Now I shall be identified, and rightly so, with the *general tendencies* of any book I translate. Therefore if I should make a false step and translate anything of whose general tendencies I disapprove, it will be an *irreparable* injury, not to me personally, but to my *usefulness*.[18]

By far the best-known interpreter of German ideas was Thomas Carlyle. He began to learn German in 1819, and developed a strong admiration for Goethe (to whom he wrote adulatory letters), Jean Paul Richter, Kant, Fichte and 'Novalis'.[19] His works contain numerous references to German authors whose ideas he claimed to follow, but in fact he adapted their thoughts to suit his own purposes. Kant's austere concept of a moral law, the 'categorical imperative' which reason could not deny, and his distinction between objects as they appear to the senses and as they are in themselves, especially appealed to Carlyle, and he turned the latter idea into a romantic and mystical concept of a spiritual world behind the visible one. Although Kant had denied that man could ever really know the spiritual world, Carlyle demanded that all men should try to be aware of it and reject materialism. Although he professed to admire German philosophy, he had no time for German universities, where he thought a materialistic scepticism had obscured faith. He described the university attended by his hero Teufelsdröckh as a 'Rational University, in the highest degree hostile to Mysticism'. He continues: 'Thus was the young vacant mind furnished with much talk about Progress of the Species, Dark Ages, Prejudice, and the like; so that all were quickly enough blown into a state of windy argumentativeness; whereby the better sort had soon to end in a sick, impotent Scepticism.'[20] Carlyle's own beliefs were far from orthodox, and he strongly criticised the outworn 'Church clothes', but although staunch Anglicans might accuse him of pantheism, his tone of religious enthusiasm made him generally acceptable as a sage, though his manner was probably more influential than his matter.

For those who could not read German, however, it was difficult to find out at first hand what 'notorious' Germans had actually written. Few publishers seem to have encouraged systematic translations of German philosophy or theology. Susanna Winkworth had some difficulty in publishing her *Life of Niebuhr*, though it was finally accepted by Chapman, who also published George Eliot's translation of Strauss and several translations of Fichte. Publishers' reluctance was probably because there was little demand for German works as textbooks, for at all the universities theological studies, such as they were, relied heavily on Butler and Paley and other English divines of the eighteenth and nineteenth centuries. Most students were recommended to read Mosheim's ecclesiastical history, but this had been written long before the dangerous period of German theology. Significantly, only German works of an orthodox nature were recommended to students; King's College, London, where theological studies were more systematic than at the old universities, recommended the works of Hengstenberg, H. Olshausen, and R. E. Stier, whose devout and orthodox commentaries were all available in English translations. The most dangerous writer on the lists of King's was Neander, whose histories of the primitive Church were suggested, but Neander was a 'mediating' theologian, who was strongly opposed to Strauss, and accepted the miracles of the New Testament.

As late as 1851 Oxford students were not required to read any German theological works except Mosheim and J. C. K. Gieseler's *Compendium of Ecclesiastical History*, though in secular history they did read the works of Neander, Schiller and Schlegel. The philosophy school did not take up Kant or Hegel properly until the time of T. H. Green and F. H. Bradley, later in the century. Most of the textbooks mentioned above were published by the Edinburgh firm of T. & T. Clark, who brought out a special series between 1835 and 1841 called *Clark's Biblical Cabinet*, including some thirty volumes, and reprints of tracts. The *Cabinet* was mainly of Biblical commentaries which were safely orthodox, though it did include philological works by Tholuck, a member of the 'mediating' school who subjected the Bible to careful textual criticism without rejecting its supernatural element. The volumes cost twelve shillings each, which was a reasonable price considering that many of them were very weighty, and there were also short lives of Kant, Niebuhr and Mme de Staël for one shilling. Clark also published a series called the *Foreign Theological Library*, which by 1875 had over one hundred volumes. This contained translations of many substantial but orthodox German works, including six volumes of Olshausen's Biblical commentaries, nine volumes of Neander's works, and three volumes of Hengstenberg. No more 'doubtful' authors were included, and the series was obviously intended for students and clergymen, who could receive four volumes a year if they subscribed a guinea.

Another and even more well-known publisher of German works was H. G. Bohn (1796–1884), son of a German bookseller. Bohn made a fortune, originally by taking advantage of the 'remainder' trade—buying unsold volumes from firms going into liquidation. Bohn began his *Standard Library* in 1846, selling solid little green editions of famous books at a popular price of three and six. During the next ten years he began eight other libraries, including the *Ecclesiastical Library* in 1851 and the *Philological Library* in 1852. By the time he sold the libraries to Bell and Daldy in 1864 they included some six hundred titles.[21] Bohn was a shrewd businessman, not scrupulous in respecting foreign copyright (as indeed few publishers were), and he was able both to commission translations and to acquire the copyright of previous translators through the remainder trade. Bohn was naturally interested in German literature, and usually chose works of lasting interest. A metrical translation of Goethe's *Faust* was still selling a thousand copies a year long after he had sold the libraries.[22] His chief work in translations was to bring the German philosophers before the English reading public at a price which even a penurious clergyman could afford, but he did not publish German theologians except for Neander and the two orthodox commentators, K. Wieseler and F. Bleek. His *Standard Library*, however, did include the major works of the Schlegels, Ranke, Goethe and Schiller, as well as Kant's *Critik*, and so did valuable service in spreading knowledge of German literature.

Many English clergymen who did not read German seem to have depended on Clark and Bohn for knowledge of German literature, and the limitations of these two firms help to explain the ignorance which prevailed. William Goode, one of the most learned of English theologians, knew no German, and his immense library contained only English translations of Bunsen, a few volumes of Clark's translations of orthodox writers, and some general histories attacking German rationalism. Bishop Christopher Sumner collected a hundred volumes of Clark's *Foreign Theological Library*, and, together with one translation of Michaelis's commentaries on Moses, this was all his library knew of German theology.

If actual translations were undertaken erratically, there was also comparatively little interest in English commentaries and reviews of German ideas. On the whole, the more politically conservative a journal was, the less interest it showed in German literature. The *Quarterly Review*, which was the most famous and successful of the serious periodicals, and also a notable bastion of conservative thought, hardly touched on German ideas except to attack them. In 1843 articles were published describing the lack of morality and the unhealthy political excitement among German university students, and the dreadful effect on the female mind of German education, which put too much emphasis on reason and not enough on faith.[23] These illustrated the general attitude of the *Quarterly* towards German ideas. Even Milman, by no means an orthodox clergyman, was alarmed by Strauss, and wrote in the *Quarterly* that he considered it inexpedient to review the *Leben Jesu*. So the *Quarterly* published no review of Strauss's work, though its contributors occasionally glanced at him in passing. After 1865, however, it took more interest in German works because of the threatening political developments in Germany. The *Christian Remembrancer*, the most solid of Church periodicals, published learned reviews of German discoveries in philology, but also produced confused and unfavourable notices of Hegel, Strauss and Feuerbach. On the whole, it reviewed translations rather than works in the original German, and this was true of most of the major periodicals, including the *English Review*, which published slashing attacks on the whole system of German scholarship.

The Whiggish *Edinburgh Review* was less conservative than the *Quarterly*, and took more interest in German literature. Unlike the *Quarterly*, it usually reviewed from the original German editions. It also treated them with more approbation, but in 1849 it published a violent onslaught on German theology, provoked by Froude's *Nemesis of Faith*, which seemed to show the danger of contagion from German ideas. As the clergy were usually inclined to the Tory party, it is less likely that they read the *Edinburgh* than the *Quarterly*. Bishop Wilberforce always wrote for the *Quarterly*, and Stanley (who wrote for the *Edinburgh*) pictured the effect on the country clergy of the bishop's *Quarterly* article on *Essays and Reviews*. 'Meetings of the clergy were held to condemn the book which most of them had never read. Preachers, rising from a Saturday's perusal of the *Quarterly* denounced the writers the next morning from the pulpit as Atheists.'[24]

The Benthamite *Westminster Review* was also sympathetic to German literature, but its circulation did not compare with the two major party quarterlies, and it probably did not attract many of the clergy. It praised Bunsen's *Bibelwerk* in 1858, and was fair to Strauss, though not convinced by him. In 1846 the *Westminster* absorbed the smaller *Foreign Quarterly Review*, which had devoted much space to German works and had received contributions from a regular correspondent in Berlin, though one contributor had remarked that the solid erudition of Germany was more important than its 'metaphysical lumber'.[25] Another quarterly, the *British and Foreign Review*, always had a section for reviews of current German literature, and was opposed to Hengstenberg's orthodox party, but this periodical was not particular successful; it lasted only from 1835 to 1844, leaving the monopoly of foreign literature to the *Westminster*.

Except for the works of Lewes and Mackay, there were few surveys by Englishmen of the development of German philosophy or theology, but a few translations of German surveys were undertaken. Clark published two from the German: F. A. Kahnis's *Internal History of German Protestantism* in 1856 and K. R. Hagenbach's *German Rationalism in its Rise, Progress and Decline* in 1865. These were devoted to explaining the faults and deficiencies of German ideas. Kahnis was a professor of theology at Leipzig, and his work was translated by a Dissenting minister, F. Meyer, who hoped to fight Germanism with Germanism. He had translated Kahnis because Kahnis believed that the works of

Schleiermacher and the other unorthodox theologians had been ephemeral and were no longer followed in Germany. This was not true, as the Tübingen school was flourishing at that time. The book also contained a hostile and distorted picture of the works of the most eminent German philosophers and theologians. Hagenbach's book was less intolerant than Kahnis's, and he recognised the nobility of spirit in great philosophers like Kant, but he too insisted that German rationalism had burned out because it did not satisfy man's spiritual needs. He also blamed the great poets, for he thought Goethe and Schiller showed a dangerous lack of specific religious belief. It was impossible to gain from such books any clear knowledge of the arguments used by German philosophers, yet such were the works on which those who did not understand German would have to rely.

In view of the difficulty in finding out what the Germans had actually said, it is not surprising that a great deal of uninformed criticism was common among the English clergy. The Rev William Cureton, one of the most learned antiquarians on the British Museum staff, wrote in 1853:

> German criticism and German research upon all subjects connected with theology are generally most censured and most reviled by those who are the least acquainted with them. We believe that the indiscriminate condemnation of almost all works of theological research in Germany by some professors and tutors in our universities, and perhaps, indeed, by some of the Bishops of our Church, who are unable to read a line of the original writings, and condemn only from hearsay, or second-hand information, is not only highly unjust, but, in this country, has been, and is, injurious to the cause of impartial research, by which alone truth can be elucidated and upheld.[26]

The first sounds of orthodox alarm were raised in 1825 by the Rev Hugh James Rose, who, in the course of his duties as select preacher to the University of Cambridge, delivered a series of sermons on The state of the Protestant religion in Germany, with the text, 'Thy wisdom and thy knowledge, it hath perverted thee' (*Isaiah*, xlvii. 10). The published sermons produced some stir in theological circles. Rose attributed the new theology of Germany to a vain belief in the power of human reason. 'But when religion is thus placed at the mercy of reason,' he said, 'it is manifest that the first step will be to treat religious matters like any other science within the province of reason.'[27] Another factor, he thought, was the weakness of the German Protestant churches, which did not have the power to control the opinions of their ministers. This should be a warning to the Church of England to guard its Articles and liturgy, and to expect every clergyman to conform to them. Rose was no expert on German affairs; his fears had been roused by a visit in the previous year during his grand tour of Europe, and he did not refer to particular German writers with much knowledge.

Rose was corrected, strangely enough, by Pusey, who had also recently returned from Germany, where he had studied Hebrew under Eichhorn and had met Tholuck, Schleiermacher, Ewald and Strauss. Pusey, then twenty-five and not yet in orders, was much attracted by the great linguistic scholarship of the Germans, and laid the foundations of his own knowledge of Hebrew and oriental languages. He opposed Rose's facile attack on German scholarship, and pointed out the learning and devoutness of many German divines, but he too had been perturbed by Eichhorn's treatment of the Bible as a literary rather than a sacred work. Shortly afterwards his own religious views changed and he withdrew his attack on Rose from circulation, to become himself in later years one of the most implacable enemies of German theology.[28]

From Rose's time until the 1840s there was a series of more or less uninformed criticisms of German literature, mainly in the orthodox periodicals. There was not a great deal of interest, probably because of the scarcity of translations. Even the publication of the *Leben Jesu* in 1835 did not arouse much comment, because most people were unable to read it. The founders of the Oxford Movement looked back to the primitive Church for inspiration, and ignored the German theology of the nineteenth century, which treated the early Church as a product of its age, not necessarily the vehicle of divine truth. Newman, one of the greatest men in the English Church, knew nothing of German, and Mark Pattison, his former disciple, recalled:

> A. P. Stanley once said to me, 'How different the fortunes of the Church of England might have been if Newman had been able to read German.' That puts the matter in a nutshell; New-

man assumed and adored the narrow basis on which Laud had stood 200 years before. All the grand development of human reason, from Aristotle down to Hegel, was a sealed book to him.[29]

During the 1840s, however, as more translations of German theologians appeared, criticism from orthodox churchmen gathered strength, inflamed by the suspicion that members of the Anglican clergy had been seduced by German ideas. The obnoxious work of Strauss at last appeared in English, and provoked several unfavourable reviews and replies. The Unitarian Beard, who edited a collection of anti-Strauss essays in 1845, stated the general fear of the unsettling of religion which such works could cause, even among those least likely to read them.

Even where the *Leben Jesu* was not known, and could not be read, a conviction had prevailed, that some great work had been put forth in Germany, which, as being destructive of the Christian religion, its ministers in England wished to keep from the knowledge of the people and were afraid even to study themselves.[30]

Beard at least discriminated between one German writer and another, but to many who could not read German all German writers were part of the same rationalist movement.

Most churchmen, ignorant of conditions in Germany, seem to have comforted themselves with the thought that rationalism prevailed there because of a feverish and unbalanced quality in the German mind which was alien to English common sense. Many thought of German universities as breeding grounds of atheism, and German scholars were considered among those who knew little of them as pedantic, over-erudite men, blinded by the conceit of their own speculations. The massive works of German scholars, often the products of several decades of research, seemed to prove only the barren and desiccated nature of German thought, divorced from true religious enthusiasm. A little book published in 1844 by E. H. Dewar, chaplain to the English residents in Hamburg, attributed German theology to the anarchy of private judgment in religion; in a Church where every minister was allowed to set himself up as an interpreter of the Bible, it was not surprising that heresies arose. He also thought he saw a general indifference towards religion among the German people, who, he said, were careless about observing Sunday, and he gave an ill-informed description of the ideas of Kant, Hegel and contemporary theologians to explain this. He recalled with relief that the doctrines of the Church of England were clear and defined and could not be tampered with by arrogant priests.[31] In spite of a contradictory work, W. C. Perry's study of German university education (1845), which pointed out the solid virtues of the German educational system,[32] Dewar's attitude towards German ideas seems to have been representative of most orthodox churchmen, and it prejudiced attempts to adopt the professorial system during the period of university reform in the 1850s.

A crucial article reflecting the wild confusion of ideas about German thought appeared in the *English Review* in December of 1848, written by William Palmer, a Fellow of Worcester College and a ritualist. Palmer was one of the first to attack the Broad Churchmen for accepting German ideas. The immediate cause of his article was Julius Hare's *Life of Sterling*—John Sterling, who died in 1844, had been Hare's curate and friend, and had succumbed to religious doubt, influenced by his reading of Strauss. Palmer's review of this book glanced at the corrupting influence of Coleridge and Carlyle, and attacked the circle of which Sterling had been a member, including Arnold, Hare, Maurice, Thirlwall, Bunsen (in Rome), Francis Newman and John Stuart Mill. As Samuel Wilberforce and R. C. Trench, afterwards Archbishop of Dublin, had also known Sterling, they were rather surprisingly dragged into Palmer's collection of Germanists. To Palmer it was clear that the heterodoxy of Sterling and his friends had been produced by reading German literature, and he listed, as the main causes of their fall, Fichte, Schleiermacher, Neander, Olshausen and Strauss, though Palmer evidently could not read German and relied for his opinion of Schleiermacher on what others had told him.[33] The *Record* added fuel to Palmer's fire by pointing out the existence of a 'Sterling Club'—in reality a dining club—to which most of the clergy Palmer had mentioned belonged, together with Stanley and Manning. Although Sterling had played a very minor part in this club, the *Record* contended that it was a den of Straussians; its orthodox members hastily withdrew, and it collapsed.

Hare published a pamphlet to vindicate himself, Sterling and the other accused, especially Maurice, and deplored the misrepresentations of German literature which were common in England. He described the English Church as sheltering behind a dyke which the German ocean was about to overwhelm: 'The rationalizing and infidel Theology of Germany has made its way into England, without Mr. Maurice's aid, and without mine. . . . We cannot build a Chinese wall and shut it out. . . . The very act of building such a wall is a proof of weakness and degeneracy.'[34] Although Hare himself was no admirer of Strauss, he believed that the benefits of German learning could be used to fight German infidelity. He also thought that English common sense would prevent German rationalism from taking root in England, but that a good understanding of Germany was needed, not a profitless denunciation. Nor did he think that the Anglican Church could shelter any longer behind divines of the past, who had no conception of the present difficulties. He cited Thirlwall, then Bishop of St David's, as an example of one who had 'assimilated the elements and products of German speculation and research with the peculiar spirit of the English mind, with our practical, statesmanly judgment'.

Palmer's article was written in a year of revolution, and the same number of the *English Review* included another article entitled 'The German Mind'. This attributed the political upheavals of Germany to rationalistic ideas in religion, leading to a general decline of religious faith. In this decline the 'quiet smears' of Goethe were listed with Kant, Schiller, Neander, Strauss and Feuerbach as the root cause. Only Friedrich Schlegel and the mystic poet Klopstock could be read without danger, the article claimed, revealing the inability of so many English critics to distinguish between German writers of widely different opinions. Many were tempted to make a connection between religious doubt and political insurrection, and Beard wrote in 1849:

> Future historians will probably find reason to state that to the combined influence of Rationalism and Pantheistic Philosophy, which has gone far to blight and uproot the positive religious convictions of France as well as Germany, was in the main to be ascribed the socially and politically destructive storm which has lately swept over the Continent.[35]

Nor was this idea entirely without foundation. Ewald, though not a revolutionary, was associated with political liberalism. Strauss was elected to the Frankfurt Parliament after the revolution of 1848 on a wave of popularity, though completely unfitted to be a politician. In the people's minds he was somehow confused with the general challenge to authority of all kinds. The episode was echoed later in the century, when Ernest Renan, who purveyed German ideas to the French in his *La vie de Jésus*, became a hero of the Third Republic, though not himself a republican.[36]

From the 1840s until the last decades of the century there was an inordinate fear of German theology among many orthodox English churchmen. The alarm persisted in 1849, when Tait, then Dean of Carlisle, had to answer a charge in the *Guardian* that German ideas were being taught at Rugby by some of the masters. Two notorious spiritual autobiographies, Froude's *Nemesis of Faith* (1849) and Francis Newman's *Phases of Faith* (1850), also added to the troubled atmosphere by describing the descent into unbelief of their authors, furthered by a reading of German literature. Henry Rogers in the *Edinburgh Review* consequently deplored the 'intoxicating' effect that a study of German was likely to have on young minds, and advised that young people postpone such reading until maturity.[37]

There were fewer outbursts of alarm in the 1850s, though the Church was disturbed by the Broad Church opinions of Maurice and Jowett. In 1855 the High Church fortnightly periodical the *Literary Churchman* was begun; it was specifically designed to keep clergymen in touch with British and foreign developments in theology. It did review German works, but only to dismiss them out of hand with much scorn. Baur and the Tübingen school were particularly despised. The *Literary Churchman* encouraged the belief that disagreements among German theologians necessarily made nonsense of all their ideas, and rejoiced that Kahnis and Hengstenberg had vindicated the old ways. To clergy who could not read German it gave a distorted and biased picture of German learning. It continued until 1892.

The attitude of the *Literary Churchman* revealed that the ritualist movement was preparing to fight German rationalism using the weapons manufactured by the German 'confessionalist' party. The affinity of Hengstenberg's party with the ritualists in

England has already been mentioned. Some of the Evangelicals were also turning towards Germany, for aid against both ritualism and rationalism, but they naturally looked more towards the revived Evangelical party in Germany rather than the confessionalists. In 1845 English Evangelicals of many denominations had met in Liverpool to consider forming an international alliance against rationalism and 'popery', whether in the form of Rome or Tractarianism. The immediate background of this meeting had been Peel's decision to give government aid to the Roman Catholic college at Maynooth. This had aroused a tremendous protest from both Evangelical Anglicans and Dissenters, many of whom came to London and unsuccessfully tried to put pressure on the government.[38] This event had revealed unsuspected powers of unity to the Evangelicals, and the same men who had formed the backbone of the anti-Maynooth committee now met in Liverpool to form the Evangelical Alliance. The chairman was Sir Culling Eardley,* a wealthy Evangelical Anglican with a passion for religious liberty; another notable figure was Edward Bickersteth, also an Anglican, who was known as a powerful preacher. The Congregationalists were well represented, as this group was the spearhead of the Dissenters against any form of government aid to privileged religious groups. The meeting decided that unity was possible among men of Evangelical views without compromising the ideas of the individual sects; and they drew up nine articles of belief, which included the right of private judgment, and the doctrines of eternal punishment for the wicked and the depravity of man.[39]

In 1846 a much larger meeting was held in London to ratify this agreement. There were over 800 members, with Anglicans, Congregationalists and Wesleyans providing somewhat less than a quarter each; Baptists made up about an eighth, while various Methodist groups and Scottish and Irish Dissenters composed the rest. There were over seventy attenders from the United States, fifteen Germans, nine Frenchmen and seven Swiss, all of various Protestant denominations.[40] The meeting accepted the nine articles, which excluded Unitarians, and declared itself in favour of Evangelical unity. The main debate was concerned

* Sir Culling Eardley Smith (1805–63), took the name of Eardley in 1847.

with the rights of slave-holders to membership of the Alliance, but the meeting finally declared itself against slavery, in spite of objections from the American group. The European members took little part in the proceedings. Although founded on principles of hostility to rationalism and popery, the Alliance succeeded mainly because of its devotional spirit; fervent prayers were raised and edifying speeches delivered which were 'evangelical' in the widest religious sense. The members were uplifted by the experience, and left to conduct their own local meetings.

The first links with Germany were tenuous, although the Alliance did take root there. In 1847 the monthly periodical *Evangelical Christendom* was begun, which purported to give news of religious developments in other countries. Every number had articles from correspondents in France, Prussia, Austria and other parts of Europe, the Middle East and the mission fields. Although its circulation was not large, it did provide a friendly summary of events in Germany, although it was uncompromisingly hostile to both Hengstenberg and the Tübingen school.

In 1857 a more direct link with Germany was made when the annual conference of the Alliance was held in Berlin. By then it was in favour with the English episcopacy, as many of the bishops were of the Evangelical tendency favoured by Palmerston. In Germany, Bunsen supported the conference, and Frederick William IV himself attended several of its meetings. Again, there was not much practical discussion; the real work of the Alliance was to press for religious freedom (including freedom for Catholics and Jews) in those countries where there was still religious discrimination. But the devotional spirit of the conference inspired the English members to seek a closer contact with Germany. A corresponding committee was set up to exchange news of theological developments with German evangelical theologians like W. A. Dorner, and the correspondence was printed in *Evangelical Christendom*. Usually, however, it was superficial and perfunctory.

The aim of the Evangelical Alliance at this time was to use orthodox German theologians to fight German rationalism, which seemed to be influencing a whole school of English writers. But the letters of the Evangelical Germans and the comments of the editors of *Evangelical Christendom*, although they helped to break down the belief that the whole of Germany was riddled with infidelity, merely bolstered up English readers in the comfortable belief that, even in Germany, rationalism had been annihilated by superior argument.[41] The conclusions of Baur were paraded with scorn, not argument, and the safety of his soul was questioned by the editors. The Alliance broke down some Evangelical prejudice against Germany, but reinforced it in other directions.

There was one other striking example of a clergyman with a literal belief in the Bible using German criticism to fight German infidelity and the Broad Church. In 1858, Henry Longueville Mansel, then a reader in moral and metaphysical philosophy at Oxford, and later Milman's successor as Dean of St Paul's, delivered his Bampton lectures. These were entitled *The Limits of Religious Thought*. Mansel, a High Churchman but not a ritualist, was well acquainted with Kant, and lectured on his philosophy in Oxford; according to Pattison he was the first to do so.[42] Mansel accepted from Kant that pure reason could not conceive of God through logical deduction, but used this idea as a springboard to show the necessity of revelation. The Broad Churchmen had gone on from Kant's premise to contend that man could recognise God's nature through his own divinely-given sense of morality, and that his moral sense enabled him to separate the necessary from the unnecessary parts of the Biblical revelation. Mansel, while accepting that this moral sense did exist, maintained that no human moral system could reveal the attributes of God. God's essence was unknowable to human perceptions, and human morality was only a pale shadow of divine morality, which could comprehend facts like the worldly success of evil men and the sufferings of the innocent; mere human morality could not understand them. The Biblical revelation did not show the essence of God, which was infinite and incomprehensible, but it was couched in the simple language which the minds of men could receive. This left Mansel with the task of explaining why the Christian revelation should be the only true one, and he had to fall back on the usual 'evidences', which included miracles.[43] Some High Churchmen like Burgon thought that Mansel's lectures had provided the ultimate answer to the Broad Church, but other churchmen of all shades of opinion were dissatisfied with them. They could not accept that a personal intuition of God was impossible, and Maurice, who was particularly certain of his own intuition, attacked Mansel bitterly.

The publication of *Essays and Reviews* in 1860 brought fears of German theology into the open again. The essayists seemed to have assimilated the thought of Germany, and to be demanding the same freedom of opinion as German pastors like Schleiermacher and Strauss. Wilberforce denounced the *Essays* as 'trains of German doubts' intended to blow up the Church, and wrote:

> What then we really have to deal with is not an unbiased criticism threatening Christianity, and compelling us in self-defence to occupy some new position, but the almost passive adoption by our own countrymen of weapons forged in the workshops of German criticism against the faith, and seized by these new assailants with such a blind greediness that they often come to the attack with weapons which have been already shattered upon German battle-fields of theological discussion.[44]

Wilberforce shared the hopeful High Church view that the school of Hengstenberg had routed the critical scholars.

For many of the clergy *Essays and Reviews* was their first introduction to the conclusions of German scholarship, and they reacted with horror. Even Stanley, to whom the book's ideas were not new, thought that Rowland Williams's essay on Bunsen was too precipitate, and that it took for granted German ideas that were new to English clergy. Stanley wrote in the *Edinburgh*: 'Conclusions arrived at by the life-long labours of a great German theologian are pitchforked into the face of the English public, who never heard of them before, with hardly a shred of argument to clothe their repulsive forms.'[45]

Hostility towards German scholars demonstrated itself in a practical way when, in 1860, just as the outcry against *Essays and Reviews* was mounting, the newly-created chair of Sanskrit at Oxford required an occupant. The election to the chair was contested by F. Max Müller, the Professor of Modern European Languages and a distinguished Sanskrit scholar, and also by M. Monier Williams, whose scholastic claims were not as great, but who was an orthodox churchman. Max Müller had not written any unorthodox works himself, but he was a German scholar and a friend of Bunsen and Broad Churchmen, and therefore suspect. The MAs, including many country clergy, came up on 7 December to vote in Convocation, and Max Müller was defeated by 833 votes to 610. According to Stanley, Pusey and others also took advantage of the gathering to begin the first organised protest against the essayists, and to petition Archbishop Sumner to act against them. A few years later Colenso, who had also been influenced by German theologians, was to cause a similar outcry. But were the Broad Churchmen really the complete Germanists that the orthodox imagined?

Notes to this chapter are on pages 248–9

Chapter 3 GERMANY AND THE BROAD CHURCH

THERE IS no doubt that the Broad Churchmen were cut off from the more orthodox sections of the Church by their knowledge of German thought, but they differed greatly amongst themselves in their response to it. In most cases an interest in Germany had been fostered by an early reading of the religious works of Samuel Taylor Coleridge. Coleridge occupied the place in English theology which Schleiermacher had in Germany because he tried to counter the assaults of the Bible critics by pointing out that the basis of religion was an internal, not an external revelation. Just as Schleiermacher tried to justify religion by claiming an innate human sense of dependence on God, Coleridge believed that the proof of Christianity lay in its appeal to man's moral sense and the way it satisfied his spiritual needs. He wrote: 'The truth revealed through Christ has its evidence in itself, and the proof of its divine authority in its fitness to our nature and needs; the clearness and cogency of the proof being proportionate to the degree of self knowledge in each individual hearer.'[1]

Coleridge accepted a Kantian idea of the internal 'moral law' upon which religion was based; orthodox churchmen, of course, believed that morality arose from religion as revealed in the Scriptures. But Coleridge confused the moral law in Kant's sense with intuitive faith in a personal God. From Kant's writing it would be impossible to conceive of a God with any attributes except severe moral justice, but Coleridge adapted Kant's idea of the practical reason into an idea of the inward knowledge which allows man to communicate directly with God. One of his chief concerns was to explain that reason need not contradict revelation because their origins were different; like Kant, he divided the mind's power into two, which he called 'reason' and 'understanding'. 'Understanding', like Kant's pure reason, was the power to deal logically with sensual experience, while 'reason' was the 'eye of the mind', which discerned spiritual truths by its own power.[2] From this point of view the Bible was invulnerable to critical attacks because its value lay in its spiritual, not its literal truth. Coleridge attacked 'Bibliolaters' who put a literal belief in the Bible in front of morality; for he said that such a course led them to defend, as divinely commanded, immoral episodes like Jael's murder of Sisera, which were irrelevant to faith. He wrote in *Aids to Reflection*: '. . . all Revealed Truths are to be judged of by us, as far as they are possible subjects of human conception, or grounds of practice, or in some way connected with our moral and spiritual interests.'[3] On the other hand, no historical or scientific criticism could dispel the moral example of the miracles performed by Jesus, and so it was permissible to subject the Bible to criticism 'like any other book' without threatening the sources of faith. His whole aim was to provide a 'safety lamp' for religious inquirers, so that they might approach their task with the feeling that their faith was secure.

Coleridge's works, *Aids to Reflection* (1825) and the posthumously-published *Confessions of an Inquiring Spirit* (1840), were widely read among young students and particularly influenced the Broad Churchmen, who, although they criticised Coleridge's lack of coherence and his inability to construct a consistent philosophy, nevertheless owed him a great deal.[4] Arnold, Julius Hare and Maurice reveal his influence in most of their writings, and Hare even imitated his aphoristic style in a youthful work *Guesses at Truth*, which he wrote with his brother Augustus and published in 1827. Carlyle, whose dislike of Coleridge was perhaps tinged with jealousy at the popularity of the rival sage, remarked on the widespread belief that Coleridge alone held the key to German 'transcendentalism'.[5] Young men admired the devotional tone of Coleridge's writings, and for this reason he inspired men as diverse as Temple, Williams, Wilson and Archbishop Thomson. Thomson approved Coleridge's piety, not his ideas about the Bible.

The relationship between the German theologians and the Broad Church was embodied particularly in one man; Christian Carl Josias, Baron von Bunsen (1791–1860). Broad Churchmen of two generations, from Thirlwall in Rome in 1819 at the beginning of Bunsen's career, to Williams in Heidelberg in 1857 at the end of it, made pilgrimages to him. Bunsen was a protégé of Niebuhr, and succeeded him as head of the Prussian legation in Rome; he married an Englishwoman and was in high favour with Frederick William IV, who appointed him to negotiate between Prussia and England on the question of the Jerusalem bishopric in 1841. Bunsen's charm and capabilities made him extremely popular, and he was made Ambassador to Queen Victoria. He lived mainly in England from 1842 until 1854. He resigned after a difference with Frederick William over Prussia's refusal to participate in the Crimean War, and left diplomacy to concentrate on his Biblical studies. He was greatly interested in ecclesiastical history, and wrote a massive *Bibelwerk* in 1858. This was a commentary on the Bible, and formed the subject of Rowland Williams's contribution to *Essays and Reviews*. Other major works were also available in English, translated with the aid of Susanna Winkworth.[6]

In his younger days Bunsen had sat at the feet of Niebuhr and Schleiermacher; from the former he derived critical methods which he applied to ecclesiastical history, from the latter a devout sense of the importance of religion in everyday life. He was an erudite scholar, particularly interested in Hebrew, Arabic and Persian, and was well acquainted with the literary development of his own country. He was drawn to Hegel, but opposed the Tübingen school and Strauss, whose doubts as to the accuracy of the New Testament far exceeded his own. Their ideas would die away, he predicted, leaving the combination of devout religion and rational argument which he believed would save the Christian churches.[7] As a fervent Evangelical Lutheran, he believed that the congregation was more important to religious life than the priest—a view directly opposed to that of the Oxford Movement—and he described the Bible as the voice of the congregation. In repeating this view, Rowland Williams fell foul of the ecclesiastical courts. In his theology Bunsen was of the German 'mediating' school, equally opposed to orthodoxy and to Strauss, and he thought some parts of the Bible were more inspired than others.

Among the Broad Churchmen, Arnold, Thirlwall, Julius Hare and Maurice visited Bunsen in Rome or Switzerland, where he moved in learned and distinguished circles. He corresponded frequently with Arnold and Hare on matters of learning and religion, sharing their desire for a Church which would include all Christian believers, and he saw them often in England, where he had a house near Hare's at Hurstmonceux. Through Arnold he met Stanley, who brought Jowett to see him in Berlin in 1844, and he introduced them to Neander. Williams sent Bunsen a copy of his book *Christianity and Hinduism* and Bunsen was delighted to find that their ideas were similar; they began a correspondence in which Bunsen amiably signed himself 'yours in Platone and in Christo', admiring Williams's courage for producing such a work in England. 'I know well', he wrote, 'how rare that virtue is in England, the land of domestic self-devotion; of civil and political courage, but of religious cowardice.'[8] Pattison offered to translate Bunsen's *God in History* (1857–8) when Susanna Winkworth doubted her competence to do so. She did undertake it after Bunsen's death. Bunsen shared the notion common to most Broad Churchmen that the nineteenth century was a time of religious upheaval akin to the seventeenth, and that most of the European Churches were making a desperate attempt to save orthodox belief by imposing various forms of ecclesiastical despotism and fettering religious inquiry. He also hoped for a second Reformation, which would sweep away all priestly despotism.

While Bunsen lived, most orthodox English Churchmen made a polite distinction between his person and his ideas. He was in great favour at Court, and mingled with churchmen of all parties. Stanley recollected after Bunsen's death: 'How often does one remember, with something of almost incredulous wonder, the time when this oracle of Christian learning, learned in all the wisdom of Germany, was heard, without offence, by prelates and by the religious world, both at Lambeth and at Exeter Hall.'[9] The ritualists disapproved of his opinions, but he was not subjected to any major attacks in his lifetime and was on amicable terms with Pusey. The English world accepted the man and disregarded his theology. He died in the year *Essays and Reviews* was published, and while his deathbed was an edifying example of Christian resignation and his personal qualities were highly acclaimed, the public was reminded by Williams's essay that Bunsen had doubted whether the Scriptures were divinely inspired throughout. There were various attacks on these opinions in the general onslaught on *Essays and Reviews*, but critics tried to preserve a distinction. 'The truth was', said Henry John Rose, 'Bunsen was better than his principles; he was not in flesh and blood what he was upon paper.'[10]

The Evangelical Alliance, which remembered with affection Bunsen's support at its conference in Berlin, passed a resolution of sympathy with his family on the death of the 'distinguished Christian statesman'. This provoked a characteristically vindictive protest from the *Record*, which deplored Bunsen's theology. The *Record* also published a letter from Thomas Birks, son-in-law of Edward Bickersteth, and a secretary of the Alliance, who had not been present when the resolution was passed. Birks had just read Bunsen's *Egypt's Place in Universal History*, which questioned the truth of the Pentateuch and which he described as 'the most mischievous attack on orthodox Christianity . . . which has appeared in the literary world for the last thirty years'.[11] The committee of the Evangelical Alliance was thrown into confusion, and the editors of *Evangelical Christendom* defended its members by publishing a detailed description of Bunsen's deathbed, with his last pious ejaculations. Sir Culling Eardley, who was at first disposed to be angry with Birks, then read Williams's essay and became alarmed at its interpretation of Bunsen. The committee finally withdrew the words 'distinguished Christian statesman', though the editors continued to maintain their belief in Bunsen's salvation. This morbid controversy at least revealed the ignorance of Bunsen's work among several leading members of the Evangelical Alliance, but to their credit their regard for Bunsen as a man overwhelmed their suspicions of his orthodoxy.

The same double standard was applied to Ewald, who made himself a popular figure in 1837 by being discharged from the University of Göttingen with six other professors for their protest against Ernest Augustus's repudiation of the 1833 constitution of Hanover. Ewald was well received on his visits to England because of his political liberalism, and the English Church separated his political from his religious views. Fortunately, perhaps, he was not as well known in translation as Bunsen was, for nothing except his Hebrew grammar was available before 1864.

The Broad Churchmen approached their German studies in different frames of mind. Coleridge first planted the German seed in the mind of his disciple Julius Hare, who encouraged Thirlwall and Arnold to learn German also. Both these men wished to read Niebuhr in the original, for they were themselves historians and discovered much from him about historical method. Tait, Stanley, Jowett and Temple all learned German as young men when they were most under the influence of Coleridge, and all spent some time visiting Germany. Pattison and Williams, who were scholars by nature, also learned as students, though Pattison did not take up German studies seriously until after he broke with the Oxford Movement. Hare and Arnold admired Niebuhr greatly, but were critical of the unorthodox theologians. Hare considered that a study of German theology had liberated him from the fear that any rational inquiry into religious matters must necessarily lead to a loss of faith, and wrote in 1820:

> To them [the German theologians] I owe my ability to believe in Christianity with a much more implicit and intelligent faith than I otherwise should have done; for without them I should only have saved myself from dreary suspicions by a refusal to allow my heart to follow my head, and by a self-willed determination to believe whether my reason approved of my belief or not.[12]

Hare kept busts of Bunsen, Schleiermacher and Niebuhr in his archdeaconry; possibly the only one in England to be so decorated. German writers like Schleiermacher, who found the source of faith in an internal revelation, were fascinating to young men who admired Coleridge and who could read German biblical criticism without feeling that their religion was being undermined. They did distinguish, however, between those German theologians who merely sorted out textual difficulties in the Bible and those who tried to alter the whole interpretation of the

Scriptures. None of the Broad Churchmen accepted Strauss; Arnold thought him deficient in learning, and Sterling, the only one of the group influenced by Strauss, moved away from the Church altogether. Hare deplored the effect that Strauss had on his friend's mind, and Baden Powell dismissed Strauss's whole theory as utterly implausible.[13]

Thirwall's relationship with Germany was much more scholarly and less fervent than Hare's, for his religion was not of the enthusiastic kind. Niebuhr was his ideal of learning and erudition, and the work of Schleiermacher which he chose to translate was not one of the impassioned treatises like the *Reden*, which really accounted for Schleiermacher's popularity in Germany. On taking orders, Thirlwall drew further away from German ideas, though he still admired German scholarships. In 1828 and 1831 he and Hare published translations of the first two volumes of Niebuhr's *History of Rome*, which were much admired although the *Quarterly Review* stated that it was unwise to translate any such work because of Niebuhr's unorthodoxy. Thirlwall rejected most of the philosophy of Germany which came after Niebuhr and Schleiermacher, especially that of Hegel, whom he described as 'the most impudent of all literary quacks'.[14] By 1857 he was completely disenchanted with German literature, and his own dislike of dogmatic enthusiasms, whether orthodox or not, made him suspicious of Germany, where scholars wrangled incessantly over their own particular opinions. Thirlwall thought that younger men like Rowland Williams were too confident of the benefits of German theology, for, he said, his own experience of it had led him to treat it with caution and reserve.[15]

The same mixture of interest and suspicion is seen in Tait, Temple, Maurice and Stanley. Tait and Temple were the least affected by German ideas, which perhaps explains why they were received back among the orthodox. Tait visited Germany as a young man and enjoyed reading Ranke and Lessing, but his career swept him away from scholarship to practical duties. His friends hoped that his mind was not entirely closed to common sense about Germany, and in 1861 Stanley asked Ewald, who was then in England, to send a commentary to Tait, explaining that Germany was not as committed to infidelity as orthodox clergymen believed. Tait, however, dissociated himself from his former pupils when he signed the bishops' condemnation of *Essays and Reviews,* though he opposed any attempts to prosecute the writers.

Temple himself was not committed to unorthodox ideas; his essay had merely suggested that the Old Testament was not a perfect guide for nineteenth-century Christians. He had read Kant and Hegel with Jowett, but, like other Broad Churchmen, had assimilated German ideas in a form which suited him. He had adapted Kant's idea of the 'categorical imperative' into an evangelical belief in Christian duty and hard work. Whereas Kant had doubted whether moral duty could ever be anything but an abstract concept, Temple interpreted the 'categorical imperative' as the voice of conscience, which was man's direct link with God, and obedience to which was true freedom.[16] Temple's essay *The Education of the World* adopted the theory which was becoming common among the 'Liberal Anglican' school, that the human race was gradually developing its moral faculties towards perfection. In contrast to the theories of G. R. Porter and other nineteenth-century political economists, Temple stressed the spiritual rather than the material progress of man. The inference from this idea was that a religion which was suited to a primitive Jewish tribe could not be satisfactory in every detail for the nineteenth century. Such a theory of development was directly derived from Lessing's *Die Erziehung des Menschengeschlechts* (1780), and was to be found in various forms in Herder, Hegel, and the English historian H. T. Buckle, though Hegel substituted it for Christianity in a way abhorrent to Temple and the other Broad Churchmen.

The Broad Church saw the hand of Providence behind all historical events, for man could only develop with the guidance of God. (Evolution could also be made to fit into this scheme.) Temple was a great headmaster, who followed directly in the steps of Arnold; he told his boys that the duty of their time was to substitute education for ecclesiastical despotism, for only in an educated community was private judgment in religion possible. He taught them that the sense of duty was the highest kind of freedom—thus Rugby imbibed Christianised Kant—and that the Bible contained God's message to man, though not any particular set of dogmas. All this was Germanic in origin, with strong modifications on the lines of Coleridge and Arnold, but Temple, like Tait, was essentially a practical man and never made any specific criticism of the Bible.

Maurice, too, read German with great caution. He would not condemn German theology, but thought that England and Germany must grow in different ways; Schleiermacher and Bunsen suited the German temperament, but were not right for England.[17] Maurice was the least doctrinaire of the Broad Churchmen, and he tended to decry all theological systems which he thought came between men and a personal sense of devotion. He ridiculed Wilberforce's faith in the power of Hengstenberg's orthodox school to rout rationalism in Germany, for he said that neither Hengstenberg nor any other theologian could save England from rationalism if men lacked a sense of inner conviction. He looked for spiritual regeneration rather than doctrinal revision.

Stanley also avoided disputes on Biblical questions, though he thought that the German critics performed valuable service by cutting away the 'dead wood' of dogma and revealing the true spiritual value of the Scriptures.[18] His *History of the Jewish Church* (1862) relied a great deal on Ewald, but he did not indulge in speculations about the authorship of the first five books of the Bible. His descriptions from personal experience of life in the Middle East were well received, but *Evangelical Christendom* reported that he was not orthodox in his ideas about the divine inspiration of the Scriptures, though he did not fall into the German error of treating them as myth. The article continued:

> It may suit the fancy of some German professor . . . to see a myth here, and a legend there, and so piece and patch the Bible narrative according to some preconceived theory of his own. But Canon Stanley can use the German critics without giving up that roundabout common sense which is the distinguishing mark of the English intellect.[19]

What Stanley seems to have admired most about the Germans, judging from his own actions, was the freedom of their pastors to criticise as they chose, and he spent much energy in demanding a relaxation of the terms of clerical subscription, so that the clergy should not be subjected to any process of uniformity.

Of the younger Broad Churchmen, Jowett, Williams and Pattison were the most influenced by German ideas, and most capable, intellectually, of digesting them. Jowett's contribution to *Essays and Reviews* was particularly frightening to the orthodox churchman because it accepted without question that many German criticisms of Biblical miracles and prophecies were indisputable, and he proceeded to argue that even if these traditional evidences of Christianity were removed, the Christian religion would be unharmed because of its moral value. Like Hare, he thought that the English Church and the universities were 'living behind the dykes', trying to ignore the roaring of the German ocean.[20] He believed that German ideas could not be kept out by force, and that only a broadening of the university curriculum could train the Church to cope with them. Jowett, unlike the older Broad Churchmen, was impressed by Hegel, but he never produced a systematic theological work of his own. His most 'Germanic' works were the commentary on St Paul and his contribution to *Essays and Reviews*, but after that he renounced controversy and retired to classical studies. It was left for later men to introduce German philosophy into Oxford. An unkind critic, Leslie Stephen, maintained that Hegel only served to befuddle Jowett's thought, and that he would never really commit himself on such matters as the literal and metaphorical interpretations of the Bible; he seemed to accept both as a kind of dialectic in which opposites existed simultaneously.[21] Jowett and other Broad Churchmen would have argued that such a committal was unnecessary as long as the spiritual message of the Scriptures was accepted, but such an answer did not satisfy those like Stephen who wanted to know whether the miracles of the Bible were literally true or not.

Williams read much German theology, and admired Niebuhr, Neander, Lessing, Schleiermacher and Hegel, as well as less radical writers like Tholuck and Stier, but his ideas will be discussed in more detail in the next chapter. He was, however, an erudite Broad Churchman and commanded respect from Bunsen and Ewald. Pattison also had a more extensive knowledge of Germany than most English scholars. He read widely, and after 1855 when he temporarily left Lincoln College he spent much of his time in Germany. He was correspondent for *The Times* in

Berlin for a short period, and in 1859 reported on German education to the Royal Commission on popular education. In 1857 he published in the *Westminster Review* an article entitled 'The Present State of Theology in Germany', which presented a well-balanced and informed view of the subject.

Whereas most orthodox critics thought that German theologians were divided merely into orthodox and infidel, Pattison rightly pointed out that there were several schools of theology, and distinguished the orthodox school of Hengstenberg, the 'mediating' school of Schleiermacher's followers, and the 'historico-critical' school of Baur. He rejected the first two schools because he opposed Hengstenberg's rigid and backward looking Lutheranism, and thought him a lackey of the Prussian government; the 'mediating' school was also at fault because it put emotional religion before critical scholarship and this was foreign to Pattison's nature. He criticised the Tübingen school because it was given to over-speculation, but thought that its methods of scholarship were basically sound and that it would eventually triumph over the others. Pattison did not admire Strauss, but thought that his failings had caused a reaction in favour of more careful scholarship among the Tübingen school and this was beneficial to theology. He argued that German theology was not, as the orthodox thought, a transient phase which was already in the process of destruction, but in the direct tradition of European thought which led from the Reformation. Only the Germans had the knowledge which would preserve Christianity from the attacks of science. Pattison's essay was characteristic of him; learned, detached and hostile to religious enthusiasm, whether orthodox or unorthodox. In this he differed from the devout Coleridgeans among the Broad Churchmen, like Hare, Maurice and Williams, who tended to favour the 'mediating' school because of its devotional tone.

From this survey it may be seen that there were certain assumptions about religion, derived ultimately from German sources, which kept the otherwise dissimilar Broad Churchmen together in defiance of orthodoxy. The first, from which all others led, was a belief in the value of private judgment in religion, especially the right of a clergyman to some freedom of opinion, as in the German Protestant Churches. The second was the belief that the traditional evidences of Christianity, particularly miracles and prophecies, the proofs on which the eighteenth-century divines had relied, were no longer sufficient, and that they must be replaced by a faith based on moral principles. From Kant and Coleridge the Broad Churchmen accepted the belief that man was possessed of an innate sense of moral justice, which he realised in the course of his education and through which he was able to judge revealed religion. Lessing, Coleridge and Bunsen taught them that Christianity survived because it was moral, not because Christ had been able to work miracles; they tended to avoid the question of whether He actually *had* worked the miracles or not. The Broad Churchmen were all concerned with education in some way themselves, and believed that man's faculties were being slowly developed by education which would lead to natural changes in his religion. Miracles were part of a childish age which had needed a sense of magic for the proofs of its religion, but educated men of the nineteenth century needed only to read the Bible to see that miracles were far less important than the spiritual message of Christ. Therefore they could pursue critical studies without fear of losing their faith.

This, then, was the 'Germanism' which identified the Broad Church in the eyes of their orthodox opponents, but it can easily be exaggerated, for in many ideas the Broad Churchmen were completely alien from Germany. Their German was largely self-taught, improved by continental tours which were mainly devoted to sight-seeing. Except for Pattison, their lives were not devoted to scholarship, for, as Pattison pointed out regretfully, the 'scholar divine' was no longer a part of the English Church now that cathedral revenues were not used to foster learning. Nearly all the Broad Churchmen were scholarly amateurs when compared with Niebuhr, de Wette or Ewald, and they all had manifold duties to distract them from learning. Perhaps for this reason the Broad Church did not produce a really great theologian, although it attracted so many gifted men. The universities which produced them did not have the philological studies in which German universities excelled, and there was not the sense of competition among a scholarly community which existed in Germany and moved, in the course of the century, from Berlin to Göttingen to Tübingen. The backbone of the English clergyman's education was classical, and the paths of Plato and Aristotle were clear to him, whereas Kant and Hegel were unexplored jungles through which there were no guides. None of the Broad Churchmen seem to have really understood Kant, from whom, through Coleridge, much of their own attitude had come. Hare even rejected the 'categorical imperative', which was not a Christian idea, as a sign that Kant's mind had decayed,[22] and yet his own ideas were based on the Coleridgean view of the moral law within each man.

The Broad Churchmen thought that they could accept the researches of German scholars and yet ignore many of their conclusions. Like their orthodox opponents, they distinguished between the 'fancifulness' of speculative writers like Strauss and Baur, and the 'solid' scholarship of de Wette and Ewald. They also believed that sound English common sense would reject all the illogical conclusions to which the German mind was prone.[23] Although the Broad Churchmen wished to encourage freedom of inquiry and the use of common sense in religion, in order to preserve the faith of the educated, they seem to have been thwarted because they did not accept some of the implications of their arguments. The criticism which Temple made of Tait, that he led his pupils into critical inquiry and then drew back from their conclusions, applies equally to most of the Broad Churchmen. They implied that certain parts of the Bible had no moral value, yet they would not name these parts, except for a few instances. Their ideas remained generalised and they would not descend to details. Arnold and Bunsen devised a plan to review all the prophecies in the Bible and show the true value of each, but they never realised it. The works of Coleridge and Bunsen, which were so influential, were also ambivalent in the same way. They never stated roundly whether they believed in miracles as a physical fact, but preferred to notice the existence of a difficulty and then explain it away by emphasising the moral issues. The Broad Churchmen would not cast the old props of Christianity completely aside in their search for new ones. Only Baden Powell, the scientist, came close to denying that miracles had actually occurred;[24] the others tried to evade the difficulties that would arise from such a denial by concentrating on the moral aspect of miracles. When it came to the point, neither Bunsen nor the Broad Churchmen would deny the supernatural elements in the Bible. Even Rowland Williams, who was considered one of the most radical Broad Churchmen, was not prepared to admit that much of the Old Testament might not be historically accurate, and wrote to Colenso that more history was preserved in Genesis than the heterodox bishop thought. Williams admitted that he himself drew back from such a conclusion:

> . . . if I pause on what, so soon as the *principle* of criticism is admitted (as I do admit it), is but the threshold of more advanced views, it may be so partly from old associations and from the duties of an office which inclined, if it did not compel, me to err, if at all, upon the side of caution and reserve, rather than rashness.[25]

Essays and Reviews was the definitive voice of the Broad Church, for even Colenso produced nothing which went beyond it. It was also the last theological work of most of the essayists, who were soured by controversy and turned themselves to less arguable subjects, except for Williams and Wilson, who continued to produce variations on the same theme. It is difficult to estimate the influence of the Broad Churchmen on the students of the day, who were the ones they most hoped to attract. Many of them were men of strong personality, who won admiration from their scholars. Of the second generation of Broad Churchmen, who felt the dangers of educated alienation from the Church more strongly, Maurice, Temple, Jowett, Williams and Wilson all had their disciples among a new generation of clergymen. Maurice, Temple and Williams also had a fervent attitude to religion which was most attractive to young men, and they inspired by their example. They relied on their own unshakeable faith to save them from any doubts arising from their studies, but did not realise that this personal and emotional sense of faith might be denied to others. The somewhat vague belief in 'innate moral principles' did not satisfy those who questioned the Broad Church view of morality. John Stuart Mill was particularly concerned to attack the 'intuitive' school of philosophy, and maintained that moral principles were not innate or unchangeable, but were a product of social conditions and were derived from practical experience. He wrote in his *Autobiography*:

> The notion that truths external to the mind may be known by intuition or consciousness, independently of observation and experience, is, I am persuaded, in these times, the great intellectual support of false doctrines and bad institutions. By the aid of this theory, every inveterate belief and every intense feeling, of which the origin is not remembered, is enabled to dispense with the obligation of justifying itself by reason, and is erected into its own all-sufficient voucher and justification.[26]

Frederic Harrison, who finally accepted the Positivist idea of a 'religion of humanity', attended Maurice's lectures but found in them only confusion. Maurice was aware of the rational obstacles to belief in miracles and other doctrines, but he could find no explanation for them save that Christianity was mysterious. To Harrison, Maurice seemed to teach only that we should 'hug our fetters, and revel in our darkness'.[27] Two other clergymen, C. Kegan Paul and Leslie Stephen, found that the Broad Church could not satisfy them for long, and they departed; Kegan Paul through positivism to Rome, and Stephen to agnosticism. Kegan Paul was not content to believe in a system which began in criticism and ended in mystery, and finally decided that Rome provided the only authoritative answer to religious doubt.[28] Leslie Stephen, although he thought that: '. . . whatever claims are still possessed by the Church of England to the allegiance of thinking men are due to the Broad Church element among the clergy,'[29] criticised the Broad Churchmen for not proceeding to logical conclusions. None of them, he wrote, were prepared to reject any traditional dogmas, but only to explain them away or to find less harsh meanings in phrases like 'eternal punishment'. Although Stephen was unfair to the Broad Churchmen in implying that they retained certain doctrines, such as hell, for social convenience, there was nevertheless some truth in his argument. They hesitated between a literal and metaphorical interpretation of the Scriptures, and could never decide for one or the other. Yet they were the first to bring the Anglican Church of the nineteenth century out of its insularity, and to seek for a compromise which should save Christianity from the steady and imperturbable attacks of science and history. In the process they caused profound disruption in the Church, but their ideas have been most influential in shaping the belief of many modern Christians.

Notes to this chapter are on pages 250–51

Chapter 4 ROWLAND WILLIAMS

ROWLAND WILLIAMS was not the most distinguished Broad Churchman. In intellectual qualities he was not equal to Jowett or Pattison; in practical piety he resembled, but did not match, Maurice. His numerous works are now almost forgotten, for they are not particularly original and are cumbered by a turgid style. His life did not differ markedly from that of any High Church clergyman of the best type; he neglected no duties as a teacher or as a country parson, he was politically conservative, observed a moderate High Church ritual in his church, and believed all his life that State-run social services were iniquitous because no charity was holy unless it came from voluntary enterprise. Yet this ordinary clergyman came to be considered a dangerous radical because of his intellectual curiosity and his desire to bring the teaching of the Church into line with the developments of nineteenth-century thought. He was a good example of a new spirit in the Church, in spite of his personal weaknesses, as an admirer wrote after his death:

> Dr Rowland Williams may indeed claim a high place among the representative men of our time; sharing to a considerable extent its liberal tendencies, occupied continually in the religious questions which are now so keenly discussed among thoughtful men . . . an eminent type and product of the Liberal, inquiring, progressive religious movement of our day.[1]

That such a storm could gather around the heads of two such pious, learned, and essentially conservative men as Williams and Wilson is indicative of the precarious temper of the Church in the mid-nineteenth century, split by party schism and threatened by rationalism and disestablishment. The ideas of Williams and other Broad Churchmen seemed only to indicate that the Church's greatest danger was internal; so indeed it was, not because of Broad Church ideas, but because of party hostilities which existed among Broad Churchmen as well as orthodox ones, and which helped to blind them all to the fact that every year it was becoming more difficult to win back the working classes to the Church. All parties had violent members who were trying to retain some form of dogmatic orthodoxy in an age when such orthodoxies were becoming increasingly repugnant to educated men. Broad Churchmen were no exception to this; the attacks they sustained from orthodox churchmen sometimes made them bitter and dogmatic. This is seen particularly in Williams, whose opinions were as vehement, as those of Denison or the *Record*; he was hardly prepared to grant liberty of opinion to those whom he believed to be wrong. His greatest opponent, Thirlwall, was by 1860 much more conservative in his religious opinions than Williams, but he only turned on Williams when provoked, and was far more tolerant towards diversity of ideas. Williams, in many ways, reveals the Broad Church at its best and at its worst.

Rowland Williams was the second son of a Welsh clergyman, who was a canon of St Asaph and had enough means to educate his children well. After a successful undergraduate career at King's College, Cambridge, of which he became a Fellow in 1839, he returned to Eton, his old school, as an assistant master for a short period. This was followed by eight years as a classical tutor at King's. He was at first a strongly conservative High Churchman, but as an undergraduate and Fellow, he was beset by religious anxieties. These did not take the form of the 'dark night of the soul' and sense of alienation from God experienced by Froude and Clough, for Williams always kept an implicit belief in the existence and goodness of God. He was seeking for a firm rational basis for his faith, and doubted whether the Church's interpretation of the Scriptures provided it. He read Coleridge, admired Thirlwall, and heard Julius Hare preach on justification by faith. He soon came to the conclusion that the writers and prophets of the Old Testament were only partially inspired, and that their works were strongly influenced by their own ideas and surroundings. He believed that private judgment, if used devoutly and humbly, was the only instrument with which to interpret the Scriptures, and that no Church could claim authority to interpret because there was no Scriptural warrant for such an assertion.[2]

These ideas developed into a belief in the 'verifying faculty', so important to the Broad Church. This was the power in each man's mind to read and accept the moral truths of the Scriptures, and to reject that part of them which was not moral or relevant to faith. Naturally this was against orthodox teaching, which stated that man's reason had been evil ever since the fall, and therefore incapable of seeing moral truths without a divine revelation. Nor could this revelation be questioned by man. Edward Hawkins, for example, wrote that private judgment could only be exercised in matters which the Church had not already defined, and that anything else was mere intellectual vanity.[3] The difficulty of this argument was that there were many conventional beliefs which had not been clearly defined by the Anglican Church.

At Cambridge Williams was deeply moved by the writings of Coleridge, who seemed to hold the answer to so many of his problems, and was led to a study of German writers and a tour of Germany. He was a capable linguist, and apart from German, which he knew well, he was considered one of the foremost English scholars in Hebrew. In 1848, at a time when comparative religion was almost unknown in England, he won a Cambridge prize for a dissertation on the comparative merits of Christianity and Hinduism, which he published in 1857. *Christianity and Hinduism*, which was praised by Bunsen and Ewald, was in some ways a halfway mark between traditional English scholarship and new German ideas. He set the book in the form of a Socratic debate, in which Christianity emerged morally triumphant over Hinduism, but he adopted a critical approach to the sources of both religions. It seemed illogical to him that the miracles of the Vedas should be rejected by Christians when equally incredible happenings in the Bible were accepted without question. He wondered why scholarly tests which applied to the religious books of the East should not be used on the Bible, and for a while he dreaded the answer.[4] His solution was not to reject Biblical miracles, but, like Coleridge, to assert that they were not the true evidences of Christianity, which survived only because it was the most perfect moral guide for man. During the fifties he wrote: 'If the great doctrines of Christianity were improbable in themselves, the mere intellectual evidence is not sufficient to prove them. But if they are in a way self-proved by their goodness, they need less logical confirmation.'[5]

Fortified by the belief that no critical investigation could destroy Christianity, he continued with his studies and read German authors enthusiastically. His own views were closest to the 'mediating' school of German theology, and he much admired Schleiermacher, Bunsen, Ewald, Tholuck and Neander, who were critical of the Scriptures without discarding any of what they thought were the essential truths of the Bible. Williams wrote in 1852:

> We ought not to be constantly driven back into untenable positions by the mere bugbear that, if we go so far, we shall be obliged to go further. Perhaps a shutting of our eyes to the light . . . may be even a worse evil than the consequences dreaded. Probably, also, a particular plant was likely in the soil of Germany to develop itself differently from what it might in England. In many cases, such as Neander, Arnold, and Julius Hare . . . no such evil appears to have followed as we are taught to dread . . . and if God does guide us more by probability and less by infallibility, such a principle seems quite clearly indicated by the Apostle—'Prove all things; hold fast that which is good.'[6]

In 1849 Williams was appointed to the position of vice-principal and professor of Hebrew at St David's College, Lampeter. He took up his post in the following year. Although Lampeter was in a remote part of Wales, his prospects were good, because the former vice-principals, Ollivant and Browne, had become bishops of Llandaff and Ely respectively. Williams might have expected a Welsh bishopric because of his academic reputation, and a Welsh bishop would have pleased the nationalists who were badgering Lord John Russell about the need for indigenous bishops, but his subsequent controversial career ended all such hopes.

The work at Lampeter was arduous. The college had been founded in 1822 by Bishop Burgess of St David's, and was intended to supply the Welsh clergy with suitable recruits. But even in 1850 Welsh benefices were usually much poorer than English ones, and so Welsh clergymen of any education left to take up English parishes if they could. The main candidates for Lampeter were therefore the sons of small farmers who could not afford a university education for them, and who thought an impecunious benefice better than farm work.[7] Neither Ollivant nor Browne had succeeded in keeping the standard of education at Lampeter very high, though Browne had made some useful reforms by importing examiners from Oxford and Cambridge and improving the college finances. These were in a tangled state because the principal of the college, Dean Llewellyn Llewellyn of St David's, was also the bursar and supplied the college with produce from his own farm to his personal advantage.

At first Williams was on good terms with his diocesan, Thirlwall, who was also the Visitor of the college. Williams greatly admired Thirlwall's scholarship and his reputation for liberalism in religious thought, and sided with him against the Welsh nationalists. This group was led by the Archdeacon of Cardigan, John Williams, and his influential friends Sir Benjamin Hall, MP for Marylebone and later Lord Llanover, and his formidable wife Augusta (who, strangely enough, was Bunsen's sister-in-law). This group set up a rival institution at Llandovery, something between a grammar school and a university, because they thought that the teaching at Lampeter was too English in character and neglected Welsh culture. They strongly opposed the appointment of Ollivant to Llandaff in 1849 because he was an Englishman. In 1851 Archdeacon Williams publicly attacked St David's College as 'the slaughter house of the rising talent of his country',[8] which naturally roused Williams to fury, and he replied with a scurrilous lampoon on the Archdeacon. Lady Augusta always considered Williams a traitor to his country, as she wrote to a friend:

> As to Mr. Rowland Williams, he *cannot be trusted*—he is sold entirely to St. David's and Llandaff and to the concealment of Llampeter . . . corruptions, and nobody . . . could ever doubt that [his] heart . . . was not *Anglo-Welsh*—a much *worse thing* than a Saxon one, because it is unnatural.[9]

So Williams was out of favour with the nationalist clique, though Thirlwall supported him and St David's College. When he later fell out with Thirlwall he found himself isolated in the diocese.

In spite of early difficulties with the nationalists, who attacked St David's College in Parliament for corrupt finances, Williams succeeded in raising the standard of the entrance examination to the college, even though this meant that it was not filled to capacity. The general standards of the college improved, and it was permitted in 1852 to grant the degree of BD. Williams, however, inevitably suffered from a sense of intellectual isolation; it was hard to attract well-qualified teachers to Lampeter because the college was not well-endowed, and, as Browne had told him, 'a post at St David's was something like a missionary station'.

In 1854 Williams was appointed select preacher to the University of Cambridge, and his sermons were published the following year under the title *Rational Godliness*. They summarised his Cambridge studies and caused great offence to the Evangelical members of the clergy in St David's diocese. Ollivant of Llandaff, whose titular chaplain he was, asked him to resign that position, which he did. Williams then published a tract called *Lampeter Theology*, which was intended to show that he was not teaching harmful ideas to his students and to clarify in a series of propositions the views expressed in *Rational Godliness*. This was a crucial step in his career, for it marked him as an unorthodox churchman, and the ideas he put forward and the tone he adopted towards his critics did not change for the rest of his life. He was as rigid and dogmatic in his own way as the orthodox clergy he attacked, but he believed that his problems were of supreme importance and must be resolved satisfactorily before the Church could make any progress.

Williams's problems reflected those of most Broad Churchmen and fell into two divisions: moral and critical. Moral difficulties arose because he could not make some passages of the Old Testament square with his own idea of right and wrong; he believed in his own moral code, but thought that God's must rise far above the most exalted conceptions of man. The new scientific developments of the nineteenth century played remarkably little part in his dissatisfaction with the teaching of the Church, although he was aware of the uneasy relationship between the natural sciences and orthodox Christianity. His critical problems were based on the philological developments in Germany.

In *Lampeter Theology* Williams tried to answer all possible logical criticisms of the Bible. He maintained that the spirit of faith in the Bible was more important than the literal word which embodied it. It was impossible that the Scriptures had been dictated by God when they bore so many marks of human passions and limited knowledge. But the moral lessons remained clear and unchangeable. Among the many passages which were merely the record of Jewish history, distorted by legend and poetical writing, were the laws that men must live by, explicitly stated by Christ in the New Testament. Prophecy did not refer to actual happenings in the future, but indicated the moral vision and understanding which came from a perfect communion with God; the miracles in the Old Testament were the creations of tradition, and, in the case of Christ's miracles, were intended as a spiritual lesson, not just a crude display of physical power.[10] Williams did not deny, however, that the miracles of the New Testament had actually happened.

Although these ideas were objectionable enough to the orthodox clergy, Williams's way of expressing them gave even more offence. He was naturally an impatient and irascible man where his favourite opinions were concerned, and his style of writing was usually emphatic and didactic. His own faith was so strong that he became exceedingly harsh with those who did not agree with him. As Kegan Paul wrote: 'Dr. Williams, though one of the most charming of men, silver tongued and kindly in speech, was one of those whose pen dripped with vitriol so soon as he began to write.'[11] Williams believed that his opponents were denying the moral significance of Christianity and supporting a false 'floating tradition' based on Hebrew fables; he also stated roundly that Bishop Ollivant had been frightened by the illiterate clergy of Llandaff into denying all responsibility for him. In a published letter to the Bishop, Williams implied that Ollivant had asked him to resign his chaplaincy because of personal dislike of his opinions, not because they contradicted the Church's teaching in any way.[12]

Williams's writings alarmed orthodox Evangelical clergy in St David's who feared that the authority of the Bible as the direct Word of God was at stake. They feared that Williams would corrupt the young generation of clergy at Lampeter, and seventy clergymen petitioned Thirlwall to restrain him. There is no doubt that Williams was a forceful teacher and admired by his students. His teaching was probably not of the kind an orthodox churchman would have approved; he warned his pupils to be ready for ecclesiastical controversy, which was painful but sometimes necessary; asked them in examination papers to show how the miracles of the New Testament differed from those in the Old, and how Christ's miracles exemplified his doctrines. He also presented Jowett's controversial commentaries on St Paul as prizes. But the books which were recommended for reading at St David's college were unimpeachably orthodox, and there was a whole examination paper on Bishop Butler's *Analogy of Religion* (1736) as part of a study of the traditional evidences of Christianity. During 1856, however, there was a strained correspondence between Thirlwall and Williams. Each man later used this correspondence to show that he had been ill-used by the other, and they failed to reach any agreement.

Connop Thirlwall, Bishop of St David's, was a man of whom much might have been expected in the task of reconciling educated doubters to the Church. He was by far the most learned of the bishops in the middle of the century, and his early career had been academically distinguished and controversial. His infant precocity and gift for acquiring languages almost rivalled those of Niebuhr, whom he much admired. After election to a Fellowship at Trinity College, Cambridge, he decided to become a lawyer, but his real interest was historical research. In the 1820s he translated works by Tieck and Schleiermacher from the German. He returned to Cambridge and was ordained, but even his devoted biographer, J. J. Stewart Perowne, admitted that it was from a desire for a scholarly life rather than any sense of clerical vocation,[13] though this does not detract from the sincerity of Thirlwall's religious feelings. He explained his decision to become a clergyman to his uncle in 1827.

> The mode in which I might best gratify my inclinations, and might lay out myself and my faculties to the greatest advantage, is a point on which I have certainly been long doubtful. . . . Nor is this, I think . . . a thing very much to be wondered at or to be violently censured. Society possesses two or three strong stiff frames, in which all persons of liberal education who need or

desire a fixed place and specific designation must consent to be set. . . . Fortunate indeed are they to whom it presents no difficulty, when the promptitude of decision arises from clearness of conviction and not from the absence of thought.[14]

Thirlwall had known some religious vacillations at Cambridge, because he could not see that Christianity had added anything to the ethical ideas of the ancient Greeks, but he seems to have convinced himself that religious uncertainty was more untenable than certainty, after a reading of Pascal.[15] In 1828 appeared the first volume of the work which brought him public notice: the excellent translation, in collaboration with Julius Hare, of Niebuhr's *History of Rome*. Six years later there was a Cambridge dispute between Thirlwall and Thomas Turton, the future Bishop of Ely, who wished to keep the universities strictly Anglican institutions. Thirlwall published two letters supporting the admission of Dissenters to university degrees: the question itself was a dangerous one, but he made himself even more unpopular by arguing that the universities were not intended to be theological colleges, and that the standards of religious training and chapel services in them were often an insult to the Church.[16]

He was forced to resign his post at Trinity, and accepted the small but comfortable living of Kirby Underdale in Yorkshire, where he spent most of his time (sometimes sixteen hours of the twenty-four, according to Perowne) working on his own history of Greece, which appeared in eight volumes between 1835 and 1844. His views had favourably impressed the Whigs, who were having difficulty in finding clergymen of suitable opinions to fill the vacancies on the episcopal bench. Accordingly Lord Melbourne, who also admired Thirlwall's scholarship, offered him the see of St David's in 1840, but prudently sounded Archbishop Howley about his orthodoxy beforehand. With typical thoroughness Thirlwall acquired the Welsh language in six months and was able to write and preach in it, but he had little in common with the clergy and people of his mountainous and impoverished diocese. His Welsh was academic rather than colloquial, and he frightened the simple parish clergymen with his diffidence and his learning.[17] They felt uncomfortable in his presence and would not visit him if they could help it. And so he remained in his palace at Abergwili, unmarried, scholarly and secluded, occasionally visited by prominent men and regularly travelling to London to speak in Convocation and the House of Lords.

His career and associates marked him as a clergyman in favour of Church reforms and conversant with modern critical research. For many years he supported alteration of the liturgy to remove passages like the damnatory clauses in the Athanasian Creed which offended many humane nineteenth-century ears in parish churches.[18] His friendship with Bunsen and his German translations, especially of a reputedly heterodox author like Schliermacher, gave him a link with German rationalism which the orthodox considered hardly proper in an Anglican bishop. Above all, he was a scholar whose intellectual opinions must be respected; unlike the peripatetic Wilberforce and most of the other bishops, the duties of his diocese could not keep him from study, and his relative lack of home and social life gave him more time for his books. He could not be accused of being out of touch with the intellectual progress of the time.

This was the man with whom Williams joined battle, with such relish that he could be suspected of deliberately provoking it. The positions of the two men were paradoxical; Williams, volatile and outspoken, was often incoherent in print, though his muddled style could not hide his basic principles or the fervour with which he held them. His religion was ardent, personal and emotional, and he used to sing and pray to himself as he rode through the Welsh mountains; yet his writings all demand that Christianity should be reasonable and satisfying to the intellect. Thirlwall, on the other hand, was an enigmatic figure because of his solitary life, but in his writings he was cold, precise and methodical; his main polemical weapon was deftly-wielded irony, whereas Williams often fell back on a heavy form of sarcasm and invective. Baroness Bunsen made a telling observation on Thirlwall as a young man, which reveals this side of his character.

> I rather suspect him of being very cold, and very dry—and although he seeks, and seeks with general success, to understand everything, and in every possible way increase his stock of ideas, I doubt the possibility of his understanding anything that is to be *felt* rather than *explained*.[19]

In short, Thirlwall was an anti-romantic, and had an eighteenth-century dislike of enthusiasm. His speeches and sermons could be witty, ironical, learned, but never emotional; and yet he was forced by Williams virtually to deny the importance of reason in religion and the conclusions of contemporary scholarship.

The acrid correspondence of 1856 between Thirlwall and Williams began when Ollivant permitted students from St David's diocese to enter his own theological college in Llandaff, which had a shorter course of study, and this drew them away from Lampeter and Williams's teaching. It is difficult to judge Thirlwall's reaction to this, because both men saw it in such a different light. Thirlwall apparently thought that Williams was endangering the interests of St David's College, and said as much without directly criticising his teaching. Williams immediately assumed that Thirlwall, in his capacity as Visitor of the college, was threatening to remove him from his position and bring him into the ecclesiastical courts.[20] He insisted that Thirlwall give his opinions on the doctrines in *Lampeter Theology* which had started the affair; if Williams's view were the right one, then truth would prevail and the fears of the orthodox clergy should be ignored.

Thirlwall was pained by the imputation that he was persecuting Williams, and replied that he had no power to remove him from Lampeter unless an ecclesiastical court had first found him guilty of heresy, which was unlikely. He objected to Williams's 'habitual' tone of violent criticism, and implied that he was deliberately courting martyrdom and that his judgment was 'clouded by an incurable prejudice'.

At this point matters rested uneasily because the college did not seem to be suffering particularly from Williams's ideas. In August 1857 Ollivant delivered his charge to his clergy and spoke his fears openly. Ollivant was a moderate, peaceable clergyman of the Evangelical school, and the first Bishop of Llandaff for many years to reside in his diocese. He was by no means unlearned, and had been Regius Professor of Divinity at Cambridge. Unlike Thirlwall, however, he was chiefly a practical bishop labouring to build churches and improve conditions in his backward diocese, and he does not seem to have had much time for study, for he published nothing except his charges after he became bishop.

His charge of 1857 was a model of orthodoxy. Williams had challenged him to discuss the points at issue, and after disposing of regular diocesan matters he produced a lengthy attack on the Broad Church in general and Williams in particular, with a stab or two at Jowett in passing. In the published version of the charge he intensified the attack in a long appendix, which tried to show that Williams's ideas were akin to those of the notorious American rationalist Theodore Parker, and he mentioned Francis Newman's apostasy as an example of the natural end of such ideas.

Ollivant did not fight Williams on his own ground. His main premise was that the Scriptures must be infallible because God would not have let His Gospel come down through the centuries in an imperfect form. He mentioned vaguely that the Church had plenty of evidence of the literal truth of the miracles of Christ, without saying what the evidence was, but he concentrated on explaining exactly what Williams's ideas were, not contradicting them rationally, probably because he knew that to his audience the mere exposition of such doctrines was shocking enough. As for Williams's view that certain parts of the Bible were not moral, Ollivant maintained that human conceptions of morality must be fallible like all other human ideas, and that fallen man was not able to understand the purposes of God. The writers of the Scriptures claimed authority for themselves and their word must be accepted. Of course the Apostles were ordinary men, and not omniscient except where their spiritual mission and writings were concerned. But Ollivant's whole conception of the inspiration of the Scriptures was cloudy; the Church had no definite teaching on the matter, he said, but this was not important, because once the fact of inspiration was accepted it was unnecessary to inquire further into its nature or limits. He pointed out that adherence to the spirit of the Bible, to the neglect of the letter, could lead only to religious anarchy, because it was impossible to interpret the spirit precisely, and he again quoted the case of Francis Newman. He had no doubts of Williams's piety or sincerity, he said, but feared for St David's College and the state of Christianity generally if such ideas spread.

Williams naturally defended himself with relish. In 1857 he took the degree of DD and preached a sermon at Cambridge on

'Christian Freedom in the Council of Jerusalem'. He said that the Church's first thoughts had been for the freedom of its heterogeneous members, but that the nineteenth-century Church would 'now bind the whole circle of Jewish ideas upon our reluctant and astounded minds'.[21] He printed the sermon together with a letter attacking Ollivant, who, he said, had answered none of his questions and had nothing better for his arguments than the loose ideas generally accepted among his clergy. He agreed with Ollivant's condemnation of Strauss and Baur, but looked for an answer, not in the unlearned orthodoxy of Hengstenberg but in the 'mediating' school of Bunsen, de Wette and Neander. He asserted that it was not his own rationalising but Ollivant's lack of it that might have sent Lampeter students astray. Some of the students in Ollivant's time had left the college and founded a mystical sect of their own, and Williams was quick to seize upon this fact. He wrote of those students:

> They began with a weak mysticism which disparaged rational knowledge as not edifying. . . . It is probable that if all cases were put together, we might look far for any theological teacher (unless we found one at Oxford), who has seen so many of his pupils as you have seen of yours, lapse into schism, if not apostasy.[22]

Ollivant's response to Williams had been a predictable Evangelical one; Thirlwall's opinions could not be anticipated in the same way. He delivered a long charge two months after Ollivant's, and the petition of the seventy clergymen of his diocese needed to be mentioned. Thirlwall's view of the Church and its doctrines was, like that of Thomas Arnold and Julius Hare, comprehensive. He believed that the Articles of the Anglican Church were elastic enough to include many shades of opinion, and all his life he resisted any attempts to restate doctrines in a simpler and more dogmatic manner. Similarly he opposed the revival of Convocation and the movements towards centralisation in the Church, because he feared that if any one body claimed the sole right to interpret the Church's teachings persecution and fanticism would result. Therefore his answer to the seventy clergymen who petitioned against Williams was negative, because he felt bound to protect the freedom which the Church granted to all its members, as long as they did not deny doctrines which he believed were clearly stated in the formularies. He would take no action against Williams, whom he believed to be a worthy man, but he could not help criticising his incoherence, his abrupt manner, and the ideas expressed in *Lampeter Theology*: '. . . not so much on account of any thing which they distinctly state, as of the difficulty of perceiving their exact drift and their collective import, and because . . . a reader might conceive a suspicion of something behind them all, which they were meant to suggest, but not to express.'[23]

Williams was aggrieved by this, but continued at St David's College until 1862, though in 1858 he accepted the King's College living of Broad Chalke with Bower Chalke in the diocese of Salisbury. *Essays and Reviews* appeared early in 1860, but the orthodox reaction was not stimulated until October, when Frederic Harrison's article in the *Westminster Review* pointed out that the volume cut away the ground from under the feet of believers, but that from a rationalist point of view it did not cut enough. Then began the flurry of indignation in the Church which resulted in the prosecution of Williams and Wilson in the ecclesiastical courts.

Williams's essay on the Biblical researches of Baron Bunsen advanced nothing on the views he had expressed earlier, but taken in conjunction with those of the other writers it received much more publicity. It was generally believed to be one of the most radical of the essays, and even Stanley considered it too rash and outspoken. There was also an irritating ambiguity over which were Williams's own opinions and which Bunsen's. Williams expressed a little more clearly the ideas of *Rational Godliness*: that revelation should be reconciled with nineteenth-century conceptions of morality; that there was need for revision of the traditions concerning the authorship of the Old Testament; that the principles of reason and righteousness in the human mind are a greater guide in religion than external authority; that miracle, prophecy, and ideas like atonement and justification by faith should be interpreted morally, not literally; and he even stated plainly that the Bible was the result of the Christian spirit and not the cause of it, 'for the Bible is before all things the written voice of the Congregation'.[24]

Williams's actions during 1860 seem to bear out Thirlwall's

remark that he was courting martyrdom. In his letters and journals his tone was often violent and enthusiastic; like other Broad Churchmen he believed that the Church was approaching a crisis akin to a second Reformation. The Church insisted on holding on to traditions which were lifeless and sapping all its power over the rising generation. Perhaps, at the back of his mind, Williams hoped to place himself in the position of a Luther, or at least a Cranmer or Ridley, who would precipitate the new Reformation and provide it with the necessary martyrs. He wrote:

> Yet surely the time must come when God will mercifully bring our spirit into harmony with our understanding. Perhaps a greatness and a place not far from the Apostles in the kingdom of heaven, may be reserved for some one, who, in true holiness and humility of heart, shall be privileged to accomplish this work.[25]

He was convinced that he was being persecuted out of his place at St David's College for views which he knew were true. It cannot have been a surprise to him that *Essays and Reviews* was received with such clamour, remembering the unpopularity of his earlier writings in Wales, but before the storm broke he made another attempt to provoke an open conflict with Thirlwall. Mrs Williams recalled that her husband was sure that Thirlwall secretly held the same views on inspiration as himself, but that he was afraid to state them because of his rank in the Church. This turned Williams's early admiration for Thirlwall into the bitterest animosity, and he was determined to wrest some theological opinion from him.

The bishop was due to deliver his next charge to the clergy of St David's in October 1860, but prior to this Williams published *An Earnestly Respectful Letter to the Lord Bishop of St. David's, on the difficulty of bringing Theological Questions to an Issue.* The letter was certainly earnest but hardly respectful, and was, said Williams, an appendix to all his previous works. He included quotations from his early correspondence with Thirlwall to show that he had been threatened without having his views discussed thoroughly. Yet all these hostilities had taken place in 1856 and 1857, and it seems strange that Williams should have waited three years before replying, unless by throwing out a challenge just after the publication of *Essays and Reviews* and just before Thirlwall's charge, he was determined to court notoriety. His tone was again aggressive towards those who, he thought, based their faith on falsehood because they were frightened of free inquiry. Like Luther he produced his theses, in the shape of ten propositions, which repeated the points raised in *Lampeter Theology*, and challenged Thirlwall to debate them. He did not dispute the doctrines of Christ, he maintained, but: '. . . the true commencement for discussion is that point at which the finite elements in Scripture, whether limitations in knowledge, or imperfectness of spiritual development, come in collision with what educated men know, or with what pious Christians believe'.[26] He proceeded to challenge the 'oracle at Abergwili', whose scholarly achievements were widely honoured, to give his own theory of inspiration, which he promised to accept as authoritative. He ended with a scarcely veiled criticism of Thirlwall's apparent pusillanimity.

> The want of commanding qualifications in those who should give the tone to our theology is not more fatal than the want of courage to use them; and the clergy are stript of their natural protectors, if those who should guide us give no guidance to our efforts, and when they should judge our results, give other men's sentence for their own. Thus . . . we are bidden say things which if we believed, we should be no longer fit for our sacred office. My lord, I desire without offence to confess my wish that Bishops who have never adopted such things in their teaching would not seem to sanction such by their judging.[27]

His whole letter rang with the conviction that the Church of England possessed a system of terrorism against those of its members who dared to think for themselves, as pernicious as that in the Church of Rome.

Thirlwall was placed in an extremely difficult position, in which any decisive move on his part would benefit Williams. To attack Williams for opinions which, in spite of the rashness of their expression, were held by many educated and pious men, would only encourage Williams's tendency to represent himself as a martyr to the cause of the truth, but agreement with him would cause a furore in the Church. Thirlwall's own theological opinions are obscure because he rarely said anything about them, but he was obviously not opposed to free rational investigation into the Scriptures, and some of his letters show that he, too, continued to feel some qualms about the morality of certain parts of Scripture. As late as 1871 he confessed to a friend that he found the story of Abraham and Isaac painful, and hoped that possibly it had not been handed down in its original form; on another occasion he wrote that prophecy presented many difficulties, and that differences of opinion about it must be tolerated.[28] What Thirlwall most disliked was that his own ideas, or those of anyone else, should be regarded as authoritative, because any kind of dogmatism could only disrupt the Church. The clue to his attitude may be found in a letter to the only woman who appears ever to have interested him, the young Betha Johnes:

> Our Church has the advantage . . . of more than one type of orthodoxy; that of the High Church, grounded on one aspect of its formularies; that of the Low Church, grounded on another aspect; and that of the Broad Church, striving to take in both, but in its own way. Each has a right to a standing-place; none to exclusive possession of the field.[29]

Naturally this position was far from Williams's dogmatic Broad Churchmanship, and Thirlwall's reply to Williams, also in a published letter, was calculated to irritate the Welshman even further. Thirlwall neither agreed nor disagreed plainly with his ideas, but merely demolished stylistic confusions with cold precision. He said that it was impossible to answer all Williams's questions in a short space, and he had no authority to make judgments where the Church did not. He accused Williams of asking his questions disingenuously, to trap his opponent, which was unfair to Williams though it was partly true. He refused to give any opinion on the inspiration of the Bible, and remarked that a belief in complete verbal inspiration did not exclude belief in the direct workings of the Holy Spirit on the minds of men. He suspected that the whole attitude of the Church throughout the ages favoured the idea of verbal inspiration but did not impose it; therefore Williams was free to believe what he liked, but not to upset honest clergymen by vilifying their opinions.[30] He did make definite statements on two moral issues—that miracles were necessary to show the physical power of Christ, because the moral power was already evident, and that a 'bad' miracle like the blinding of Elymas by Paul (*Acts* XIII. 8), which Williams had cited, was nevertheless beneficial because it commanded belief in the beholders and because, for all we know, it might have caused Elymas's spiritual awakening.

Williams wrote a *Critical Appendix* to Thirlwall's letter, complaining that the bishop had failed to answer any of his questions and producing more learned, abstruse and rather confused arguments. He did not, however, do more than restate his case, and brought forward no new ideas. In fact, there was little reasoning in any of Williams's works; he simply stated his opinions and expected that they would be instantly acceptable to common sense. When Thirlwall, whose mind he respected, was unmoved, Williams was reduced to anger. In a sense, he had exhausted his armoury in his first pieces of writing, and had no new weapons to produce. He continued hostile to Thirlwall all his life, and his anger was increased when Thirlwall joined with the other bishops in condemning *Essays and Reviews*. The reason Thirlwall gave for this was that the only alternative to condemning the book was to agree with it, or ignore it, which would seem to amount to the same thing in the atmosphere of clerical hysteria which had arisen.[31] Williams thought that Thirlwall had betrayed him and the Broad Church cause for selfish motives. He wrote in a letter:

> My great difficulties in South Wales arose, not from my own countrymen, who are generally a truth-loving people, but from having a Diocesan with a mind far more sceptical, but less ingenuous than my own; and when Dr. Connop Thirlwall imputed to me 'scepticism' . . . I felt that a practical paradox was being enacted, in which inconsistency was not on my side.[32]

He believed that Thirlwall was denying his own earlier opinions, and that he was trying to suppress the translation of Schleiermacher. An anonymous pamphlet produced quotations from this work to show that it anticipated *Essays and Reviews* on several points, and Thirlwall was forced to confess in the press that this work of his younger days was 'imperfect', although the pamphleteer had taken statements out of context. He repeated his belief in the 'latitude of opinion' which the Church allowed its ministers.[33]

Thirlwall's charge of 1863 brought him out more openly into the orthodox camp. He defended the literal truth of miracle, and attacked *Essays and Reviews*, which, he said, would not win back unbelievers to the Church but drag the whole Church down to the level of the members with the least amount of Christian belief. He disparaged scientific inquiry, because he thought it led to 'excitement of mind' which did not foster the proper attitude towards religious truth. Thirlwall was not particularly shocked by the essays of Jowett and Pattison, probably because their attitude was academic and detached and so closer to his own; he even defended Jowett's opinions on the inspiration of the Bible as not incompatible with revelation. Jowett had rejected verbal inspiration but did not think that the Bible was a purely human work, and maintained that a close textual study was necessary to sift out the various elements in it. Thirlwall revealed that this view approached his own. Now this opinion did not differ materially from that of Williams or Wilson, and Thirlwall made it clear that it was their manner rather than their matter which was disagreeable to him. Unlike the other essayists they were pastoral teachers, and their irresponsible vehemence would only serve to upset simple believers. Thirlwall did not think it necessary to refute their views, because this would only renew old conflict within the Church.

Thirlwall was universally respected as the most learned member of the episcopate at that time, and his opinions were anxiously awaited. Most of his colleagues were delighted with his attack on *Essays and Reviews*, especially Tait, who was far from narrow-minded but shared Thirlwall's belief that the book would upset the honest faith of many clergy and laity. In his charge Thirlwall had also deplored any attempt to narrow the doctrines of the Church to keep critical inquirers outside, and this also pleased Tait, as he wrote in his diary. 'The Bp of St. David's . . . seems to have awakened as from a dream and to have shaken off Oxford's influence*—and to be ready to do what with his great learning . . . he ought. There is no other Bishop who seems to me of the slightest use for this good purpose.'[34]

Yet Thirlwall refrained from any definite theological commitment, and during the thirty-five years of his episcopate, in spite

* Thirlwall was a close friend of Samuel Wilberforce.

of all his study, he produced no further major works; a strange end to a career which had promised so much in his earlier years. In matters of practical policy, like the disestablishment of the Irish Church, he spoke out on the Liberal side, but he avoided religious arguments when he could: he hated a narrow dogmatic attitude to religion, and it was Williams, the disciple of free inquiry, who wanted to bind men to his own opinions and sneered at those who would not agree. Perhaps there lay more hope for the future in Thirlwall's belief that the Church must be weaned away from the dogmatic orthodoxies which disrupted its corporate life in the nation.

Meanwhile, Williams had found his martyrdom at the hands of his third bishop. This was Walter Kerr Hamilton (1808–69), who had become Bishop of Salisbury in 1854, the first English bishop with Tractarian sympathies. In his youth he had been a pupil of Arnold and adopted the earnest piety which Arnold inculcated, but at Oxford he was influenced by the Tractarians, particularly Newman, and accepted many of their ideas. He was a close friend of Bishop Denison of Salisbury and became a canon in Salisbury Cathedral. Denison pressed Lord Aberdeen in a deathbed letter to make Hamilton his successor; Aberdeen was naturally unwilling to do this, because of Hamilton's opinions and because he did not want to create a precedent for such requests, but at last he consented. The Queen was most annoyed when she found out what Hamilton's views were. Hamilton accepted the appointment only after a long and emotional discussion with his friend Gladstone, because he knew the difficulties his views might cause in the diocese and because he always distrusted his own motives, but Gladstone at last persuaded him. Hamilton decided to proceed cautiously and to avoid shocking any of his clergy by overt ritualism.[35] He was a conscientious bishop, immersed in the affairs of his diocese and performing his duties diligently. Even his well-wishers could not make any claims for the strength of his intellect, but he was undeniably a good and earnest man.

He first met Williams in 1858, when Williams was presented to the living of Broad Chalke. There was an immediate practical problem: the vicarage was in disrepair and Williams wished to be non-resident while a new one was built. He came to see Hamilton about this in November, and found that the bishop was nervous about instituting a man with such unorthodox ideas. Williams fired up immediately. 'He said', recollected Hamilton, 'that if I determined not to accept the presentation & institute him, he was too poor a man to carry his case into a law court & should on other grounds not be disposed to litigate the matter with me.'[36] Hamilton was distressed at the mention of litigation and asked Williams to recall his statement. Williams agreed to modify it. Afterwards the matter was settled, and in December Hamilton wrote in his diary. 'I have this day written to Dr. R. Williams that there is not I believe any legal objection to his institution. But what a very dangerous man he is & his temper is vile—no self control.'[37]

Until 1862 Williams spent his time between Broad Chalke and Lampeter. As the hostility towards *Essays and Reviews* increased, pressure was put on Hamilton to begin proceedings against him in the Court of Arches, which he finally did. The Judge of the Arches, Sir Stephen Lushington, decided from amongst several charges of false teaching that Williams had erred in calling the Bible the 'expression of devout reason', and the 'voice of the congregation', and in interpreting justification by faith as the peace of mind which comes from trust in a righteous God. Broad Churchmen disliked the idea of justification because it implied that God was a wrathful being who needed to be reconciled. Lushington considered that these opinions were against the doctrines of the Church as embodied in the Articles and liturgy, though he did dismiss several other charges, including those which alleged that Williams had denied Biblical prophecies and the authorship of the Old Testament; either because Williams's views were ambiguous or because the Church's teaching was not specifically defined. In December he was suspended from his living for a year.

Williams, while appealing from the Court of Arches to the Judicial Committee of the Privy Council, preached a sermon at Lampeter on the subject of *Persecution for the Word*, reiterating all his views, and condemning a Church which persecuted a clergyman for speaking out. 'The office of critic', he complained, 'must be subordinate to that of clergyman; the clergyman should not contradict his Bishop, or unsettle his congregation.'[38]

His attitude was self-pitying, but behind the rhetoric was a certain satisfaction that those who opposed his doctrines had placed themselves in the wrong, because, he said, that side of a controversy which first resorts to coercion to prove its point betrays itself as the false one. At last he was able to speak as a martyr to his cause.

Hamilton refused to have anything to do with the appeal because he did not think the Judicial Committee had sufficient authority in such matters and did not represent the Church. He did not wish, he said, to ascertain the doctrine of the Church on these vexed questions, but to save one of his parishes from any false teachings.[39] Williams wasted few words on him; he does not seem to have aroused his animosity as a worthy foe like Thirlwall. When the Judicial Committee reversed the sentence in 1864 Hamilton was deeply disturbed, and it confirmed his fears about the imperfections of the Church's legal machinery. He explained to his clergy that although the sentiments of *Essays and Reviews* might be commonly held in the nineteenth century, clergymen could not accept them without disloyalty to the Church. He had hesitated, characteristically, before beginning any legal proceedings, because he had feared that it was his personal zeal which prompted him, but the declaration of his fellow-bishops had urged him on. He could not accept that religion was a matter of personal sentiment only; like other Tractarians, he believed that the Church relied on definite dogmatic teaching which appealed to both faith and intellect. He determined that the next generation of clergy should be sent in the right direction, and in 1861 he instituted a diocesan theological college to train them.[40]

After the judgment, Williams, justified, retired to Broad Chalke, where he continued to expound his theories without any modifications in his parish church. He wrote poetry, a play defending Owen Glendower, and commentaries on the Hebrew prophets, and was visited by Harriet Martineau and Ewald. He denied that he had intended to undermine the Church in any way, and supported clerical subscription to the Prayer Book and Articles as long as no one attempted to define them too precisely. He taught his flock the Broad Church ideas that Leslie Stephen found so infuriating; for example, that priests should have the choice of omitting the more bloodthirsty Psalms, but that the content of the Psalms could also be used as a figure for holy war and the defeat of sin. In the same way he softened the doctrine of the atonement by emphasising the self-sacrifice and obedience of Christ rather than the actual bloodshed. Williams always denied that he was a member of any Church party, and maintained that the opinions of the other essayists, whom he hardly knew, were not his. When Temple was appointed to Exeter, Williams wrote to his sister:

> Now that Dr. Temple is safe, it may be time to point out, what his friends have been in their eagerness willing to forget, that he is not the only Essayist who would be well contented to stand alone, and who would gain something by standing alone, if the entanglements of (even a temporary and literary) combination permitted it.[41]

Nevertheless, Williams was considered a leading member of the Broad Church, because his writings were incurably partisan. In 1867 the Unitarians James Martineau and J. J. Tayler joined with friends of other free-thinking groups and a few Anglicans to form a 'Free Christian Union', which they hoped would unite all liberal-minded Christians on an undogmatic basis. They wrote to all the prominent Anglicans who they thought would be interested, including Voysey, Goldwin Smith and Williams. Kegan Paul joined enthusiastically and took part in the society's undenominational religious services, but Williams politely refused to join, affirming his own belief in the value of the Anglican teachings. He replied to the secretary of the society:

> There is hardly any doctrine of the Church of England, and here I include all such as the Trinity, and Baptismal Regeneration, which I do not systematically teach, and continue to teach: though it has seemed to me a sacred duty to avoid the exaggerations and misinterpretations with which these doctrines have been too often associated. . . . When I have been dead a century, somebody will discover that, upon the hypothesis of the Church of England being properly conservable, my method was the most logically conservative.[42]

Williams always suffered from a sense of isolation, not only at Lampeter but also at Broad Chalke, which was a secluded country village, and he lamented that he had little rational society. His reputation prevented him from making friends among orthodox clergy, and in the diocese of Salisbury his best friends were men who shared his opinions: Kegan Paul, then incumbent of Sturminster, and Robert Kennard, vicar of Marnhull in Dorset, a former pupil of H. B. Wilson. The presence of such men in his diocese perturbed the unfortunate Bishop Hamilton, but as long as they remained quiet and continued to perform their clerical duties he could do nothing about them. The visitation returns which Williams sent to Hamilton were invariably insulting; he described the greatest hindrance to his ministry as episcopal litigation and despotism, which 'had lessened in him that spirit of confiding obedience which is so charming an ingredient in the ministerial character'.[43]

Williams's congregation numbered about 200 out of the estimated 800 inhabitants of Broad Chalke. (Bower Chalke had a population of 400 and was attended to by his curate, John Owen.) Like other ministers, he found that the poorer members attended both Church and meeting-house without discrimination, and they had an unhappy tendency to prefer extempore sermons to the ritual of the church. They seem to have been undismayed by his ideas, and were pleased when he was acquitted by the Judicial Committee. His sermons, unlike his polemical works, were clear and simple, and he had the gift of appealing to simple village people. He was renowned in the parish for his attempts to visit and teach the scattered shepherds in the hills and the gypsies in the countryside, and this aspect of him is the one which survives in the parish today, not his reputation as a controversial figure.* But his life was spent in country districts, and he had little knowledge of the problems of the industrial towns; like many of the Broad Churchmen he was intellectually remote and thought that the solution to religious indifference among the masses lay in theological compromise.

He was disappointed with the slow progress that his ideas seemed to be making in the nation, and wrote in 1868:

> Now, for too many years my mind, knowing its inmost desires to be at variance with the great tendency of the age, has resigned itself in too Cassandra-like a manner to see, suffer, and lament;

* According to the present incumbent, the Rev H. J. Treasure.

> only having suggested the best preventives. Henceforth, I will see, *Deo adiuvante*, if I cannot adapt myself more to the future, and work what fresh issue we can out of fresh circumstances.[44]

He died in 1870. His funeral service was read by Kennard, who was to perform the same office eighteen years later for H. B. Wilson. His friends set up a window in Broad Chalke Church to his memory. It shows Williams in his different roles as professor, preacher, divine, and parish clergyman, under a figure of St Michael destroying the dragon of falsehood. Underneath is his favourite text:

The Letter killeth: the Spirit giveth life.

Notes to this chapter are on pages 251–2

Chapter 5 H. B. WILSON AND THE NATIONAL CHURCH

WHILE ROWLAND Williams expressed the Broad Churchman's concern for the moral and rational aspects of religion in the nineteenth century, H. B. Wilson continued faithfully the tradition of Coleridge and Thomas Arnold in trying to find a new relationship between Church and society. This involved a critical approach to the basic assumptions of Anglicanism and its relationship to the Bible, the Articles and the Prayer Book. Coleridge's *On the Constitution of the Church and State According to the Idea of Each*, first published in 1830, was the model for Broad Church thinking on the subject. He distinguished between the ideal of a Christian Church which could embrace all men irrespective of national divisions, and the Church as it must necessarily exist in human society. Organised Christianity was bound to differ from nation to nation; the problem was to find unity within each national Church. Coleridge thought that the main duty of the national Church was to preserve civilisation and ensure the spiritual progress of the nation.[1] The instrument of this was the 'clerisy', which consisted of all learned men, not necessarily priests, who undertook the task of education. Education could not make everyone intelligent, but it could preserve civilisation by producing a healthy religious tone in national life. The true temporal head of the national Church was the king, and the Church should not be subject to the whims of changing governments, but Coleridge was not sure how this was to be achieved. Church property should be national property, in the national trust, to be used for providing each parish with a clergyman and schoolmaster, a church and a school. The task of the clerisy was to teach the Christian truths which were the basis of social and religious duty.

Coleridge's work was no plan of action but a vision, and he postulated a Church whose foundation was undogmatic. Thomas Arnold adapted the vision into a more detailed plan. He, too, thought that Christian unity must be encouraged within each nation, and that, because all Christians accepted certain basic doctrines, these doctrines must be made the centre of national life, and no others enforced. His ideal was:

> . . . to constitute a Church thoroughly national, thoroughly united, thoroughly Christian, which should allow great varieties of opinion, and of ceremonies, and forms of worship, according to the various knowledge, and habits, and tempers of its members, while it truly held one common faith, and trusted in one common Saviour, and worshipped one common God.[2]

Like Coleridge, Arnold accepted that the king must be the head of such a Church, and hoped, unlike Coleridge, that Roman Catholics might enter into it, if they could allow the king's supremacy instead of the pope's. The only difficulty he foresaw was with Unitarians who steadily refused to recognise Christ's divinity, but he said: 'If an Arian will join in our worship of Christ, and will call him Lord and God, there is neither wisdom nor charity in insisting that he shall explain what he means by these terms.'[3]

Arnold conceived of a Christian ministry on an undogmatic basis, which would be a true reflection of society; this would close the gap between clergy and laity which was responsible for mass apathy to religion. The clergy should be drawn from all ranks of life; the chief ministers would need to be educated men, but there was also room for less educated 'assistant ministers', men of earnest mind drawn from the working classes, who could speak directly to their fellows. These men might be subsidised by Easter contributions. The Church should allow more power to laymen in its government, and services should be varied enough to satisfy all. Arnold, like Coleridge, was not sure how these reforms were to be carried out, but he thought that both government and clergy should have a hand in them, and stressed that they should not be left to the clergy alone.

These two ideas were very influential among Broad Churchmen, who all agreed that toleration and compromise were necessary. Stanley accepted the ideas of his masters with enthusiasm, and caused a scandal later in his career by allowing a Unitarian member of the committee for the revision of the Prayer Book to take communion with the other members in Westminster Abbey. The main obstacles to this kind of national Church were the Articles and Prayer Book, to which each clergyman had to subscribe, and the Broad Churchmen could not agree on what to do about them. Stanley wished to do away with subscription but keep the Articles in the rubric; Maurice, Williams and Wilson tried to argue that the Articles were more ambiguous and gave more room for differing opinions than orthodox clergy would allow. They wished to retain Anglican traditions, and yet realised that they were an obstacle to comprehensiveness. They did, however, begin a tentative search for an ecumenical system, which is being carried on more openly in the Church today.

To orthodox churchmen the Broad Church attitude towards the relationship of Church and State, and towards doctrinal authority, was unacceptable. Coleridge and Arnold taught their disciples that Church and State should be indivisible, and that it was the State's duty to ensure that the Church did not become exclusive by enforcing rigid orthodoxy on its members. High Churchmen, on the other hand, were convinced that a government in which many beliefs were represented threatened the spiritual life of the Church. Arnold's views were particularly unacceptable to High Churchmen because he wanted Church and State to control Church affairs jointly. Orthodox clergy also tended to see the rejection of any dogma as a step towards infidelity. High and Low alike could not accept a religion in which private judgment was supreme and there was no dogmatic certainty, for they needed some form of external authority. The Rev Frederick Meyrick, an Evangelical preacher, expressed this view in the university pulpit at Oxford: 'There must be certainty somewhere. There must be authority somewhere. There must be an appeal to something which shall be final in its declarations of truth and falsehood, of right and wrong. Else we are of all creatures the most miserable.'[4]

It was the misfortune of Henry Bristow Wilson that, academic and retiring by nature, he should be thrust into the vanguard of Church controversialists. He hoped to bring peace by adapting the ideas of Coleridge and Arnold for churchmen in the 1860s, but to preach comprehensiveness to a Church already divided, threatened by rationalism and militant dissent, was only to divide it further. He spent his life developing the idea of a national Church, but the temper of the Church in the 1860s was exclusivist, not comprehensive, and his ideas were unacceptable to most churchmen. His name has been linked with that of Williams ever since their joint trial, but they knew little of each other before it, and Wilson did not thrive on controversy as Williams did. He has left few personal records, but the development of his ideas can be clearly seen in his published writings. His friend Kegan Paul enthusiastically compared his style to Newman's, but this is a great exaggeration, for he was not an original thinker or a master of prose. Yet his works show the attempts of an intelligent clergyman to solve the problem of how the Church was to survive in a literate and inquiring society, and so he is worth some attention as a true representative of the Broad Church movement, though not one of its greatest men.

Wilson came from a clerical and scholarly family which was closely connected with the solidly middle-class Merchant Taylors' School in London. His father, Harry Bristow Wilson, was second master at the school and also its historian. He was an antiquarian of some note, and it is likely that his son owed some of his religious liberalism to him, for in 1849, at the age of sixty-five, Harry Bristow Wilson was preaching that it was false to believe that the majority of mankind was damned. He did not deny that some men were lost, but said it was unjust to think that God had not the power to save most of His creation. He attacked the Calvinistic view shared by most Evangelicals as a 'gloomy and unscriptural system'.[5] His son was later accused of heresy for expanding on this idea.

Henry Wilson followed in the academic footsteps of his father; he attended Merchant Taylors' School and went from there to St John's College, Oxford, where he was elected to a Fellowship in 1825. He remained at St John's for twenty-five years, and was Rawlinson Professor of Anglo-Saxon from 1839 to 1844, though he was probably no serious scholar of the language. In the days before university reform, the chair was held for five-year periods only, and passed to St John's automatically every fifth turn. As tutor at St John's, Wilson became involved in the uproar over *Tract XC*, and with three other college tutors, Tait of Balliol, T. T. Churton of Brasenose and J. Griffiths of Wadham, he wrote a public letter to Newman on 8 March 1841, beginning the outcry against the Tractarians. The four tutors' names carried some weight in Oxford, though they hardly knew each other and had been brought together for the purpose of drawing up the letter by C. P. Golightly, perennial opponent of ritualism.[6] Wilson, like Tait, was to find that this letter would be held against him in his future career, and he was later charged with inconsistency because he demanded that his own unorthodox ideas be heard, though he had denied the same right to Newman.[7] The letter which he signed included this passage:

> We readily admit the necessity of allowing that liberty in interpreting the formularies of our Church which has been advocated by many of its most learned Bishops and other eminent divines, but this 'Tract' puts forward new and startling views as to the extent to which that liberty may be carried.[8]

Wilson expanded his own position in a pamphlet letter to Churton after the Hebdomadal Board had condemned *Tract XC* and Newman had written that the four tutors had misunderstood his ideas about the Articles. Wilson repeated the views which had appeared in the tutors' letter: that the *Tract* was cunningly ambiguous and implied that anything not specifically condemned in the Articles might be permitted by the Church. On this pretext, Wilson said, Newman was offering apologies for the doctrines of purgatory, pardons, image worship and invocation of saints. Wilson's reaction was straightforward and conventional; he said that such suggestions were against the principles of the Reformation; that the Church's strength depended on a legitimate formal constitution, and that its teaching was based entirely on Scripture. He even referred to the Bible as the 'Word of God', a phrase which most Broad Churchmen, including Wilson himself at a later date, repudiated because it implied a superstitious reverence for the Bible itself and not the moral ideas contained in it. There was a hint of his future thinking at the end of the letter, however, when he stated that the ultimate interpreter of Scripture was the reason and religious sense of the reader, and that each man must find Christ in his own way.[9]

The pamphlet addressed to Churton was not particularly distinguished, and said nothing more than did many opponents of the Tractarians, but from that point Wilson's ideas began to move along a more distinctively Broad Church path. Like Williams, he spent most of his intellectual energy searching for a coherent theology, which he found by the beginning of the 1860s to his own satisfaction; from then on he tended to repeat himself.

The influence of Coleridge began to show most plainly when in October 1843 Wilson preached in the University pulpit on 'The Independence of Particular Churches'. This sermon was the first published indication of his interest in the idea of a national Church which was thereafter to engross his work. Like Coleridge and Arnold, Wilson accepted that a universal Church was not possible, except as an idea, because of unavoidable national differences, and that a comprehensive national Church was needed within each society. Private judgment in matters of religion was to be the basis of such a Church, and every man should be allowed to exercise his reason without provoking controversy.

The sermon was mainly a plea for understanding and charity, and merely touched on the idea of a national Church. Wilson developed the idea much more thoroughly in his Bampton Lectures of 1851, which were entitled *The Communion of Saints*. Even in these, however, there was a certain tentativeness in his thought, which suggests that he was still groping for the truth. In the lectures he tried to establish the basis on which a national Church might rest, and to do this he had to dissect the assumptions which lay behind the various sects of Christendom. The lectures were therefore mainly destructive, to show the weakness of readily-accepted ideas of authority. First, he rejected the belief in authority claimed by traditional dogmas and creeds, supposedly derived from a divine revelation, and sanctioned by centuries of use in the Church. He said:

> Although objective truth, the truth of all things, and of divine realities, in the most eminent sense . . . must ever in itself continue the same, not only may our perceptions and judgments of it

> vary, but the expression of it in languages may be, at one time or another, inadequate, and that which is adequate in one age may cease to convey . . . its object to another.[10]

In this Wilson was close to Coleridge (and to Kant) in suggesting that all knowledge is relative to the knower; that although absolute truth exists, it is not possible for man to grasp it with his limited intelligence, and so to dogmatise is folly. Of course this was in opposition to those who believed that one particular church had been chosen to preserve the truth originally given in a divine revelation.

Secondly, he criticised the notion of 'private judgment', which he maintained was the basis of the teachings of Luther and Calvin. Private judgment was indeed the duty of every Christian, and was closely connected with the Protestant idea of justification by faith, but clearly these ideas could not draw a church together, and churches which were based on individual opinions were either ephemeral or tended to become dogmatic. Wilson was obviously uneasy about the role of private judgment; later, when his own freedom of speech was attacked, he asserted the claims of private judgment more defiantly, as necessary to the national Church.

The third principle of authority which Wilson considered and rejected was divine 'grace', exercised either through the immediate spiritual influence of God on the Christian, including the agency of miracles, or by such influence received through the Sacraments. On this point Wilson differed markedly from orthodox churchmen, because he could not believe that the relationship between God and man was that of divine giver and passive receiver. To him, grace was not a specific spiritual influence on the soul, but 'an elevation of the internal powers of man to their highest possible functions', though he conceded that this was impossible without the Bible, because without it man could not know of his relationship to God.[11] Wilson did not directly attack Biblical miracles, but said that it was degrading to the notion of a perfect and omnipotent Deity that He should have to intervene personally to upset the order of the universe from time to time, merely to convince man of His power. This was a childish idea of divinity, which did not suit a more civilised age.

All this led up to Wilson's chief argument, which was that the main source of possible Church unity lay in man's moral sense, which bound him both to God and his fellows. This idea also came largely from Coleridge,[12] and through him from Kant's idea of a moral order in the universe. Every man had an innate sense of morality, which enabled him to receive Christianity, for Christ had presented in Himself the most perfect system of morality. Christ had founded the Church as an instrument for moral purposes, and only a belief in this duty would give it a sense of unity to override individual difference of opinion. Coleridge had thought that the latent moral sense in every man needed to be stimulated into reflection before it became aware of itself (hence the aim and title of his book *Aids to Reflection*). Wilson shared this idea, and believed that such an awakening was the chief duty of the Church. He thought that the moral sense was universal.

> The modification of our moral nature, when we are placed in relations of moral action and passion, are as uniform under their variety, as are the impressions made on us through the senses. Here arises no question of the extent or nature of the corruption of man, or of the remains of the divine image and similitude which still abide in him; for whatever the depression of his natural state, all alike inherit it; whatever are his capabilities of elevation, in all are the same rudiments of improvement.[13]

Every man, he said, had a sense of his own imperfection, and this was the dynamic principle of Christianity; once the heathen had been aroused to feel moral uneasiness, they too would be drawn towards Christ. Like Williams, Wilson accepted the idea of the innate moral sense of man; both men relied on this sense to provide an accurate guide to the valuable parts of revelation and thus to provide the focus for the life of the national Church.

Like Williams, Wilson had a strong element of both theological and political conservatism in his thought. He wanted to reject part of the Scriptures, but not to reject the need for a revelation altogether. The lectures were delivered three years after the last outbreaks of Chartist agitation in 1848, and Wilson may have had these in mind when he maintained that a greater interest in the teaching of morality would help the Church to replace socialism ('the demoralising selfishness of socialism') in the minds of the people, instead of being identified with the ruling classes.[14]

Maurice tried to solve the same problem by helping to found the Christian Socialist movement in 1849 and by stressing the value of co-operatives in the spirit of Christian brotherhood as an alternative to secular socialism. Wilson said that Christianity did not enjoin community of goods, but that each man held his possessions in trust to be used for the benefit of his fellows. The social principle which arose from man's moral sense was the theory of duty, which should appeal to more people than socialism ever could, and would draw Christians closer to each other. Like Williams, he relied on individual voluntary effort to solve social problems.

The Bampton Lectures offered no solution to the problem of forming a national Church, for Wilson had nothing more constructive to suggest than that confirmation should be held at a later period of life than usual. The lectures were weighty and diffuse and probably were not read much outside Oxford, though the *Record* accused Wilson of denying the importance of creeds and formularies, which were the backbone of the Church, and cited the religious decadence of Germany as the result of such ideas.[15]

In 1850 Wilson accepted the St John's living of Great Staughton in Huntingdonshire, a small and comfortable country parish where he appears to have been an energetic vicar, restoring the church and building a new vicarage. In 1854, during the arguments over university reform, he published a pamphlet urging more representation for members of the university in university government. He was not nearly as liberal in his outlook on this matter as Jowett, and thought that the blessings of open Fellowships had been exaggerated, for they tended to encourage cramming schools. Nor did Wilson favour the German system of professorial teaching, but thought that a reformed university government might be left to manage its own affairs.[16] In fact, Wilson's opinions on most matters were those of many moderate clergymen; even some of the least intellectual sections of the Church were beginning to question traditional values, and Wilson, perhaps more than the other essayists, shows a fairly ordinary mind rising on a current of opinion.

In 1857 he contributed to a book called *Oxford Essays*, which, like *Essays and Reviews*, was a loose collection of essays without an editor. Wilson was in distinguished company, for the other contributors included Gladstone, Sir Edward Grant Duff and Richard Church. The book was a learned work without much reference to current theology except for two essays: 'The Study of the Evidences of Christianity', by Baden Powell, and Wilson's 'Schemes of Christian Comprehension'.

This essay was in many ways Wilson's most interesting production on the subject of the national Church. He discussed two theologians, J. A. Turretin and F. Blackburne, who had both proposed schemes for comprehensive churches, on the assumption that all Protestants agreed on 'fundamental' principles. Wilson wondered why their schemes had failed, and decided that it was impossible to draw up a list of 'fundamentals' which would be accepted by everyone. He extended the argument of the Bampton Lectures: if man's apprehension of divine truths varies according to the intelligence of his age, then dogmatic belief is impossible. Wilson was prepared to state the problem more bluntly than most Broad Churchmen; if the accuracy of both the Scriptural record and man's interpretation of it were in doubt, then man must accept that his religion did not rest on dogmatic certitude but on 'probability', and that in each age man was seeking for a religion which was more 'probable' according to his sense of reason and morality. Wilson did not believe that faith and reason could be separated; reason must judge faith, and faith elevate reason.[17] He did not, however, suggest how this might be done, other than by saying that reason should be tempered with humility.

Like most other Broad Churchmen, Wilson was supremely confident of the truth of his ideas. He was willing to believe that men could live without the certainty which dogma gives, and face the consequences without fear for their faith. All dogmatic illusions were ultimately harmful, and if churches could accept 'probabilities' instead of certainties, then communions could respect each other's principles without conforming to them, and tolerance would become the basis of the national Church. Much of this theory was not new, but was borrowed from Arnold and Bishop Butler.

Like Coleridge, Wilson was aware of divinity immanent in everyday life, and thought it impossible to say where the natural ended and the supernatural began. On the one hand, many 'supernatural' experiences could be explained scientifically; on the other, the ordinary world was full of wonders. This, according to Kennard, was one of the most attractive features of Wilson's teaching, and drew young men to him.[18]

The *Oxford Essays* seem to have inspired Wilson to think of a theological review with topical reference. He received promises for articles from Williams and from Jowett, who took up the idea enthusiastically and asked Temple for contributions, while Williams also asked Goodwin. The origins of *Essays and Reviews* are still somewhat obscure, but Wilson must have been acquainted to some extent with Baden Powell and Mark Pattison, for they had all been at Oxford for many years. Baden Powell was called in at the last moment, when there did not seem to be enough material for the book. The essayists did not see one another's work before publication, and were distressed when their views were treated as identical by orthodox critics, although they refused to repudiate one another. Temple's essay was a hastily rewritten sermon, which he sent to the publisher to meet the deadline. Williams afterwards referred to Wilson as the 'editor' of *Essays and Reviews*, which suggests that Wilson may have known something more than the others about the contents of the book before it went to print, but each writer chose his own subject. The firm of James Parker in Oxford, who had published the *Oxford Essays*, also handled this book. In 1861 pressure from Parker's orthodox friends forced him to hand over the book to Longman's after publishing three editions. Wilson's connection with Williams was tenuous; they had not met by 1860, though Williams was already a well-known Broad Church writer, which may have caused Wilson to approach him.

Wilson's contribution to *Essays and Reviews* was considered by most people, including Stanley, to be the most offensive in the book. Stanley defended the essays of Temple and Jowett, and thought Wilson's the ablest of the remainder, but he wrote: 'Wilson has committed the unpardonable rashness of throwing out statements, without a grain of proof, which can have no other object than to terrify and irritate.'[19] Stanley did not really disagree with Wilson's ideas, although he was not as openly sceptical about miracles, but he always objected to works which provoked controversy. Once the two essayists were in court, he aided them as much as he could and subscribed to the fund for their defence.

Like Williams, Wilson said little in his essay that he had not said in previous works. His views on inspiration of the Scriptures and the basis of religious belief were much the same as those in the *Oxford Essays*, but the essays on 'Séances Historiques de Genève. The National Church', in *Essays and Reviews*, was more outspoken in its tone than the more academic one of 1857, and it naturally drew more attention because of its company.

Wilson's essay followed Coleridge closely in his description of the national Church. Wilson was concerned at the alienation of both educated and uneducated from the churches, and at the common tendency among the orthodox to attribute this alienation either to sinfulness or to the spread of 'German' ideas. Wilson thought that sin and Germany had very little to do with mass apathy, and that men were in fact recoiling from doctrines taught in the churches which they could not reconcile either with their moral feelings or their common sense. He repeated plainly the Coleridgean idea which lay under all his philosophy: 'With respect to the moral treatment of His creatures by Almighty God, all men, in different degrees, are able to be judges of the representations made of it, by reason of the moral sense which He has given them.'[20] To a modern reader Wilson's interpretation of working-class alienation seems naïve. It was one of the weaknesses of the Broad Churchmen that they knew little of the working classes, although they were deeply concerned at their lack of religion. Wilson thought, like Jowett, that once the educated had been reclaimed—which meant a revision of doctrines—the masses could be converted. This view did not, of course, take into account the social differences between educated and uneducated, or understand the difficulty of communication between them. Wilson acknowledged that the problem was more complex than many people thought, and did not think that working-class apathy was due to sinfulness, but he was scarcely aware of its real depth. He had little personal contact with the working classes in the towns and did not realise that the cause of their disaffection was not doctrinal but social and economic.

Like most Broad Churchmen, Wilson applied his moral criticisms mainly to the Old Testament, and found little fault with the New, because he considered the words of Jesus completely in harmony with men's moral sense. He did claim, however, that the purpose of Christ had been to teach not dogma but morality. He argued that the Bible was not the 'Word of God' in the sense that every word of it was inspired, but men should distinguish 'between the different kinds of words which it contains between the dark patches of human passion and error which form a partial crust upon it, and the bright centre of spiritual truth within.'[21] This was close to the ideas of Williams's essay, and was blunt enough to be particularly objectionable to the orthodox, whether High Church or Evangelical. The whole tone of the essay was forthright and made a strong claim for freedom of opinion among the clergy. Subscription to the Articles Wilson saw as one of the greatest barriers to comprehensiveness in the Church, for, he said, the Articles did not claim to interpret or develop the Scriptures, and were obsolete tests against heresies which had long since died. He wished to break down this artificial barrier between clergy and laity. He roused the orthodox to fury by quibbling with the phrasings of subscription and saying that they were capable of a very wide interpretation, yet he himself had objected to Newman's stretching the Articles to permit Anglo-Catholic beliefs. Although he was critical of the Articles, Wilson never suggested that they be removed from the formularies altogether.

Wilson's plans for the comprehensive national Church included Coleridge's idea that ministers should come from every part of the population, regardless of status and education; be paid by national endowment, and be concerned with the ethical development of the people, not with dogmas. Like Coleridge, he saw the Church as a national trust, and deplored the sale of livings. Coleridge's view of mutual toleration Wilson applied particularly to the two schools of Biblical interpretation in his own period; he said that the literalist and the idealist should not condemn each other, and he even essayed a mild defence of Strauss, who, although extravagant in his conclusions, nevertheless explained some details of Jesus's life which were difficult for the literalist. Wilson had no suggestions for implementing his ideas; both he and Coleridge tended to think that once their ideas had become current they would be put into practice. Coleridge, Arnold and

Wilson never thought that the Church could embrace everyone, for human perversity was boundless, but it could become more truly national.

Wilson's allegiance to Coleridge may also explain his earlier hostility to Newman's interpretation of the Articles, because Coleridge was not prepared to allow a Roman type of clergy within the national Church. Those who owed allegiance to a foreign authority, or who deliberately remained celibate, had no real share in their country, and were self-excluded from the national Church.[22] Coleridge had opposed Catholic emancipation; Wilson objected to an interpretation of the Articles which might in fact make the Church more exclusive. This might be inconsistent, but it has always been difficult for a democratic or comprehensive society to account for minority groups who do not recognise democracy or comprehensiveness.

Wilson concluded his essay with a few remarks on the difficulty of living according to Christ's law; he said the Church ought not to occupy itself with dogma, but with teaching men to lead good lives and preparing them for death. He mentioned here his hope that there might be some chance for men to save their souls after death, even if their lives had not been virtuous enough.

> The Roman Church has imagined a *limbus infantium*: we must rather entertain a hope that there shall be found, after the great adjudication, receptacles suitable for those who shall be infants, not as to years of terrestial life, but as to spiritual development—nurseries, as it were, and seed grounds, where the undeveloped may grow up under new conditions . . . and the perverted be restored.[23]

This short statement aroused almost as much hostility towards Wilson as everything else he had said, and it was one of the charges against him. Like Williams, Wilson tested Christian doctrines by his own moral standards, and found that the idea of eternal punishment for the wicked was not consistent with the idea of a loving and merciful God.

Williams always thought that much of the organised attack on *Essays and Reviews* came from Pusey's desire to be avenged on Wilson for *Tract XC*. This was hardly fair to Pusey, who would have been as alarmed and disgusted by Wilson's ideas had he never heard of him before, but the ritualists did tend to think of Wilson's trial as a judgment on him. Like Williams, Wilson became more dogmatic and defiant when under attack. In 1861 he published a lengthy introduction to the work of a lay Broad Churchman which argued against the infallibility of the Scriptures, and defiantly restated his ideas.[24]

Wilson had been invited by John MacNaught,[25] who sympathised with his ideas, to preach at St Chrysostom's Church in Liverpool in May 1861. He prepared three sermons, but was prevented from delivering them by John Graham, the elderly Evangelical Bishop of Chester, who sent a monition to MacNaught forbidding Wilson to preach in his diocese. By this time Wilson was in the same irascible mood as Williams, and he promptly published the three undelivered sermons with a preface attacking the Bishop's legal right to inhibit him and maintaining the right of the clergy to freedom of opinion. Wilson was by now a forthright champion of the right of free inquiry and private judgment, not as ends in themselves, but as indispensable conditions for the discovery of religious truth. He thought that private judgment was the essential principle of Protestantism, and that the Church was becoming 'papal' by trying to remove clergy with unorthodox opinions. Like Jowett, Wilson demanded the right to interpret the Bible like any other book. After the preface, the three sermons themselves were innocuous enough, but Wilson did state in them that the Church was made for man, not man for the Church, which was capable of teaching morally unsound precepts. The second sermon denied the doctrine of original sin as Scripturally untenable and incompatible with morality.[26] MacNaught read the sermons in St Chrysostom's himself.

On 16 December 1861 proceedings began against Wilson in the Court of Arches. Many passages of his essay were cited to prove that he had taught doctrines contrary to those of the Church of England, all of them concerned with Wilson's views on the inspiration of the Bible, except for two passages where he had said that not only Christians would be saved and that there might not be eternal punishment for the wicked. Williams's case was heard immediately before Wilson's, and Sir Stephen Lushington decided to pronounce judgment against both defendants at the same time, which annoyed them because they thought they were entitled to separate treatment. Wilson was found guilty on the three charges mentioned.

Both men were heard together before the Judicial Committee in June 1863. The legal proceedings had now been under way for nearly two years, and were a severe strain for the defendants, neither of whom was in good health at the time. They had become friendly by this period, although Williams disagreed with Wilson's ideas on future punishment and his tampering with the Articles. Williams wrote in his diary in April: 'Wilson's perfect calmness, as well as his deliberate wisdom, in the midst of all turmoil is quite refreshing.'[27]

Both men spoke in their own defence before the Judicial Committee, and Wilson prepared an immensely long and elaborate defence which had to be substantially cut before he could deliver it. He brought all his erudition and eloquence to bear, with the result that the subject of the defence was occasionally lost from view under a great mass of words containing Wilson's opinions on several matters. He contended that he had not taught any doctrines contrary to the Articles and Prayer Book, which were elastic enough to permit a great many diverse opinions. He further claimed that his ideas had been misinterpreted. His speech was delivered in June 1863, and he had only to defend his ideas on eternal punishment and inspiration, as the third charge had been dropped on a technical point.

Westbury, pronouncing judgment in February 1864, upheld Wilson's claim that the Articles did not define 'inspiration' or teach any definite doctrine of the future punishment of the wicked. Orthodox clergy were horrified that a doctrine which they considered indispensable to social morality should be thus put aside. A wit wrote a mock epitaph on Westbury:

> In the Judicial Committee of the Privy Council
> He dismissed Hell with costs,
> And took away from orthodox members of the Church of England
> Their last hope of everlasting damnation.[28]

The immediate results of the trial in orthodox Church circles were a synodical condemnation of *Essays and Reviews* by both houses of Convocation, and a great declaration addressed to the Archbishop of Canterbury, and got up by Pusey and Denison, who for once were able to enlist the support of the Evangelical clergy. The declaration, which had over 11,000 clerical signatures, maintained the clergy's faith in the doctrines which the Judicial Committee was presumed to have overthrown, especially miraculous inspiration and everlasting punishment for the wicked. Part of it was worded as follows:

> We, the undersigned Presbyters and Deacons in Holy Orders of the Church of England and Ireland, hold it to be our bounden duty to the Church and to the souls of men, to declare our firm belief that the Church of England and Ireland, in common with the whole Catholic Church, maintains without reserve or qualification the plenary Inspiration and Authority of the whole Canonical Scriptures as the Word of God, and further teaches, in the words of our Blessed Lord, that the 'punishment' of the 'cursed', as the 'life' of the 'righteous' lasts for ever.[29]

Broad Churchmen like Stanley maintained that few really responsible clergy signed the declaration, and that many of the signatories were curates who had been forced to sign in case their chances of promotion were blighted, but the number did account for 58 per cent of the clergy, most of whom were in the countryside. Thirlwall and Maurice were also scathing about the declaration, and the bishops received it coldly because they did not want the clergy to set themselves up as an independent tribunal.

The Judicial Committee had not tried to show whether Wilson's view of these doctrines was right or wrong, for this was not its function; it merely pointed out that the Church had no formularies clear-cut enough to allow a definite decision. The main result of the judgment was a widespread dissatisfaction with the Judicial Committee as the final court of appeal in ecclesiastical matters. Wilson, who had hoped that the Church might become truly national because comprehensive, had in fact helped to widen the rift between Church and State and to increase the anxieties of orthodox churchmen over the whole constitution of the Church as a national establishment.

After the trial Wilson retired to his parish at Great Staughton. He wrote no more controversial works and concentrated on parish duties. Presumably in such a parish his duties were social as well as pastoral, for there were county families like the Duberleys occupying great houses near by. He cut himself off from

Oxford, but corresponded occasionally with Mark Pattison; in 1867 he grumbled that High Churchmen were having things all their own way in the university. He wrote to Pattison in 1869 that Temple's appointment to Exeter had created a slight demand for *Essays and Reviews* again, which warranted the printing of extra copies. A year later came an extraordinary letter. 'Jowett and I have determined to get out another volume of *Essays and Reviews* and hope you will join us. . . . Our object is to have a much better volume than the last.'[30] There is an incomplete list of the contents of this prospective volume in the few Jowett papers which survive. From the contents, it appears to be an expansion of the first book. Wilson was to write on 'The Principle of Protestanism', Jowett on the lines of 'The Evidence for miracles, the reign of Law, the moral and historical nature of religion', Pattison a sequel to his former essay; Stanley on his favourite subject, the reformation of the liturgy; Edward Caird (the philosopher and future Master of Balliol) on 'The History of Doctrine, Protestant and Catholic', and Max Müller on eastern religions. Lewis Campbell, later Jowett's biographer, was to write on 'Mistranslations and Misreadings of the New Testament'. Jowett conjectured about other possible subject and contributors.[31] All this was purely speculative, and there are many possible reasons why it was never realised. Pattison was soured by controversy, and decided that the English, unlike the Germans, did not have a public sophisticated enough to understand new theological developments.[32] Wilson himself was stricken with paralysis shortly afterwards. Another volume might have embarrassed Temple, who had just been appointed to Exeter, and Jowett himself probably lost interest in the idea because he could at last see before him the prospect of becoming Master of Balliol, which he did in 1870. More controversy might have spoiled his chances.

Yet although there were numerous personal motives for abandoning the project, the central fact remains that the Broad Church had lost its original impetus by 1869 and could not go much further. The Broad Churchmen were inquiring by nature but essentially conservative; they had pushed their inquiries as far as they could without actually denying the inspiration of the Scriptures or the existence of hell or the actuality of prophecy and miracle. To an observer like Edward White Benson, Jowett and

Stanley seemed to have reached the end of their work by the mid-1860s. Benson hoped for more from Temple, whom he greatly admired, but this hope was not fulfilled.[33] Williams, the only essayist who continued to write controversial religious works, only repeated himself, and Maurice produced no new thoughts. One of the difficulties was that none of the essayists, except perhaps the reticent Pattison, was a theologian of first rank, and their notoriety was disproportionate to their attainments, reflecting the unsettled state of the Church rather than the revolutionary nature of their own opinions. More solid work in textual criticism was being done at Cambridge by Benson's friends, Lightfoot, Westcott and Hort, who evaluated the text of the Scriptures without the preconceived notions of the Broad Churchmen or their sense of mission, and so received much less publicity.[34] These were the founders of a solid, learned school of theology, on which the authors of the famous *Lux Mundi* built. *Lux Mundi* (1889) did not come to conclusions much different from *Essays and Reviews*, but the basis of the argument had become much less speculative by then, and the later descendants of the Tractarians sought for a synthesis between Anglo-Catholicism and liberal theology, to the dismay of the embattled ritualists who survived from the 1860s.[35]

Unlike Rowland Williams, Wilson has left few traces of his character behind. By the time of *Tract XC* his singlemindedness had gained him a reputation in Oxford for being 'crotchetty' and one of Tait's friends was rather alarmed to find Tait's name coupled with Wilson's in the protest of the four tutors. As a tutor he invited students to private Sunday lectures on St Paul, and they admired him for his 'Protestantism' and opposition to any form of spiritual tyranny.[36] He won the lasting devotion of at least one of them, R. B. Kennard, who considered him one of the greatest minds in the Broad Church. This is probably true, but it rather points out the general scarcity of brilliance in the Church on this side. He was incapacitated for sixteen years by his paralytic stroke of 1870, which prevented him from carrying out his parish duties. He lived until 1888, when *Essays and Reviews* was largely forgotten except by the generation of older churchmen, like Denison, whom it had so distressed. In Wilson was seen most strongly the Broad Church's desire for tolerance and freedom of opinion within the national Church, and for him, as for many Broad Churchmen, the result of his ideas was to increase the party divisions within the Church. Yet his views would be accepted by many churchmen today; had they been more generally received in his own time the fate of the Church might have been different.

Notes to this chapter are on pages 252–3

Chapter 6 CHARLES VOYSEY

AFTER THE acquittal of Williams and Wilson, Broad Churchmen hoped for more freedom for clergymen to express criticism of the Scriptures. Stanley, who was in the court when the judgment was pronounced, believed that the Church was no longer committed to outworn doctrines, especially those of the verbal inspiration of the Bible, and of eternal punishment for the wicked. 'I hope that all will now go on smoothly', he wrote, 'and that the Bible may be really read without these terrible nightmares.'[1] Yet the essayists had escaped mainly because their criticism of the Scriptures was generalised and could be interpreted in such a way as not to contradict the plainer parts of the Articles and liturgy. This Broad Church tendency to stop halfway did not satisfy everyone who started off on the same critical road. Charles Voysey determined to push Broad Church criticism of the Scriptures to some definite conclusion and to demand the right to use such criticism as part of his everyday pastoral teaching.

All the Broad Churchmen approached the Bible in the light of their own conceptions of morality, but none more directly than Voysey. His criticism was hardly related to the new scientific and philological arguments, although he was aware of them, but his method was to subject the Bible to the uncompromising test of his own idea of what was morally acceptable. Because his criteria were as simple as this, it will not be necessary to deal with his ideas at length; unlike the leading Broad Churchmen he was not an academic writer but a hard-working and underpaid perpetual curate. He was not more learned than most country clergymen, though probably he was more inquiring than many. His published works are clear, direct and not scholarly. Voysey became notorious because he insisted on forcing his opinions on public notice, but he always maintained that his ideas were not unusual, and, indeed, that they were shared by many clergymen who were more shy of expressing them openly. In 1870 he wrote to a well-wisher:

> If I cannot reckon on more than two or three men as outspoken as myself, I can reckon by the hundreds, clergy who are deeply influenced by what has been said this last five years. And so the leaven works, not quickly, but surely.[2]

It is impossible to say whether Voysey was exaggerating in his estimate of the numbers of clergy who sympathised with him, but there were certainly many people, including clergy, who supported him financially in his legal battles and saw no reason why he should not remain in the Church. Voysey's own life shows the effect which the ideas of Coleridge and the Broad Church could have on a thoughtful and practical-minded parson. Like Williams, he courted martyrdom for his opinions, and was prepared to renounce material benefits for the sake of ideas. He also reveals the spirit of dogmatic certainty which afflicted the Church at this period; like Pusey or Archbishop Thomson or Williams, Voysey was certain that his own ideas were the only correct ones, and that anyone who contradicted them must be morally wrong. Like other Broad Churchmen, he succeeded only in accentuating the party divisions within the Church, and was prepared to carry his own notions to the point of founding a church of his own in which to express them.

Charles Voysey, born in 1828, was the son of an architect who died when he was ten years old. Voysey then began the struggle against poverty which was to continue for over thirty years. He was brought up to hold strict Evangelical opinions, and managed to obtain money from an Evangelical foundation in order to read for his BA degree at St Edmund Hall, Oxford. Voysey was a student in the late 1840s, at a time, he recalled, when the diversity of opinion on religious matters was very marked in the university, but before it had crystallised into the kind of personal hostility which was common in the 1860s.[3] Voysey heard sermons with contradictory views preached week after week in the university pulpit; he became sceptical of his early beliefs but was never in danger of losing his faith. With the straightforwardness which was characteristic of him, he informed the society which supported him financially of his conversion to liberal opinions, and they withdrew their grant. He managed to finish his studies only with the help of the vice-principal of St Edmund Hall, the Rev John Hill, who gave him financial aid although he did not agree with his opinions. He took his degree in 1851 and was ordained.

Voysey then undertook a series of poorly-paid curacies. He worked in a parish in Hull for seven years without a fixed stipend, and then spent eighteen months in Jamaica. At some time during this period he was brought to the notice of Stanley, who became his friend and helped him to obtain a curacy at Great Yarmouth in 1860. He left this parish after six months because he disagreed with the incumbent over *Essays and Reviews*, which he supported. Stanley again helped him to find another curacy at St Mark's, Whitechapel. Here he preached against the doctrine of eternal punishment for the wicked and antagonised some of the parishioners. He was forced to leave this curacy also, and Tait appointed him to another in the Victoria Docks area—there was, after all, a shortage of curates willing to work in poorly-paid benefices in London. After six months Voysey was invited to become curate of the parish of Healaugh, about nine miles from York. The perpetual curate of Healaugh, the Rev Edward Hawke Brooksbank, was also the patron of the benefice and had held it since 1813. He had apparently heard of Voysey and approved of his opinions.[4] When Brooksbank retired from the cure in 1864 he offered it to Voysey, who accepted it and so became perpetual curate at a salary of £108 a year. Voysey never earned more than £120 a year in England, and on this he had to support his mother, his wife and his eight children. Domestic responsibility therefore weighed far more heavily on him than on most of the other well-known Broad Churchmen, nearly all of whom were bachelors or childless, with comfortable incomes.

Healaugh was a small parish, with a population of only 260, most of whom attended church. Voysey soon made his ideas plain to his congregation and to the clergy of York. On 10 July 1864, only five months after the Judicial Committee had acquitted Williams and Wilson, Voysey preached a sermon which was published shortly afterwards as *Is Every Statement in the Bible about our Heavenly Father Strictly True?* Voysey had been encouraged by the Judicial Committee's decision, and had taken it as a legal precedent to allow clergy to criticise the divine inspiration of the Bible openly. According to the Church Calendar, the lessons for the day on 10 July were *2 Sam* XXI and XXIV, in which it is asserted that God sent a plague upon Israel after Saul's death as a punishment for Saul's sins. It is also stated that God had incited David to number the people, in contradiction to *1 Chron* XXI. 1, where the incitement is attributed to Satan. To Voysey these passages were not consistent with his own idea of a just and merciful God, and he decided that if they were immoral they could not be true. He therefore preached against them, and denied that either story was the word of God. Voysey's sermon sold three editions, but he withdrew it from circulation when a fellow clergyman, who had paid for it to be printed, was reprimanded by Archbishop Thomson.[5]

In 1865 Voysey began to publish some of his sermons in a monthly series called *The Sling and the Stone.* At first they were little more than Broad Church criticism of the Bible on moral grounds, though more specific in their references than the criticism of Williams. Voysey picked out certain parts of the Bible and said they were of no value. One particular passage which aroused his anger was *2 Kings* X, which relates that God commanded Jehu to murder the priests of Baal by treachery. Williams, at almost the same time, was preaching on the same passage in Broad Chalke; he explained that God had not really 'commanded' the murders, but that human agents had somehow fulfilled a divine purpose while furthering their own ends. The story was not a divine injunction on nineteenth-century readers, Williams said, but showed the developing ideas of justice and sanctity which were expressed only crudely in the Old Testament but fully and clearly in the New.[6] This was a good example of how the Broad Churchmen tried to find something edifying behind the darkest passages of the Old Testament. Voysey, on the other hand, denied that the story had any significance for contemporary Christians at all, and maintained that it had helped to obscure man's knowledge of God as a just and merciful Father for centuries.

Voysey sent a prospectus of his sermons to Archbishop Thomson in 1865, and Thomson noticed with disquiet that they were published by Thomas Scott. Scott was a well-known freethinker, and ran a private press on which he printed at his own expense tracts by other freethinkers, including F. W. Newman. Thomson warned Voysey that Scott might be using him to test how far latitude of opinion might be carried in the Church of England, but Voysey replied that Scott was not a biased man and that no Church publisher would accept the sermons. He said he was determined to speak the truth as he saw it, and deplored the attitude of many clergy, who resembled the priesthood of the pre-Reformation Church in denying freedom of opinion to their fellows. He contended that many clergy agreed with him, but were too afraid of legal and social reprisals to speak out: 'Many clergy and laity think with me, but cannot face the kind of treatment to which such men as Professor Jowett, Mr Wilson, and the Bishop of Natal have been exposed.'[7]

William Thomson, Archbishop of York, was utterly opposed to Voysey in his theological opinions, so it is surprising that he took no action against him for several years. Although in his youth he had admired Kant and Coleridge, Thomson was a most orthodox Evangelical in his ideas. From being a popular Evangelical preacher he had become Provost of Queen's College in 1855 and Bishop of Gloucester and Bristol in 1861. A few months later he was translated to York. He was a powerful man, both in body and in his diocesan government, and one of the first bishops in the nineteenth century to appeal directly to working men, with whom he became immensely popular.[8] He was known to be most hostile to ritualists, and did all he could to keep them out of his diocese, but he did not bring any lawsuits against them until after the passing of the Public Worship Regulation Act, of which he was one of the chief supporters. He was equally opposed to the Broad Church, and contributed to *Aids to Faith*, a conservative reply to *Essays and Reviews*. After the Judicial Committee's judgment on the essayists, in which he had been overruled by the other judges, he published (as did Archbishop Longley) a pastoral letter to his clergy to explain that the Judicial Committee had not been able to judge the book as a whole, but only extracts. He affirmed his belief in the divine inspiration of the Bible and in the doctrine of eternal punishment for the wicked.[9] In spite of his disagreement with his fellow judges, Thomson strongly supported the Church's legal machinery as it was, but did not like to use the law against recalcitrant clergy because he thought it gave them undesirable notoriety. As a trustee of the Colonial Bishoprics Fund, Thomson acquiesced in the withdrawal of Colenso's salary by that body; at the same time, Voysey was privately collecting money in his parish to aid Colenso's defence.

Voysey continued to publish his sermons. In 1865 and 1866 he elaborated his ideas on the doctrine of future punishment, and said, like Wilson, that it was in man's nature to hope that even after death God could save sinners. This was a subject very much debated after the Judicial Committee's decision on Wilson. The Declaration of the Clergy had affirmed orthodox belief in the necessity of the doctrine, and churchmen of all parties had written to defend it. Keble collected all the passages in the Bible and liturgy which mentioned hell, and published them together with prayers for deliverance. Pusey wrote to Tait that if the doctrine were discarded social anarchy would result. 'I am persuaded', he said, 'that such a decision would be most demoralising to our unhappily too demoralised country. I am sure that nothing will keep men from the present pleasures of sin, but the love of God or the fear of Hell; and that the fear of Hell drives people back to . . . God.'[10]

Even the Broad Churchmen were divided in their attitude towards this doctrine. Wilson had only expressed a pious hope that all men might be saved; he had not openly denied the existence of hell. Williams told his parishioners to lead good lives and not to speculate about the future state, but he thought that the parable of Dives and Lazarus showed that Christ's teaching did not forbid the idea of eternal punishment. Maurice, who had been forced to resign from King's College because of his opinions on the subject, was also disturbed. He had come to reject the orthodox doctrine, but could not ignore the fact that the Bible mentioned 'everlasting fire' for the wicked. He could only escape from this dilemma by asserting that the Greek word for 'eternal' used in the New Testament did not mean 'everlasting' but 'indefinite', and that therefore the pains of hell might be only temporary.[11] In 1864 Maurice urged the clergy to teach about God's love, not His wrath, in order to win back the people to the Church, but he could not deny that wrath was also part of the Scriptures. Stanley, however, rejoiced because he thought the clergy were no longer bound to teach the doctrine.

Voysey went much further than most Broad Churchmen in his view of this doctrine, and also in the conclusions which he drew from it. He said that no human sin could be great enough to deserve endless torments, for this would not be consistent with the idea of a benevolent God. Voysey's concept of God was drawn from the standards of morality which he believed to be innate in every man; all Broad Churchmen believed in natural morality to some extent, but they did not deny that the Bible was necessary to awaken this moral sense. Voysey, however, decided that religion was entirely an internal matter, and that most external aids could be abandoned, as he said in one of his sermons. 'God need no longer be sought in books, or among ecclesiastics—in the musty libraries of the fathers, or in the scarcely less incoherent gibberish of modern Christianity; but in the deep secrets of a man's own heart, where God dwells.'[12] On such grounds Voysey was able to reject the idea of hell, but from this he also concluded that, if hell were not real, then salvation in the commonly-accepted sense was not necessary either. He thought that men were sinful but that they were capable of perfection, and that the only salvation men need ask of God was salvation from sin, which carried with it its own misery on earth. Voysey's ideas gradually developed along these lines until, in 1868, he denied that Christ's sacrifice was necessary for man's salvation. Other Broad Churchmen, particularly Jowett and Williams, saw Christ's sacrifice as a voluntary offering to God, which was pleasing to God not because of the pain Christ suffered but because of the unselfish devotion it showed. This was not the teaching of the orthodox, who thought that Christ had died as a vicarious sacrifice to appease the wrath of God against the human race. Voysey came to deny that Christ's death had been necessary for man at all, for man needed no justification to the God who had created him. To Voysey, salvation was the gradual progress of the human spirit towards perfection.[13]

Voysey had obviously gone far beyond any of the teachings of the Broad Church of his day, and he caused great alarm among the neighbouring clergy. They asked Archbishop Thomson to prosecute him, and their pleas were reinforced by several petitions to Convocation by both private groups of clergy and organised bodies like the Church Union. The Convocation of Canterbury decided in 1868 that Voysey's works were so patently blasphemous that it was unnecessary to issue a synodical condemnation as they had done in the case of *Essays and Reviews*; Voysey would hardly be able to escape the law. Voysey maintained that he was obliged by his sense of honesty to speak out, and that his views caused very little disturbance among his parishioners, only ten of whom, he said, openly disagreed with him, and of these only four stayed away from Church.[14]

With great pressure on him to prosecute, Thomson allowed Voysey to be arraigned in the Chancery Court of York, and his case was heard in December 1869. He was accused on 38 points, most of which concerned his denial of Christ's atonement, denial of original sin, the inspiration and authority of the Scriptures and the divinity of Christ. Voysey was defended by James Fitzjames Stephen, Leslie Stephen's older brother, who had successfully defended Williams and Wilson. Voysey argued, as the essayists had done, that the doctrine of the Church of England was flexible on such subjects as inspiration, atonement and eternal punishment. He did, however, set out his own ideas more plainly than the essayists had. He said that he did not deny Christ's divinity, but maintained that all men partook of divinity equally with Christ. He relied heavily on the judgment in the essayists' case to show that the Church had already decided that the Bible was not divinely inspired throughout. Furthermore, he said: 'It has thus been judicially determined that a clergyman of the Church of England may lawfully affirm that parts of the Bible . . . are false and wicked; and it has never been decided how far he may go in this direction.'[15] Voysey contended that he was only saying with more specific detail what Wilson had said in general terms. He did not try to gloss over his ideas, or to show that they were capable of an orthodox interpretation, for, he said, it was not he but the Church which was on trial to prove whether or not it was devoted to a rigid interpretation of obsolete doctrines. Voysey was found guilty of false teaching and deprived of his living.

The trial had occasioned much excitement, especially among Broad Churchmen, who, although they did not accept all Voysey's ideas, believed that their own liberty of opinion would be in danger if he were found guilty. Stanley, who had corresponded with Voysey for many years, deplored his outspokenness, which he did not think was needed to instruct a rural congregation. 'Do what you can to drive out error by stating the truth', he wrote, 'and not . . . secure the truth by always attacking error.'[16] Stanley, as in the case of *Essays and Reviews*, disliked controversy, but nevertheless helped Voysey in his difficulties. He believed that Voysey was an honest and devout man and that the Church should not try to restrain freedom of opinion. Stanley, thus true to Arnold's teaching, became a member of a committee which was set up to raise funds for Voysey's legal expenses. Jowett was also on this committee. Neither of them, nor Maurice, questioned Voysey's right to stay within the Church. When Voysey decided to appeal to the Judicial Committee of the Privy Council, however, both his solicitors and the defence committee urged him to withdraw for his own sake and that of the Broad Church; there was still a slight chance of his obtaining a living in another diocese if he did not push his opinions to the extreme test in law. But Voysey still hoped that the cases of the essayists and Colenso would be precedent enough to save him, and determined to vindicate his opinions at all costs.[17]

Voysey received aid, not only from Broad Churchmen but from free-thinkers, including Bradlaugh. He was also given financial help by Thomas Allsop, who had been a friend of Coleridge and was an avowed atheist. Voysey, like all Broad Churchmen, greatly admired Coleridge, and during the year in which he waited for his appeal to be heard he corresponded frequently with Allsop. His letters reveal that, like Williams, he was determined to be a martyr for the sake of his principles. He also wished to justify himself for the sake of all those clergy who, he thought, were labouring under a sense of restraint and could not express their true opinions. 'My hope is', he wrote, 'by staying in the Church, to burst its horrid mental fetters for thousands besides myself.'[18] Allsop hoped that Temple might give Voysey a living in the diocese of Exeter, but Voysey was contemptuous of Temple because he considered him too mild and cautious and afraid of pursuing inquiry to its logical limits. Temple did not aid Voysey's defence fund, probably because Voysey's opinions were far more extreme than his own, and his sense of episcopal responsibility would in any case have precluded such an action.

In February of 1871 the Judicial Committee pronounced judgment. It consisted of only one clerical member, Tait, and three laymen. Voysey's main defence had been that he was not teaching against the doctrines of the Church, but against 'popular glosses' on them, which had given rise to doctrines like that of eternal punishment. He said that the *Essays and Reviews* judgment had laid down that clergy should be allowed freedom of opinion in such matters. The Judicial Committee, however, decided against him unanimously, and the judgment, which was largely Tait's work, found him guilty of having denied specific doctrines; inspiration of the Scriptures, salvation, Christ's atonement and His divinity, and the doctrine of the Trinity. He was deprived of his living after he refused to retract his errors. Voysey was not dashed by the judgment, and wrote to Allsop:

> All I hope is that I shall cling to what is *true* & find out more of what is true than I knew already. Nothing else will satisfy me, but I believe I am leagues & leagues away from turning atheist, for I believe in God quite as much as I do in my own dear wife & children and do not mind being thought a fool for it by those who cannot see God for themselves. I am not aware of any change in my condition since my condemnation, I have only been a little more emphatic than I was before; but even then my own parishioners were well seasoned long ago in all I am teaching now.[19]

Voysey lived for more than forty years after the judgment, and his later career was as active as his work as an Anglican clergyman, though more financially secure. He was a man of attractive personality and an excellent preacher; his case therefore aroused considerable personal sympathy among unorthodox thinkers. London in the later decades of the nineteenth century was a hive of freethinking congregations, some of which were prepared to give generous financial help to their ministers. Immediately after the judgment Voysey was invited by two freethinking patrons to come to London and preach his own ideas; they also guaranteed him a salary of a minimum of £50 a year.[20] Voysey accepted and began his own theistic church in July 1871 in St George's Hall, Langham Place. He lectured in this hall to a loyal audience, and continued to publish his lectures as the *Sling and the Stone.* In these lectures and in other works he explained his idea of religion, which finally moved away from orthodox Christianity altogether. He openly denied the divinity of Christ, and said that religion rested entirely on man's own sense of morality and that the central axiom of all religion must be that 'God is at least as good as we are'. He also conducted his own form of worship, using a version of the Prayer Book which he had prepared himself, with all the parts he considered morally objectionable cut out of it. Voysey's congregation finally found a chapel of their own in Swallow Street, Piccadilly, where they remained from 1887 to 1912. After Voysey's death the theistic congregation split into two, but survived well into the twentieth century.

The Broad Church's ideas had failed to satisfy Voysey, and he demanded more liberty of opinion than the Church could allow him. He wished to push Broad Church ideas of a comprehensive Church to their limit, and it is to the credit of Broad Churchmen like Jowett and Stanley that they accepted his right, as an honest and devout man, to stay within the Church, even though they did not agree with his ideas. Yet Stanley may have been right when he said that Voysey was unnecessarily vehement in his opinions; his duty was to preach the spirit of Christianity, not to involve himself in doctrinal disputes. The opposition he encountered from orthodox clergy led Voysey into more and more extreme opinions, and he was forced by the intolerant atmosphere of his age into his own form of intolerance, which encouraged him to seek martyrdom even though it would help to prolong party division within the Church. Stanley himself was not free of controversy, especially in defence of his friends, but he thought that the truth would prevail in its own time and that meanwhile the Church should not diminish its energies by splitting into dogmatic factions. But pacifying voices like Stanley's were lost in the clamour that arose over the opinions of militants like Denison, Williams or Voysey; and in the event of open hostilities most churchmen were forced to take sides.

Notes to this chapter are on pages 253–4

Chapter 7 THE AUTHORITY OF THE BISHOPS

IN GOVERNMENT

WHILE BROAD Churchman like Williams, Wilson and Voysey demanded freedom to pursue religious inquiries as they wished, the forces of orthodoxy were gathering to restrain them. Broad Churchmen hoped for a second Reformation in which they would be the leaders, but many orthodox clergy were trying to organise various forms of counter-Reformation. The High Church party in particular were trying to draw the Church together behind a solid barrier of dogmatic authority, preferably with the help of the State, but they were prepared to do without this, if necessary. The Broad Churchmen denied traditional authority, whether of Church or Scripture, and this helped to provoke the orthodox into a more desperate search for a final authority which could preserve their doctrines. There were other dangers which forced the Church into introspection and revealed to it the need for improved organisation at national and local level; especially the threat from Dissent towards Church privileges. But behind much Church organisation was fear that rationalists, among whom the Broad Churchmen were included, would destroy the traditional authority of the Scriptures and the teachings of the Church. In the face of this common threat, some Evangelicals relinquished their apathy towards centralisation, but the old division between High and Low, exacerbated by the excesses of the ritualists, continued to frustrate reorganisation. Centralised government was needed to direct the Church's activities to some purpose and enable it to meet the challenges of the nineteenth century, but the supporters of centralisation tended to advocate it for partisan reasons rather than the general good; and this caused others to reject it for equally partisan reasons.

In such a period of introspection and reorganisation, it was natural that the function of the bishops as leaders of the Church should be reviewed. Some hoped that they would become the national executives of a more tightly organised Church, and some even wished them to have more power over the opinions of the clergy. Some of the bishops themselves shared this idea, and made an attempt to assert themselves at both a national and a diocesan level. The most active champion of these centralising forces was Samuel Wilberforce, who saw his three brothers, William, Robert and Henry join the Church of Rome because, like Newman, they were deeply suspicious of the State's ability to interfere with the teaching of the Anglican Church. Samuel Wilberforce remained behind to fight for what he believed to be religious consistency, even at the cost of disestablishment. In the long run the bishops proved incapable of the kind of central reorganising which orthodox High Churchmen believed was necessary, but some of them did valuable work in their dioceses, where they were less impeded by their relationship with the State. But for a while there were high hopes that the bishops might succeed in becoming the defenders of orthodoxy, and this chapter will show how they met the challenge. The divisions of opinion among the bishops themselves reflect to a large extent the divisions within the whole Church, and it will be seen that party hostility prevented the bishops from uniting, even on obvious and useful reforms like the creation of new sees and the revival of diocesan conferences.

In spite of opposition from Dissenters, the bishops retained their seats in the House of Lords, though since 1847, when Russell had created the new see of Manchester, the most recently appointed bishop had to wait for the death of one of his seniors before taking his seat. Social ideas about the bishops' functions, however, were changing, and this also affected their parliamentary work and the attitude of the State towards them. Prime ministers had the power to nominate new bishops, and still tended to choose men of their own party, but by the middle of the century the bishops were more independent of party politics than their predecessors in the eighteenth century had been. The ideals of the age rejected bishops who did not reside in their sees and who spent their time in London society and secular politics. In 1836 the Ecclesiastical Commission had adjusted episcopal incomes to prevent the undignified spectacle of poorer bishops scrambling for translation to the wealthy sees. Nor were bishops permitted to hold other livings together with their sees. Bishop Phillpotts of Exeter, who was in his eighty-second year in 1860, had been one of the last to insist on supplementing his income in this way, and he had relinquished a wealthy living only when bribed with a stall in his own cathedral. The Act of 1836 took property from the wealthy sees to supplement the poorer, but this could only take effect on the deaths of the men who occupied them at the time of the Act, so in 1860 Sumner of Winchester was the last bishop to have the magnificent Hanoverian income of his see.

Expansion of the press brought the bishops, like all other public officials, far more popular notice than before, and even less than secular officials could they afford adverse publicity about their private or professional lives. Bishops were no longer chosen only because of their political affiliations; they needed at least a modicum of learning, and to be earnest churchmen of exemplary life, likely to be efficient and conscientious in their work. During the frequent debates on a possible increase of the number of bishops, Wilberforce objected to the creation of suffragans to aid the holders of large sees, because it might tempt them to spend too much time on worldly affairs in Parliament, to the neglect of their spiritual duties. Some also felt that it would be unnecessary to pay newly-created bishops the minimum salary of £4,200, because if they were deprived of a seat in the House of Lords they would not have to leave their dioceses and maintain a London residence. Lord Ebury said that the clergy 'wanted Bishops who would be nearer to themselves, and not Prince Bishops'.[1]

The bishops of the mid-century lived up to this idea of episcopal duty, and did indeed spend most of their time in their dioceses. The Welsh sees especially benefited from resident bishops for the first time in many generations. Welsh bishops had usually shunned their poor and inhospitable sees for more comfortable livings elsewhere. Although the Victorian bishops had to cope with the great increase in population, they were particularly zealous in the duties of visitation and confirmation, and better roads and new railways enabled them to reach distant parts of their see. Some rarely left their dioceses; it was difficult and expensive for many of them to travel to and reside in London, and those who did tended to come up after Easter, in the middle of the session, so ecclesiastical affairs were usually debated then. Old age also prevented bishops from travelling, and Phillpotts did not come to take part in London affairs between 1860 and his death in 1869. Between twelve and nineteen bishops usually voted in any one session, except in 1862 when six was the largest episcopal vote raised on any debate.* Nor did the bishops appear in the House in these numbers all at once, and very few of them actually debated. They confined themselves to voting on ecclesiastical matters and on social policies which affected the Church, such as Sunday closing, though Tait as Bishop of London was also active in preventing the Imperial Gas Company from enlarging its premises, which threatened the health of many Londoners (and also the atmosphere of Tait's palace at Fulham). Wilberforce carried on his father's tradition by strongly supporting the abolition of public executions.

The bishops were more than usually quiescent in the politics of the mid-century, not only because of popular opinion but because of the deliberate policy of Lord Palmerston. Although bishops were no longer chosen for blatantly political motives, a prime minister naturally did not wish to promote a man who would oppose him, and Palmerston, influenced to some extent by Shaftesbury, usually appointed sober Evangelicals with no particular bias and no great distinction in character or learning, who would put their sees before their politics. In 1861 ten of the bench were his nominees. Apart from Tait, Thomson and the orthodox Evangelical Whigs Ellicott of Gloucester and Waldegrave of Carlisle, the Palmerston bishops were silent and often absent from the House of Lords.[2] Palmerston's opponents thought he was sapping the strength of the Church by such appointments, as appears in a hostile notice in the *Saturday Review*:

* Throughout this chapter, numbers of bishops in divisions refer only to English bishops, unless otherwise stated.

> The rulers of the Church of England are not required at any time to be profound and recluse students; their work is of a different kind. But they are required, at such a juncture as the present, to be on a level with their age in point of knowledge, liberal-minded, and capable of sympathising with different schools of thought, to the full extent of the range which a Church avowedly comprehensive permits within her pale. If they are such men as, till his last appointment, Lord PALMERSTON had generally given us, all the safety valves of opinion will soon be closed, and the final explosion will inevitably ensue.*

Palmerston's six appointments from 1860 to 1865, except for Thomson, were undistinguished. Of the remaining bishops in 1861, six had been appointed by Russell; these tended to be more learned divines than Palmerston's, but after the unpopular choice of Hampden, Russell had been careful to pick more orthodox men. Four had been chosen by Peel, three by Aberdeen, two (including Thirlwall) by Melbourne, one by Wellington, and C. R. Sumner by Liverpool at the express wish of George IV. Naturally on such a bench there were a large number of Whigs, who revealed themselves in the only division in the 1860s in which they were called on to vote by party. In 1864 the Conservatives moved a vote of censure against Palmerston's government for not supporting Denmark against Prussia in the Schleswig-Holstein question. Fifteen bishops voted with the government, eight of them by proxy, and only two, Wilberforce and Campbell of Bangor, against it. The motion was defeated in the Lords by 177 votes to 168, so the episcopal support was some help to Palmerston.[3]

The bishops avoided the Reform Bill of 1867 almost entirely; only Wilberforce, Graham of Chester and Jeune of Peterborough appeared occasionally to vote during the discussion of the amendments. This revealed the decline of the bishops' interest in purely political matters. During the debates which led up to the passing of the first Reform Act, the bench had made itself extremely unpopular by its opposition to the Whig reforms. In 1831, twelve English and four Irish bishops had voted against the second reading of the Bill, with only one bishop voting for the

* *Saturday Review*, 23 March 1861, p 286. The last appointment was Thomson.

government.[4] As the bill had been only narrowly defeated in the Lords, the bishops found themselves the focus of popular agitation. Phillpotts, newly-created Bishop of Exeter, laid the foundation of his great unpopularity by his unswerving opposition to reform. Inside and outside Parliament the bishops were subject to vehement attacks; their carriages were assailed on their way to Westminster, and windows of episcopal palaces were broken. Phillpotts was burned in effigy, and the Bishop of Bristol's palace was set on fire. When in the following year the Lords were forced to pass the Reform Bill, nine bishops voted for the second reading and eight against. Their unpopularity was increased by the weakness of the Church at that time, with all its old abuses of plurality and non-residence and unequal incomes. The politics of the 1830s were much taken up with Church reforms, which most bishops did their best to block, but the Church was forced to turn its attention to its internal problems, and there was a strong reaction against episcopal interference in secular matters.

Hence the episcopal lack of interest in secular politics in the mid-century, but statesmen who had appointed them could still rouse the bishops if necessary. During the debates on the third Reform Bill of 1884, when Gladstone felt he needed episcopal support, he gathered together his nominees to vote. He had classified eleven bishops, together with the Archbishop of Canterbury, as 'A' and thought he could rely on them. He also hoped that others, graded 'B', might vote with him though he had no claim on them. He sent a circular to them, urging them to vote.[5] As a result, the two archbishops and nine of his 'A' bishops voted with the Bill, and one 'B' bishop. Only one voted against. Archbishop Benson gave a short formal speech in support of the Bill, but no other bishop spoke; it was not really part of their affairs.[6]

Evangelicals predominated on the bench, partly because they were favoured by the Whigs and partly because the High Church was becoming increasingly identified with ritualist practices. During the mid-century the accidence of episcopal deaths did not give the Conservatives much chance to appoint to the bench; but between 1868 and 1870 Gladstone had to appoint nine new bishops and was conscientious in his task. Unlike his Whig predecessors, he was not drawn towards quiescent Evangelicals, and tried to choose men who suited the inclinations of the vacant diocese and who represented a particular section of Church opinion. Nor was he afraid to appoint men with very High Church tendencies, like Christopher Wordsworth, whom he sent to Lincoln in 1869. In the same year Gladstone appointed the Evangelical C. A. Hervey to Bath and Wells and Frederick Temple to Exeter, though their ideas differed from his own, and Temple was still partly under the shadow of *Essays and Reviews*. Gladstone outlined his principles of selection to Arthur Kinnaird.

> I quite agree with you that what may be called sectional men should be sometimes appointed Bps: and at the same time they should as a rule be the milder specimens. It was on this footing as I thought that both Ld. A Hervey & Dr Temple stood: & so, I may say to you they are recognised by the Archbp. of C. I was astonished when I read in the Record that Ld A Hervey was not to be recognised as an Evangelical Clergyman. . . . If you have an opportunity of reading or looking at Dr. Temple's sermons *Pray do so*. My recollection impresses me with the belief that you will find them those of a pious *Low Churchman.*[7]

To later observers, especially ritualists, the bishops of the mid-nineteenth century seemed far too pale and complaisant. 'For a while the bishops clogged the wheels of the Church. They originated nothing, they had no programme, no definite aims, no organising power,' wrote Baring Gould, a prejudiced ritualist, in 1914.[8] But the state of ecclesiastical tension at that time prevented a prime minister from appointing any man with too decided views. Gould's ideals were Benson, Gore, Lightfoot, and enlightened Anglo-Catholics whose ideas were only developed later in the century. Had an extreme ritualist been appointed to the bench instead of mild ones like Hamilton and Wordsworth, there would probably have been a storm in the Church greater than that over Hampden.

Yet numbers of intellectually mediocre bishops did affect the quality of the bench, and this meant that one or two able ones dominated them in Parliament. The two archbishops attended regularly, and the Archbishop of Canterbury was expected to give some indication of the Church's opinions of the government's work, a task which the modest Longley performed quietly but diligently. Thomson was a more forceful man, and interested in legislation for the education of workers and children in industrial areas. Waldegrave of Carlisle also spoke frequently, mainly about the need to eradicate ritualism. Thirlwall was much respected by the House for his learning, but spoke at length only on occasions which strongly affected him; several times he went against the opinion of the rest of the bench in supporting emancipation for Jews and Dissenters and the disestablishment of the Irish Church.

By far the most active participants in debates were Wilberforce and Tait, the latter having, of course, the advantage of living in London, which enabled him to attend Parliament frequently. Tait believed firmly in the mutual dependence of Church and State, and thought that disestablishment would deliver the Church up to party strife and anarchy. On the other hand, he wished the Church to be fully represented by the bishops in Parliament, and he spoke on all important ecclesiastical matters. Wilberforce was his natural opposite and rival for the see of Canterbury, though more his equal in talent and energy than any other member of the bench. The tide of disestablishment seemed to be flowing gently but inexorably at this time, which saw the abolition of compulsory Church rates in 1868 after years of argument, the disestablishment and partial disendowment of the Irish Church in 1869, and the admission of non-Anglicans to the electorate and government of the universities of Oxford and Cambridge in 1871. Although both Tait and Wilberforce voted for the first two measures after a period of opposition, their motives for capitulation were different. Tait believed that the establishment might be saved by timely compromise with non-Anglican forces, while Wilberforce was affected by the judgments on the essayists and Colenso, and came to believe that disestablishment was preferable to State interference in Church doctrine. For these reasons the two bishops inevitably voted on opposite sides in measures which concerned the integrity of the Church. Wilberforce opposed the admission of Dissenters to the MA degree to the last, and was against any relaxation of clerical subscription, while Tait believed that the pressures towards these actions were irresistible and could only be met by compromise to save the Church's popularity, and, in the end, some of its authority. Tait's ideas led him to a less liberal attitude towards the Church's relations with Romanism and ritualism than Wilberforce, and in 1863 Tait was defeated when he voted against an act to allow Roman Catholic chaplains to be appointed officially to prisons where the number of Catholic prisoners warranted it.[9]

The Victorian bishops' power to affect parliamentary legislation on ecclesiastical matters varied according to the case. During the 1860s the bishops themselves did not bring forward any major Bills until 1868, when Tait, newly promoted to Canterbury, presented a Bill for the reform of the ecclesiastical courts, at the same time as a similar one was introduced by Lord Shaftesbury which would have limited the bishops' judicial powers considerably. The reform was very complicated and was delayed until the next decade. Indeed, the bench of the 1860s presents a spectacle of caution and delay which worried those who thought that decisive action was needed to preserve the Church. The bishops' influence was mainly conservative. From 1857 to 1866 they were badgered annually in the House of Lords by Lord Ebury, who was particularly anxious to keep wavering clergy and laity within the Church by relaxing the terms of clerical subscription, reforming the liturgy to exclude tedious and unedifying lessons, and altering the burial service. Ebury believed that many clergy suffered pangs of conscience from being forced to read a service which expressed hope of eternal blessedness over men whom they had known to be hardened sinners. By sheer persistence Ebury gained himself some following, and was president of a society for the revision of the Prayer Book. His speeches in the House of Lords bristled with indignation and with anecdotes of clergy who were in anguish because the Church refused to sweep away obsolete forms and services. He had managed to move the omission of ancient State services, such as the celebration of Guy Fawkes Day, from the liturgy, but when he proposed other reforms Archbishop Longley usually persuaded him to withdraw his motion and give the bench time to think about it.

The Clerical Subscription Act of 1865 resulted largely from Ebury's efforts, and its passage illustrates the power the bench might exercise in some matters. Ebury first presented a Bill in 1862. He argued that not only were the forms of clerical subscription inconsistent, unwieldy and old-fashioned, but that many conscientious young men were deterred from entering the ministry because they could not assent to every word in the Articles and Prayer Book, as required by Charles II's form of subscription. Viscount Dungannon objected that relaxation of subscription might give rise to the unorthodoxy of the German churches, and that the doctrines of the Church of England would be destroyed by internal enemies. This was at the time of the *Essays and Reviews* prosecutions. Tait supported Ebury because he thought the terms of subscription were not logical; a parish curate had to subscribe, but a high university official need not. Wilberforce, supported by Hamilton, believed that any relaxation would allow the clergy to interpret the Prayer Book in any way they liked, as long as they used it in their service.[10] Ebury withdrew his motion, seeing that he would not get any support, but brought it forward again in 1863, pointing out that rigid subscription did not prevent dissension in the Church, even though the clergy were obliged to subscribe and take the oath of allegiance every time they received preferment. Longley argued that shortage of clergy was not due to difficulties over subscription, but to the number of opportunities opening in other professions, and he opposed any kind of change which might allow loopholes for heresy. There was certainly a decline of candidates for the ministry,* but Longley's reasons for it were more plausible than those of Ebury; the ministry was no longer one of a very few 'gentlemanly' professions, for other opportunities were opening, especially in the civil service. The Church still had great inequalities of income, and promotion still depended to some extent on influence rather than personal zeal. Yet it was also likely that a small group of intelligent young men, whom the Church could ill afford to lose, might be deterred by its clinging to uncompromising doctrines. Ebury, however, was defeated by 90 votes to 50, with only two bishops, Tait and Thirlwall, voting for him and twelve against.[11]

In the following year Ebury managed to gain the appointment of a Royal Commission to consider the whole question of subscription. The bench was well represented on the Commission, which included Longley, Thomson, Tait, C. R. Sumner, Thirlwall, Wilberforce, the Deans of Ely and St Paul's (Milman), the Archdeacon of Coventry, the Regius Professors of Divinity at

* See Chapter 9.

Oxford and Cambridge, two Irish bishops, and twelve others. The report was substantially the work of Joseph Napier, former attorney-general for Ireland, who managed to produce something acceptable to all after a great deal of argument; it was presented to the House of Lords in 1865. Several drafts had been discussed, but, as Thomson wrote later, 'Bishop Thirlwall applied his critical faculty with his utmost vigour, and no form of words was found able to stand before it.'[12]

The report, approved by Convocation, suggested minor changes to give the Irish Church the same form of subscription as the English Church, and shortened the oath against simony. It recommended that the oaths of allegiance and supremacy be taken before the ordination service and not during it. The form of subscription to the Articles and Prayer Book was condensed into one paragraph instead of the two separate oaths imposed by Elizabeth I and Charles II. Formerly, priests and deacons had been obliged to swear that they gave their unfeigned assent to every word of the Prayer Book and Articles, and to accept that the doctrines in them had 'nothing contrary' to the Word of God; now they were asked to say that the doctrines were 'agreeable' to the Word of God, and that they would use the form of service prescribed, and no other, 'except so far . . . as shall be ordered by lawful authority'.[13]

The changes were mild enough not to upset the most orthodox churchman. Ebury himself was content, and the Bill, substantially in the form recommended by the Commission, passed both Houses without trouble. Longley and Thomson were pleased that the Commission's recommendations had been adopted, and felt that the Act allowed a little freedom without permitting any heterodox ideas. The Act also gave a loophole for liturgical reform, for clergy were asked to receive changes made by 'lawful authority', although 'lawful authority' was not defined. In the House of Lords, only the Irish Bishops were dissatisfied, because they wanted to revive an Irish Convocation to arrange such changes. Outside Parliament, Broad Churchmen considered the changes trifling and a mere quibbling with words. Stanley thought that subscription was stultifying and ought to be abolished altogether. Milman had much the same idea, but was overwhelmed by the rest of the Commissioners, whose differences of opinion came to light when both Milman and Napier published their private reports, the latter's sanctioned by Longley.[14]

In the end the bishops had been able to guide events their own way, and continued to block Ebury's more radical proposals. He was not able to push through any reform of the burial service, though he brought it up session after session. Longley maintained that to give clergy the power to judge the lives of their parishioners after their deaths could lead to great legal complications, and he quelled Ebury by stating that a large meeting of bishops had been unable to find any solution. It is indicative of the puritanism of the period that no bishop argued that even a notorious malefactor ought to be allowed some hope of eternal salvation in his burial service; instead they dwelt on the legal difficulties. Not until 1867 was Ebury able to move the appointment of a Commission to report on possible reform of the liturgy, to make it more practical and popular. By then the subject had become confused with the problems of ritual practices, so the Commission investigated both subjects together, producing three reports from 1868 to 1870.[15] Some revisions in the Prayer Book were finally passed by Parliament in 1871, but by this time Ebury had given up the struggle in favour of his own Prayer Book Revision Society, which produced a version in 1874. He was disgusted at the inertness of the bishops at a time when activity seemed to be so sorely needed.[16]

Ebury, however, was a private member of the House of Lords and could not depend on party backing. The bishops' influence in Parliament was put to a severer test when measures came up from the Commons with all the weight of party and electoral support behind them. It has already been noted that the bishops were unable to stem the tide towards disestablishment, as embodied in the abolition of compulsory Church rates and disestablishment of the Irish Church. They were allowed to influence matters concerning the spiritual life of the Church, but they had far less control over its relations with the State. Supported, however, by a House of Lords which was still conservatively Anglican on the whole, they were able to modify the more radical demands of the Commons. The bishops accepted the abolition of compulsory Church rates only after they had rejected it for decades, including a Bill in 1867 which proposed the total abolition of the rates. They realised that a large section of public opinion was against them, and finally accepted a Bill which abolished compulsory rates but maintained the old vestry system intact, with power to vote a voluntary rate for Church members. As Tait said, the main areas affected would be small country parishes, because in towns compulsory rating had usually been dropped in practice because it had become impossible to enforce. The bishops all acquiesced in the Act of 1868, except Ellicott of Gloucester, who objected to giving up the just claims of the Church to popular clamour.[17]

Similarly, on the disestablishment of the Irish Church, the bishops were definitely overwhelmed, although they managed to exert some influence on the details of the Act. Gladstone first tried to suspend the power of the Irish Church in 1868 as the first step towards disestablishment, but the Bill failed to pass the Lords on the second reading by 192 votes to 97, with 17 bishops voting against it and eloquent speeches by Longley, Tait, Thomson and Wilberforce.[18] But when Gladstone was returned with a triumphant majority in the election which followed soon afterwards, it was clear that a large proportion of the country supported his policy towards the Irish Church and he was able to raise all the forces of Dissent behind him. Tait, in his first year as Archbishop of Canterbury, devoted himself to saving as many of the temporal possessions of the Irish Church as possible, for though he believed its spiritual life could not be affected by disestablishment, he was too much of a realist not to see the dangers threatening a clergy suddenly forced to rely on voluntary support in an impoverished country where only a minority accepted their Church. Only Thirlwall was really for the Bill, and in a crisp and logical speech he defined his idea of Protestantism as an intellectually superior creed which could defeat Rome by the power of its own logic, not by force.[19] Tait did not vote on the second reading, hoping by this to influence the amending of the Bill when it came into committee; it passed by 179 to 146, with 13 bishops voting against it.[20] Magee of Peterborough defended the social usefulness of the Irish Church, aided by the usually reticent Bickersteth. When the House went into committee, Tait, Wilberforce and Magee fought for as much money for the Irish Church as they could, and Lord Salisbury managed to pass an amendment handing over the glebe houses to the clergy without charge, but Tait failed in an attempt to increase the amount of the endowment left to the Church and to let the existing Irish bishops keep their seats in the House of Lords. The Bill finally passed and was sent back to the Commons, who rejected the amendment on glebe houses, but Tait was finally contented with a higher figure of settlement than Gladstone had first proposed, and a major clash between Lords and Commons was averted by Tait's realism and the intervention of the Queen, who was nervous of flouting the country's wishes.[21]

The bishops of the mid-century were therefore in a most difficult position, acting as a bridge between Church and State and unsure of the best policy to follow in the situation. Hamilton wrote to Gladstone in 1868: 'The Determination by Statesmen of their conduct is not so perplexing, it seems to me, as the determination of theirs by us Bishops—a necessity of acting is laid upon you, which is not laid upon us.'[22] In politics the bench was perpetually tempted to remain inactive and let the initiative come from the State, and Hamilton, who had already come to accept Gladstone's view that disestablishment was inescapable, revealed his belief that 'the future of the Church of England depended very much on the wisdom with which her bishops conducted, or at least assisted, in the operation'. His words show that he realised the extent to which motive power had passed out of the hands of the bishops, though he and Wilberforce wished to postpone disestablishment for as long as possible by using Convocation and diocesan synods as a barrier against the power of the State.

Thus the parliamentary power of the bishops was limited. In legislation for internal changes in the Church they had some influence, though during the 1870s Parliament became increasingly unwilling to spend time on such legislation.[23] The bishops were also impeded by dissensions among themselves and by the popular idea of a bishop, not as a practical politician, but a zealous worker in his diocese. Wilberforce and Tait were among the few with sufficient ability to carry out both roles with some success, though Wilberforce's willingness to plunge into any dispute, such as the Darwinian controversy, with little preparation, earned him a reputation for superficiality and hypocrisy from which he has only lately been rescued.[24] Most of the bishops were content to attend Parliament only as duty occasionally demanded, and preferred to try and build up a personal influence and authority over the clergy in their dioceses.

They were given more opportunity to assert their Church leadership than their predecessors had had, for in the early 1850s the Convocation of Canterbury was revived after more than a century of inactivity. At the beginning of the 1860s its position in the Church was ambiguous, and the clergy regarded it with a mixture of hope and distrust. It is not necessary here to give more than a brief description of the movement for revival, which was led by Wilberforce and Henry Hoare, a wealthy banker who spent much of his time working for greater unity in the Church.[25] The provincial Convocations of York and Canterbury were parliaments of the Church, with upper houses of bishops and lower ones of archdeacons, deans and proctors, of which only the last were elected by the clergy, and only beneficed and academic clergymen could vote for them. The elected proctors were outweighed by the non-elected members. Henry VIII had forbidden Convocation to make or alter canons without the consent of the Crown, but even this slight measure of activity was disrupted by the Civil War. Convocation had not been active since 1717, when it was prorogued by the Crown after bitter hostilities between the two houses which reflected the social and political differences between them.[26] From that time it had gathered formally at the opening of a new Parliament to present a loyal address to the Crown, and was then dissolved.

The Tractarians, who were interested in the early history of the Church, looked on Convocation as the historical instrument of spiritual power which would prevent the Church's government from falling into secular hands. After the Hampden and Gorham cases, High Churchmen thought the State no longer fit to have control of spiritual affairs, and they began to demand the revival of Convocation as an active debating and legislating body. In 1850 Wilberforce and Henry Hoare started a society for the revival of Convocation; most members of the lower houses of the dummy Convocations favoured it, but Archbishops Sumner and Musgrave and Bishops C. R. Sumner and Thirlwall were hostile. Evangelical and liberal clergy feared that the ritualists might gain too much power in the Convocations, and use them to turn the Church into an authoritarian institution with Romish practices, purging it of all who did not agree with them. The 'papal aggression' of 1850, however, brought more people to favour the historical Anglican institutions as a defence against Rome, and Wilberforce proceeded cautiously, encouraged by the discovery that Convocation could debate without a royal writ as long as it did not legislate. Pressure was brought to bear on Archbishop Sumner and the government, until Lord Aberdeen finally permitted the Convocation of Canterbury to debate in 1854 without being dissolved on the first day that it met. Archbishop Musgrave resorted to locking the door of the chapter-house on the Convocation of York, and it was not able to debate until after his death in 1860.

At first, moderate bishops like Tait and Thirlwall treated Convocation with some suspicion, but their fears were lessened by its quiet and cautious behaviour. With other opponents like Sumner of Winchester and Stanley, they began to regard attendance as part of their duty. The Convocation of Canterbury was always more independent than York, a smaller body, where Thomson proved himself as intimidating as Musgrave. He insisted that both houses sit together, ostensibly to save time when one house wished to communicate with the other, but also because he liked to control the discussions among the clergy and prevent any signs of ritualism.[27] The debates in Convocation were widely reported in the newspapers when they touched on important Church matters, and it also had its own journal, the *Chronicle of Convocation.* Inevitably there was a conflict of Church parties and personalities. The conservative position in the upper house was defended energetically by Wilberforce, supported by quiet but determined bishops like Hamilton, against Thirlwall and Tait. The lower house frequently witnessed bitter hostilities between Stanley and Denison. The bishops seemed to regard Convocation rather than Parliament as their natural home, for in 1862, when only six bishops voted in parliamentary proceedings, there were twelve bishops present at the Convocation of Canterbury. This was about the average yearly attendance of bishops, though there were twenty-one bishops in the province.

By 1861 Convocation had won enough parliamentary confidence to be permitted to alter a canon on a minor point, and it was considered an important source of Church opinion, although it was not truly representative of the clergy. It debated freely on all Church matters, but had not clarified its relation to the Church as a whole, and it had yet to test its strength against the power of the State. A significant debate, which led to a real sounding of Convocation's position, took place in 1864, shortly after the Judicial Committee had acquitted Williams and Wilson.

In February 1861, under the guidance of Wilberforce, the bishops had all signed a declaration expressing disapproval and doubt of the honesty of the writers of *Essays and Reviews*. Tait and Thirlwall both signed because they did not agree with the book's more revolutionary ideas, but that was as far as they were prepared to go.[28] There had also been a move in Convocation to condemn *Essays and Reviews* synodically, but this was suspended while the trial was in progress. The conservative clergy were horrified by the Judicial Committee's decision and by the way in which the bishops' declaration had been set aside by Lushington in the Court of Arches. In April 1864 certain members of the lower house, led by Denison, presented a petition to the upper house, asking that a synodical condemnation be considered. The petition was taken up by Wilberforce, and Thirlwall did his best to oppose it because he thought it was a plan to make Convocation pronounce some doctrinal judgment on what the Church believed about the inspiration of the Bible and eternal punishment for the wicked. As a liberal churchman he objected to any attempt to create a central dogmatic authority, and declared that any statement Convocation could make which opposed the Judicial Committee's judgment would be foolish, ineffective, and illegal. 'It is impossible', he said, 'for this house, by any act of its authority, or any judgment which it can pronounce, to cause that to become the doctrine of the Church. And I deprecate every attempt that can be made to effect such an object.'[29]

Wilberforce thought that the Judicial Committee's judgment would shake the confidence of all ordinary clergymen in the power of the Church to maintain its doctrines against the State, but Thirlwall argued that the Church had weathered similar storms over the decisions in the Hampden and Gorham cases.

Tait supported Thirlwall because he believed that the danger was exaggerated, and preferred to let the matter die down rather than present a spectacle of the bishops warring amongst themselves over it. The cautious bishops Jackson, Lonsdale and Browne did not wish to provoke legal strife by opposing the Judicial Committee. Finally they voted on whether to proceed with the petition, and found that they were equally balanced, five to five, with Ollivant, Hamilton, Ellicott and Longley voting with Wilberforce. As Longley also had a casting vote, the matter was referred to a committee of all the bishops.[30] The committee decided that synodical condemnation was needed, and in June the bishops voted for it, with only Tait and Jackson dissentient; Thirlwall was not present.[31] The eleven bishops who were not present apparently saw no reason to object.

The decision was given to the lower house, and Stanley and Denison argued it hotly. Stanley did not defend the book itself, but maintained that Convocation must not be taken to approve of all works which it did not specifically condemn. He mentioned as examples his own *Life of Arnold* and Denison's work on the Eucharist, both of which had been attacked by different sections of the Church.[32] Denison was victorious by 39 votes to 19, and the book was synodically condemned in a declaration carefully worded by Wilberforce. It is significant that throughout the debates the question cut across party loyalties in the Church. In the lower house Denison, in 1861, had been able to enlist the support of his nethermost opposite, the Evangelical leader Dr Alexander McCaul. Party spirit among the bishops was less heated, because men of extreme opinions were not usually chosen for the episcopate, but Wilberforce, who was always suspected of ritualism, gained the support of several of his Evangelical colleagues. High and Low Churchmen resented any attempt to upset the authority of the Bible, and Wilberforce's condemnation was expressed in general terms, against the book as a whole, without attacking the authors personally or attempting to pronounce a doctrine which might have been unacceptable to either Church party. He had won the more cautious bishops over to him by consulting a lawyer on the legality of the condemnation, though the law officers of the Crown had refused to give him an opinion.

Convocation's boldness could not pass unchallenged in Parliament because it could have been a threat to the authority of the Crown in ecclesiastical matters, and in July Lord Houghton, formerly Richard Monckton Milnes, brought it up in the House of Lords. He alleged that in framing the condemnation Convocation had flouted the Act of Henry VIII which forbade it to legislate without royal consent; Convocation had no authority to condemn because it was not part of the legal framework of Church courts, as there was no way of appealing from it. He hinted that if Convocation overreached itself it could be checked by the usual method of dissolution.[33]

Westbury, the Lord Chancellor, replied in a speech which was widely circulated; he ridiculed the hopes of High Churchmen to make Convocation a legal voice in ecclesiastical affairs. Urbane and ironic, Westbury poured contempt on the pretensions of Convocation. The synodical judgment, he said, had been worded so carefully that it did not fix on any particular author or point of doctrine, and dissolved in a vague cloud of disapproval. Had the bishops actually tried to judge one of the authors they might have been themselves suspended and forced to appear in Parliament in sackcloth and ashes, according to the ancient law, but, he continued: 'I am happy to tell your Lordships that what is called a synodical judgment is a well-lubricated set of words—a sentence so oily and saponaceous that no one can grasp it.'[34]

Wilberforce replied with dignity that Convocation had tried, not to prevent freedom of opinion in the Church, but to set the minds of many troubled clergymen at rest. He was pained by Westbury's flippant treatment of such an important subject. Longley maintained that the Judicial Committee had been able to judge only certain extracts from the book and could not grapple with the alarming tendencies of the whole work, which was clearly a premeditated and concerted attempt to undermine the foundations of the Church.[35] Tait could not support this last assertion because he knew the authors had written independently of one another, but he complained that Convocation had not been able to obtain legal advice from the proper law officers before issuing the condemnation. Even though he thought Convocation had lost dignity, as he had foreseen, he felt bound to support it. To those who read of the debate it seemed a triumph for the ironical Westbury; his words were obviously intended as an insult to

Wilberforce, who already had the unfortunate nickname of 'Soapy Sam'. The Lords, however, many of whom disliked Westbury's acerbity and ambition, received his speech coldly, and Wilberforce's friends thought that the bishop had had the best of it. It is likely, too, that conservative clergy were comforted by the synodical judgment.

Clearly, Convocation's claim to a synodical power to judge was tenuous in law, but Westbury could not destroy the growing influence it had on parliamentary opinion, as was demonstrated in the following year. In May 1865 Convocation was invited through the bishops to consider the suggestions of the Royal Commission on clerical subscription. In 1863 Convocation had decided to oppose any changes in the terms of subscription, except for a mild relaxation of the Act of Uniformity. As this accorded with the recommendations of the Commissioners, many of whom were members of Convocation, they must have felt safe in referring them to Convocation in 1865. The recommendations were accepted by both houses with little difficulty, and the upper house urged the lower to consider them with all possible speed and make the most of the opportunity. Even Denison, though he did not agree with all the suggested changes, did not oppose them, because he was unwilling to reject this sign of parliamentary confidence. The clergy were pleased at being consulted on subscription, which was altered by Parliament much as they had desired.[36]

A further collision occurred in 1867, during the early investigations of the newly appointed Commission on ritual. To reassure some of the clergy, Longley had stated publicly that the government would consult Convocation before any of the findings of the Commission became law. Questions were asked in the House of Lords, and Longley defensively produced historical precedents to justify his statement.[37] Tait agreed that it was right to consult Convocation, though he thought this might possibly slow down legislation, because Convocation's proceedings were notoriously dilatory. Waldegrave of Carlisle objected strongly that Convocation would always be too tardy and lukewarm to be consulted; he himself was a fervent Evangelical churchman, and feared that ritualists in Convocation would cause intolerable delay to the anti-ritualist legislation he desired. Lord Derby would not commit himself when questioned, but stated warily that it was probably better to find out what Convocation felt, and it ought to express itself.[38] Again, in 1870, Lord Ebury, as one of the chief anti-ritualists, was disturbed by the preamble of the Prayer Book revision Bill, which stated that the Bill's provisions had the support of Convocation. Such support, he contended, was unnecessary and threatened the independence of Parliament. Lord Chancellor Cranworth and Archbishop Thomson considered that the approval of Convocation, though it had no influence on Parliament, was likely to conciliate most churchmen, but the reference was finally cut out of the Act of 1871 to the annoyance of High Churchmen.[39] So Convocation remained, if not a legal authority, at least a force to be reckoned with, though its usefulness was severely limited by extremists in the lower house and over-cautious bishops in the upper.

Apart from their meeting in Parliament and Convocation, on the Ecclesiastical Commission and the Board of Queen Anne's Bounty, of which they were all members, there had grown up since Archbishop Howley's day a habit of private meetings of the bishops in London. They met during the parliamentary session, apparently after meetings of the Bounty Board, and in 1857 Hamilton suggested that these gatherings should become more formal. The bishops also took Communion together and dined together on Ascension Day. Any Irish or colonial bishop who happened to be in London also attended, and they conferred on current political issues affecting the Church. It was at two such meetings in February and March of 1861 that they decided by nine votes to five to express the bench's disapproval of *Essays and Reviews*. The dissentients were Tait, who did not care to have the essayists all lumped together, the Sumner brothers, Pelham and Baring, who were all worried that the declaration would have no real force. Thirlwall thought at first that such action would only expose the bishops' real powerlessness to act against heresy, but as he did not think it would be possible to prosecute the essayists, and silence might leave the Church in an awkward position, he finally decided to join the protest. The others were brought round to the idea that the bishops could declare the essayists' opinions were not those of the Church without seeming to persecute them. Hampden, with a strange lack of sympathy, stated roundly that the bishops had a plain choice between Christianity and heresy, and that their course was clear.[40] After conferring with his fellow bishops, Hamilton had enough support to decide to prosecute Williams in the Court of Arches.

Hamilton regarded the meetings as a chance for the bishops to come together and show a united front to the world. He was therefore rather shocked at Tait's first appearance in the circle as Bishop of London in 1857. Tait promptly supported the Divorce Bill, which Hamilton abhorred, and attacked Wilberforce, Hamilton's friend. 'Bishops ought to speak in a tone of Brotherly feeling for one another,' Hamilton commented in his notes, and, on another occasion: 'The Bishop of London is evidently captious —& very unfriendly to any free action of Church—He is no match for the Bishop of Oxford.'[41] Finally Hamilton proposed that important topics should be postponed until the following year when the whole bench might receive more definite notice of meetings, but he wrote privately that he hoped 'the new Bishops might be less unecclesiastical in another year'.[42]

A more important and more publicised attempt to bring the bishops together to discuss Church affairs took pace in 1867, when the first conference of English and colonial bishops was held at Lambeth. The *Essays and Reviews* case, followed so rapidly by that of Colenso, played a large part in bringing this about, because many churchmen began to desire Church unity for defensive purposes, though the initial idea came, not from England, but from the bishops of Canada. The details of the conference have been thoroughly examined by Dr Stephenson, but it is relevant to note that High Churchmen hoped the bishops might be able to pass judgment on matters of doctrine and so bring some authority among the doubts and dissensions of the period. Robert Gray, Bishop of Capetown, wanted the conference to condemn Colenso, and did manage to have an unofficial pronouncement signed by several bishops, with Wilberforce's help.[43] The Evangelical bishops, including Thomson, opposed the conference, and Thomson refused to attend because he thought it an attempt of the High Church party to set themselves up as a final authority in the Church. Thirlwall protested that the conference was not representative of the whole Church and could not pronounce on doctrine, though in the end he attended.[44] In such an atmosphere the actions of the conference could hardly be anything but cautious, and the bishops were carefully guided by Longley not to overreach themselves. The meetings were held in secret, but at the end a pamphlet was published containing Longley's address at the beginning of the conference, the resolutions passed, and an address of the bishops to the faithful. The conference had met, said Longley, not to pass canons, but to discuss matters of importance to the Church, especially the reunion of Christendom.[45] One of the resolutions encouraged more synodical action in the Church and suggested a system of due subordination of lower synods to higher. The High Churchmen were disappointed that it did not attack liberalism; the Evangelicals that it did not denounce ritualism. But on the whole it was considered a success, and became the first of a series which has continued to the present day as an expression of the Anglican desire for unity.

At the other end of the scale from these large meetings were small private ones, where a few bishops gathered together to discuss matters on which they felt strongly. Wilberforce frequently held such meetings at Cuddesdon, which was convenient to London. In 1856 he met with six other bishops, including Hamilton and Thirlwall (who remained Wilberforce's good friend in spite of many differences of opinion), and they discussed internal Church administration, the possible appointment of coadjutor bishops, Sunday observance, the Bounty Board and other matters of the same nature, before departing together for the opening of Parliament.[46] 'The meeting was most harmonious,' wrote Hamilton. He went to Cuddesdon often during the 1860s, and Wilberforce influenced his ideas very strongly. Gladstone had an equally strong influence on him, and he was in the habit of noting down the views of these two forceful men on important points.

An even more private little group met at Cuddesdon in 1865, after the acquittal of Williams and Wilson, to discuss the final court of appeal in ecclesiastical cases. Apart from the three bishops, Wilberforce, Hamilton and Ellicott, there were Robert Wilberforce, Archdeacon Bickersteth, Sir Charles Anderson and H. Majendie, members of the Wilberforce circle. They declared that cases concerning matters of doctrine ought to be removed from the Judicial Committee of the Privy Council and referred to a council of bishops, who would be able to say what the precise doctrine of the Church was on any point.[47] Both Wilberforce and Hamilton were dead before this was partly achieved in the reforms of 1873, but they were instrumental in encouraging the idea among High Churchmen.

In 1866 the East Anglian bishops also began to hold annual conferences. The idea seems to have come from Bishop Browne of Ely, who met his colleagues from Lincoln, Norwich, Peterborough and Rochester to discuss the particular problems of their dioceses.[48] These seem to have been purely practical gatherings, for the East Anglican bishops were not politically active.

The bishops, then, were not able to guide the destiny of the Church from their central positions in Parliament or Convocation; nor could they protect it from the encroachments of the State for long. Nor did all of them desire to do so, for peaceful Evangelicals on the bench did not wish to upset the existing relationship between Church and State. During the 1870s it became increasingly difficult for bishops to force doctrinal problems on the notice of Parliament, and yet major changes could not be made without parliamentary legislation. Therefore those bishops who responded to the idea that it was their duty to regulate the spiritual orthodoxy of the clergy had to concentrate on their own dioceses and make sure they held the reins of diocesan government firmly. They were unable to make pronouncements as a central authoritative body, but in the dioceses there was much more opportunity for a more subtle manipulation of power.

IN THE DIOCESE

Although regular meetings kept the bishops in touch with one another and strengthened their resolve, it was as individual workers in their own dioceses that they could exert most influence, though even here there were great difficulties to surmount. As the numbers of the clergy increased and new churches were built, it became very difficult for a bishop to superintend each clergyman personally. In the past this had not been considered really necessary, especially when the bishop was separated from many of his clergy by birth and the social advantages of wealth. Now the social gap was closing to some extent. Although the bishops were wealthy men as far as income went, the expenses of their administration, upkeep of the large palaces, and the many charitable and missionary demands made on them depleted their revenues considerably. Charles Baring, whose family were bankers, was a rich man in his own right, but Hamilton was not, yet both lived simply and Hamilton did not even keep his own carriage. Nor were the bishops as closely connected with the peerage as before. Eden of Bath and Wells and Pelham of Norwich belonged to old aristocratic families, but the bench was open to the sons of gentlemen without wealth or influence. Tait was the son of a Scots gentleman of small means, and had to support himself from an early age; he rose through his own ability. Hamilton was hauled into the episcopate by the dying wish of Bishop Denison, without wealth or family connections. Phillpotts and C. R. Sumner were the last of a generation of bishops who had been appointed through their connections with the powerful; Phillpotts by his wife's relations and his own timely political manoeuvres, Sumner by the influence of the Marchioness of Conyngham, whose son he tutored and who introduced him to George IV. Jackson, Bickersteth of Ripon, and Philpott of Worcester had been popular preachers. Lee and Tait had been great headmasters; Turton and Browne professors of divinity; Short and Thomson heads of university colleges.

The bishops were expected to have some reputation for learning, and Thirlwall was an outstanding example of a bishop appointed because of scholarly merit (and political Whiggery), but originality of thought was not particularly in demand. Mark Pattison lamented that the bench was no longer the refuge of scholars like Burnet and Hooker; once a man was nominated to a bishopric, he must forego scholarship and take up the humdrum activities of the public official. 'A modern Bishop', Pattison wrote, 'is a mere vicar-general, having a peculiar department of official business to transact.'[49] Pattison also maintained that bishops had become the slaves of public opinion, and it cannot be denied that changes in public opinion had forced the episcopacy to apply itself to running the Church more efficiently, and had stamped out the old abuses of pluralism, nepotism and scrambling for wealthier bishoprics. Thirlwall was the last Victorian bishop to be a scholarly recluse, though he did not neglect the duties of his office. The episcopate was no longer a reward for scholarship or political loyalty, but an arduous social task, and the bishops were gradually being turned into professional men.

Doubts about the exact nature and social function of the bishop did continue during this period, though the Evangelical view of him as devoted incessantly to the duties of his see was steadily gaining. The ideas of Thomas Arnold were also influential, for in his work on the 'national Church' Arnold had advocated that the bishop be reduced in status and salary, and that there ought to be a bishop in every town. This would keep up a close personal contact between clergy and laity.[50] *The Times* demanded more and cheaper bishops, as unlike Phillpotts as possible,[51] and Parliament debated the subject while considering an extension of the episcopate. Many dioceses, particularly London, Exeter and Lincoln, were obviously too large for one bishop to supervise properly. Only one new diocese had been created in three hundred years, so the bishops could hardly be expected to keep up with the growth of population. The diocese of Exeter was enormous, and contained remote areas of Cornwall which even an active bishop would hardly be able to penetrate, let alone the aged Phillpotts.

Lord Lyttelton proposed a scheme in 1861 by which the Ecclesiastical Commission could set up a new diocese if enough money were raised locally to support a bishop and his diocesan officers. Although the bishops themselves were all agreed that more bishops were needed, their difficulties reflected the dilemma of the Church about the nature of their office. Not all of them could contemplate the creation of a body of bishops with low salaries and no seats in the House of Lords, especially as this might give the Dissenters and other anti-episcopalians a chance to argue that wealthy and privileged bishops were not necessary at all. Waldegrave also put forward the view, which Thirlwall and Baring shared, that it was not really the duty of a bishop to interfere too much in the affairs of his clergy. Some of the more Evangelical bishops, strangely enough, although they believed that a bishop should devote himself earnestly to his particular duties of confirmation, visitation and ordination, did not think he ought to be too close to his clergy, and that it was possible for a diocese to be 'overgoverned'. Waldegrave said:

> In proportion as you multiply Bishops, in the same proportion do you withdraw them from the censorship of public opinion. In the same proportion do you increase the need for that censorship, for you increase their opportunities of intermeddling with the clergy.[52]

Tait was not particularly interested in the subject at that time, thinking that the Church might be better served by reforming the ecclesiastical courts and activating dormant deans. In the end the bishops modified the Bill to provide new sees by stipulating £120,000 as the minimum figure to be raised before a new see could be created.[53] This was what provoked Ebury to say that the clergy did not want prince bishops. Lyttelton realised that the Bill could not possibly pass the Commons, and so withdrew it at that stage, but produced it again in 1867. Again the chief problems were the position, titles and income of new bishops, and the way of raising money for new sees. Lyttelton, with the support of Lord Derby, argued that a bishop should not be reduced to a mere administrative official by overwork, but should be able to exert a personal influence on his diocese. Longley quoted Arnold ('not a man of an especially ecclesiastical turn of mind . . .'), on the necessity for subdivision of sees. The bishops were unanimously in favour of the Bill, but could not agree on whether funds should be provided by the Ecclesiastical Commission or whether everything should come from voluntary contributions. They decided for the latter course, Longley, Waldegrave, Jacobson, Ollivant and Bickersteth (mostly Evangelicals) fearing that any use of Ecclesiastical Commission funds would deprive the poorer clergy of money intended for their relief; though they had also decided, amid arguments, that the new bishops should not have lower incomes than the minimum given to the present bishops.[54] Wilberforce, however, managed to persuade them to change their minds and to ask that half the fund should come from the Ecclesiastical Commission, and although Waldegrave was still not convinced, the Bill passed in this form. Lyttelton doubted whether it could ever command popular support if it required money from the Ecclesiastical Commission. In the Commons the scheme was amended into one of voluntary contributions once again, and Sir Roundell Palmer successfully moved an amendment to make the bishops' incomes dependent on the decision of the Ecclesiastical Commission, which meant that they could possibly be set at a much lower level than those of the existing bishops. The moral indignation of the country, said Palmer, would be enough to prevent the system of translations from recurring if the bishops were unequally paid.[55] Nor would the Commons accept more bishops in the Lords, but insisted on their sitting in rotation, the junior bishops not having seats. The Lords could not agree with this, and the Bill was lost. Lyttelton tried yet again the following year, but was defeated by 43 votes to 20 in the Lords.[56] As a result, no new see was created until 1876, when the pressure of population in several dioceses was overwhelming. The pressure was relieved a little, however, by a long-awaited Bill enabling old and infirm bishops to retire from 1869, at a time when four bishops were unable to perform their duties through age or illness.

The government and the bishops themselves had failed to agree on whether bishops were to maintain their social dignity, or whether a new class of poorer administrative bishops should be created. For the time being things remained as they were, though the demands made on a bishop by his office were really impossible to meet. Most of them answered their enormous correspondence themselves, though Wilberforce used to organise a circle of friends and visitors to help him. Hamilton calculated that he himself wrote 2,913 letters a year. Wilberforce, who was more in the public eye, would have had an even greater number. Jackson of Lincoln explained that improved communications had increased the bishops' burden.

> For one letter we received previously we get thirty now. . . . One letter [the Bishop] takes up asks for advice on some point of ecclesiastical law; the next on some question of common law; the next, on some point in architecture; in the next, he is called upon to arbitrate between two persons who have a difference; the next, probably, will call for his deepest sympathy and commiseration; the next, perhaps, requires him to administer a stern rebuke; and the many matters of minor importance . . . entail upon him a very serious burden.[57]

The confirmation tours became more and more demanding, and many bishops whose dioceses contained remote regions still had to travel on horseback to perform this duty. One clergyman asked Archbishop Thomson to consider holding the visitations in each rural deanery for three or four days at a time, for confirmations and full conference with the clergy, the whole to take up six months. 'Episcopacy might then begin to be *felt* by the Church at large as a living and spiritual ministry. At present nine-tenths of the people care little more for their Chief Pastor than for the Emperor of China.'[58]

Inevitably the bishop remained remote from most of the laity. Thomson did his best to communicate with the working classes by holding mass meetings, especially in Sheffield where his commanding personality earned him great popularity, though other parts of his diocese were jealous and complained of neglect. Thirlwall, on the other hand, thought rather that the bishop should be at the head of affairs without wasting so much time on personal visitation or having his finger in every minor pie. '. . . While it was the business of a Bishop to organise, direct, and stimulate every good work going on within the diocese, it was not necessary or even desirable that he should personally lay his hand to the work.'[59]

Within his diocese the bishop could exert personal influence according to his abilities. He had to make sure that the clergy led upright lives and conducted the services regularly and properly, but he had also sworn at his consecration to drive out strange doctrines. The bishops were leaders in the church militant, as Earl Nelson said in 1869. '. . . It was just as absurd for the Church to go to war against infidelity without bishops as it would be for an army to be sent against the enemy with a deficiency of officers.'[60]

Some bishops were better fitted for this task than others, but few could escape the problem of unorthodoxy among their clergy. The relation between a bishop and his clergy, especially in questions concerning doctrine, was a delicate one, and the bishops needed to exercise great discretion.

A clergyman could only be arraigned for false teaching or moral offences with his bishop's consent. A bishop could adjudicate in his own diocesan court with the aid of his chancellor, and the accused, if found guilty, could appeal first to the Court of Arches and then to the Judicial Committee. Williams was prosecuted in the Court of Arches because Hamilton had previously signed the bishops' declaration against *Essays and Reviews* and did not wish to be accused of bias if he tried the case himself. Cases of false teaching were notoriously complicated and difficult to prove, and even if the offence were a more flagrant one of moral depravity the ecclesiastical courts were very slow and costly. Apart from the bad publicity for the Church if these cases were brought to light, a bishop had to think carefully before prosecuting, for he had to bear the expenses of the prosecution himself, and if he were to lose his case the costs were likely to be extremely heavy. Hamilton consulted his colleagues on the bench before proceeding against Williams, and the two Sumners and Jackson immediately offered him financial aid, which he refused, unwilling to create a precedent which might be criticised.[61] He did, however, accept assistance from the clergy of his diocese to help him meet the costs when he lost. Also it has been mentioned that several bishops were dissatisfied with the constitution of the court of final appeal and resented the presence of laymen on a bench which could judge cases of doctrine, especially when the Judicial Committee began to build up a series of legal precedents on which to work. The judges also pronounced as one, although it was known that in the *Essays and Reviews* trial the two archbishops had dissented from the final judgment. Tait, who had agreed with the judgment, considered the court a fitting one for an established Church, and was unwilling to let it become purely clerical. In 1865 he encouraged the publication of a legal work on the judgments of the Judicial Committee and wrote an able preface to it,[62] but High Church clergy remained suspicious of the Church's legal system.

Thirlwall supported Tait on this matter, because he believed that once the secular and ecclesiastical members of the court were separated the latter would lose all their power, but this idea was decried by Wilberforce and his supporters, who wanted to see the Church with sole power to try doctrinal cases. When the shock of the Gorham judgment was intensified by the judgments of the 1860s, the court's reputation was at its lowest with orthodox clergy. What Wilberforce and Hamilton really wanted was a court to try the truth of ideas, but both the Court of Arches and the Judicial Committee maintained that they tried, not divinity but ecclesiastical law. A clergyman could not be condemned for teaching dubious doctrines unless he openly contradicted the Articles and liturgy.

With these difficulties in their minds, the bishops hesitated to resort to the law unless they were particularly conscientious or litigious. Phillpotts had a bad reputation for spending great sums on court cases—*The Times* put it at £20,000 at his death.[63] Lord Ebury's solution was to simplify the Prayer Book and Church ritual to make it harder for a clergyman to err; another solution, favoured by Lord Shaftesbury, was to reform the working of the ecclesiastical courts, where officials were often holders of sinecures, but neither of these suggestions could be implemented very rapidly because of party differences within the Church and the unwillingness of powerful Dissenting groups in the House of Commons to spend much time patching up the affairs of the Church. The situation was altered in 1874 when the terms of the Public Worship Regulation Act decreed that a group of parishioners had the power to prosecute a clergyman if his bishop consented; this, of course, was aimed at ritual practices among the clergy, but could presumably be taken to apply to all eccentric ideas or behaviour. But the process was still slow and expensive, and the bishops usually preferred to resort to many less official methods to make sure that their dioceses contained no unorthodox teaching.

As it was so hard to deal with the clergy once they were installed in their livings, the bishops could start at the bottom and weed out all the dubious applicants for curates' licences or ordination. A bishop could refuse to institute a clergyman who had been presented to a living in his diocese, though in practice it was easier to refuse to ordain than to refuse a patron's recommendation. Wilberforce, as Dr Pugh has pointed out, liked to choose his own men, and during his episcopate managed to obtain the patronage of 86 benefices, bringing up the number in the gift of the Bishop of Oxford from 17 to 103. This meant that he had much greater power in selecting his clergy.[64] He also questioned his ordination candidates on their orthodoxy, as one of his least orthodox ones discovered. Jowett took orders at the age of twenty-eight, and described his examination to Stanley in the form of a dialogue.

Bish. One more question I wish to ask. In what sense do you sign the Articles? Certain modes I consider dishonest, without at all wishing to narrow their limits.

Cand. (a pause). In Paley's sense.

Bish. What does Paley say?

Cand. That it is an absurdity if the Legislature meant to say that you assented to four or five hundred disputed propositions. It only meant that you were an attached member of the Church of England.

Bish. No, I don't mean that I require assent to four or five hundred disputed propositions, &c. &c.

Jowett added his own comment. 'The Bishop is an excellent man, overflowing with goodness; but I doubt whether anybody can do him perfect justice who has not a spice of humbug in his composition and therefore a sympathy with that sort of thing.'[65]

Hamilton, as we have seen, wavered over accepting Williams, and took a decision which he later regretted. Thomson was vigilant to see that no ritualist came into his diocese; he accepted none that he knew of, and was exceedingly angry if one slipped through the net. In the 1870s he began to inquire what religious societies his candidates for ordination belonged to, and tried to discover if they had joined any of the numerous ritualist groups.[66] A bishop, however, could not afford to be too particular in his choice, especially if he were trying to fill badly-paid benefices, nor could he afford to reject many ordination candidates, even if their opinions were ignorant or eccentric; this will be discussed more fully in the final chapter.

Because the bishop himself could not investigate every detail of his diocesan administration, he depended to a large extent on his archdeacons and rural deans to keep him in touch with the clergy. The archdeacons, particularly, were responsible for reporting on the state of the church buildings, and held visitations during the two years when the bishop did not hold his. The rural deans, who presided over smaller subdivisions of the diocese, were in a better position to point out the views of the clergy to the bishop, and by the middle of the nineteenth century there was increased emphasis on meetings of ruridecanal chapters and subsequent meetings between the bishop and his rural deans. Wilberforce selected his archdeacons carefully, and relied on their information a great deal. He also considered the chapters the unit of his administration, and saw that the rural deans held chapter meetings four times a year to discuss subjects which he provided for them. They also communicated his decisions to the clergy. The rural deans themselves stayed at Cuddesdon for three days every year to confer with Wilberforce on the administration of the diocese.[66a]

Soon after he was elected to Salisbury, Hamilton also began holding meetings with the archdeacons and rural deans, who lodged with him for three days every year. They talked about current political affairs which affected the Church, and about internal matters such as the hymnal and dilapidated churches.[67] In 1856 they decided to hold ruridecanal chapters twice a year, to which all clergy should come. Some of the rural deans wished to exclude matters of doctrine from the chapters, but Hamilton was not in favour of this.[68] In the following year he began to make a report of the year's activities to his rural deans: '. . . that as far as I can I may lead Clergy to believe that Episcopus is not simply a Governor but the Head of their Ministrations & further to give occasion to receive & answer q's about work & to take counsel & get strength.'[69] In 1863 they discussed relaxation of clerical subscription, and decided that nothing would be achieved by it. An elderly prebendary attacked Stanley as the cause of all dissension. The meetings performed a useful function in allowing this section of the clergy to speak their minds, though as all the rural deans were appointed by the bishop they were unlikely to oppose his point of view. The ruridecanal chapters were revived successfully enough, but Hamilton was disappointed at the low attendance. Nevertheless a chain of communication had been forged, and Hamilton, in spite of the suspicion of ritualism under which he continually laboured, was honoured by most of his clergy, with the exception of the incumbent of Broad Chalke.

The bishop met his clergy mainly in the course of his special duties of confirmation and visitation. The former tended to be a hurried affair, even for a bishop with the best of intentions. Wilberforce confirmed 217 times between 1857 and 1860, and had 18,747 candidates.[70] Hamilton confirmed nearly seventy times each year. Thomson was struggling with an enormous diocese containing many pockets of rural and industrial poverty, and made herculean efforts to reach as many people as possible; he held annual confirmations in the large towns, biennial in smaller ones, and less frequently in villages, though he wanted to meet the wishes of the clergy if he could.[71] By holding more confirmations the bishops hoped to make the service as dignified as possible, for an overcrowded church full of children was rarely in keeping with the solemnity of the occasion. Nor did most bishops of that period care for their predecessors' practice of confirming whole railfuls of children at once; they believed that each child should receive the laying on of hands separately.

But the bishop could not visit every small parish in the course of confirmation tours, though he would come to them on special occasions, usually to consecrate buildings and churchyards. Wilberforce was a tireless traveller, and had a habit of appearing suddenly on horseback to attend the services at parish churches, no doubt disconcerting the unwary incumbent. Both Wilberforce and Hamilton, as High Churchmen, were particularly interested in seeing that their churches were furnished as well as possible, and encouraged gifts of church furniture; Hamilton also used to present solid Communion tables to needy churches at his own expense. In 1867 both were accused in the House of Lords of encouraging 'popish' practices by dedicating new church bells. This was mainly an unsuccessful attempt by the anti-ritualists in the House to force Wilberforce's resignation from the Ritual Commission.[72] But both bishops believed it was their duty to encourage by personal appearances a closer attention to the church buildings, and to bring the episcopacy closer to clergy and people.

Visitation was the other traditional way for the bishop to guide his clergy. In most dioceses the visitation took place every three years, and every clergyman was bound to attend or give a good excuse. The difficulties of gathering all the clergy of the diocese together at one time were naturally great, and Ellicott found it impossible to report three years' activities in a charge which should not make too many demands on the attentiveness of his hearers, so he decided in 1868 to print a yearly report in the two intervening years.[73] Ellicott was a particularly merciful bishop; Tait at first did not spare his clergy or himself, and his first charge lasted five hours, while Thirlwall's charge of 1857 lasted three hours and twenty minutes. Tait later decided to deliver the charge to several groups of clergy instead of trying to cram them all into St Paul's. Except for very retiring bishops like Lonsdale of Lichfield, it was customary for the bishops to print the charges afterwards at their own expense and to circulate them among the clergy. The charges were critically reviewed in many newspapers, and were both official reports of diocesan work and statements of personal opinion. Hamilton defined the subject of the charge.

> It belongs to the Bishop's office to oversee everything which pertains to the Ministration of the Word and Sacraments, and to the maintenance both of a sound Faith, and of good morals in that part of the Church over which he has been set. He has therefore the gravest responsibilities about the state, condition, and ability of the Clergy, about their houses of residence, about the Churches and Chapels of his Diocese, about their furniture and Ornaments, and about all things which, whether charitable foundations or not, help to fit men for the discharge of their duties to GOD and man, such as Schools, Reformatories, and Penitentiaries.[74]

These were the matters on which the bishop was expected to speak, but the time he allotted to each subject depended largely on his own inclinations and his conception of what a bishop's position was. Thirlwall usually disposed speedily of diocesan matters, and settled into a learned discussion of important ecclesiastical topics of the day. In 1857 he attacked Williams's *Rational Godliness*, and gave his views on the Immaculate Conception and the doctrine of the Real Presence in the Eucharist, for which Denison was then being tried. In 1860 he discussed Church rates and the burial service; in 1863 he dealt with *Essays and Reviews*, and in 1866 with education and diocesan synods. When challenged by someone who disagreed with his views on the last point, he replied, 'if I had considered an Episcopal Charge as a document like a Papal Allocution, too sacred for criticism, none of mine would have been delivered'.[75]

Ollivant of Llandaff held the opposite view; he said in 1863 that it was the bishop's duty at such a time to lead the clergy into solemn deliberation on the welfare of the Church as a whole, as well as local concerns.

> Under such circumstances, a Bishop should feel that anxiety . . . when he is compelled, as it were, to forget himself, and to magnify his office, and by virtue of it, as a Father in God, to 'speak, and exhort, and rebuke with all authority', though conscious at the same time that he is addressing many who may be wiser and better men . . . than he knows himself to be.[76]

Some bishops did eschew more general questions and were content to reflect on the progress in their own dioceses and to urge their clergy to apply themselves to the task in hand. In fact the way the charge was received depended mainly on the individual clergyman. The English parson was traditionally an independent figure, and not used to much episcopal interference. However much Ollivant might insist on his authority at the time of his visitation, his clergy were not forced to agree with his views, even on such limited matters as a weekly collection, which he tried to initiate in the diocese. Thirlwall might insist that he spoke without authority, but to scholarly clergymen his voice carried more weight than many of his colleagues. It is doubtful, however, if his extremely long and closely reasoned charges really penetrated to the simpler Welsh clergy. Some clergymen did expect their bishop to guide them in Church affairs, as one revealed at a Church congress when he said that episcopal charges should be the fruit of much observation of socicty, and learning gained from a close study of ancient and modern authors.

> Thus only can [the bishop] satisfy the great expectations of a clergy, who would fain regard their Bishop as their great authority in the controversies which are daily agitating the theological world, and which they, perhaps, have little opportunity of so studying as to be able to form a safe opinion.[77]

Considering that nearly every Victorian bishop except Thirlwall was forced by the pressure of other duties to give up study, it is not surprising that few of the charges of the period are noted for originality of intellect.

The charges of the mid-century reflected the problems of the times, and especially in the period between 1860 and 1865 there was a preoccupation with the questions raised by the Broad Churchmen. Many of the bishops tried to reassure clergy who, they believed, were troubled by these signs of rationalism actually within the Church and the apparent encouragement given them by the Judicial Committee's judgments. From 1860 to 1865 the cathedrals rang with denunciations of the essayists, from the turgid rhetoric of Waldegrave to the lucid ironies of Thirlwall. Baring impressed upon his clergy the virtue of humility in Biblical studies. Bickersteth deplored clerical errors with poetic melancholy, and bade the clergy beware of the seeds of original sin within themselves.[78] Jackson argued hopefully that reaction against the new movement would bring the Church back into unity,[79] while Wilberforce maintained with his usual eloquence that to relinquish one jot of Holy Scripture would be to lose all, and that no clergyman could honestly hold the views of the essayists while remaining in the Church.[80]

It is difficult to say how the clergy reacted to this, or even how far the bishop was able to reach his clergy and to understand their private thoughts on religious and practical subjects; but it is possible to generalise to some extent from the experiences of individual bishops, taking Hamilton, Thomson and Thirlwall as representative of various sections of opinion within the Church.

The visitation period was a time when most bishops made every effort to understand the problems of their clergy. The visitation returns, forms of inquiry which each clergyman was required to complete, provided the bishop with a great many of the statistics which were then becoming so important at every level of administration. Many of the questions were purely formal, dealing with the population of the parish, whether the incumbent had been resident for the requisite number of days in the year, the distance he lived from the church, the state of the church buildings, parochial education, and the number of services and Communions. The returns are a fruitful source of information for historians, in showing the difficulties the Church experienced in dealing with people of all occupations in different dioceses. Hamilton and Thomson also left space on the forms for any comments or complaints which the incumbents cared to make, and many of them took the opportunity to bring their grievances before their diocesan. Others gave the barest details, and Hamilton found one independent priest who refused to return his form at all, and had to threaten him with indictment for contumacy.[81]

The way in which a bishop's personality influenced these returns may be clearly seen in the replies from the three sees of York, Salisbury and St David's. Thomson asked his clergy to make complaints and suggestions, and from 1871 began to inquire how often a minister desired confirmation to be held in his parish, and whether consultative bodies of clergy and laity were of any use. He was interested in education, and left plenty of room for a description of parochial education at all levels. His diocese contained large numbers of both Dissenters and Roman Catholics, and many complaints were about other denominations. Sometimes the ministers took the occasion for a little self-interest, and asked Thomson to remember them with favour, while one parson described his success in attracting Methodists to church, in terms which he knew must please the Evangelical Thomson: 'I attribute this to a hearty service, plain & often contemporaneous (*sic*) preaching, & a careful avoidance of all opposition.'[82]

In the returns of 1865 there was no inkling of the troubles brewing at Healaugh; Voysey sent in a perfunctory return. There were complaints of the immorality of the labourers and the indifference of farmers, the absence of gentry interested in the Church, clerical poverty, contemporary materialism, the 'slowness of the Agricultural mind', over-large or over-populated parishes, the iniquities of pew rents and dilapidated churches and vicarages, but these were common to all dioceses to some extent. Suggestions for remedies were few, and none would have dared to suggest to Thomson any more startling innovations than prayer and hard work. The Vicar of Cowesby did suggest a return to diocesan synods, 'the original platform of Church government', while another suggested excommunication for immoral people[83] and a third that the services were not suitably arranged for farm labourers who had to work on Sunday.

As far as York was concerned, the ritualists might not have existed, and the clergy steered away from doctrinal matters, on which their archbishop was notoriously partisan. They barely mentioned the spiritual life of the Church, but obediently acknowledged their missionary duties and the ideal of devoted labour.

The returns to Hamilton in 1864 were different in tone, though his questions were much the same, except that he was more interested in the frequency of the offertory and the purposes for which it was collected, and also in the precise delivery of the services. To Hamilton the Rector of Chilfrome could dare to suggest that parishioners should seek private discussion, confession and absolution from their priest, whereas none could have said this to Thomson. On the other hand, this was not merely an attempt to reach Hamilton on his weak side, for he was known among the clergy to be fair towards the Evangelicals in a way Thomson was not to High Churchmen, and the Rector of Durweston wrote: 'I am satisfied in my own mind—that the quarrels of Ch. men—the over valuing ritual & dogma, is weaning the poor from the Church.'[84] Another confirmed Hamilton's worst fears by stating that the Catholics in his parish had taken advantage of the Judicial Committee's decision on Williams to misrepresent the doctrines of the Anglican Church.[85] The Rector of Whaddon thought that his flock did not really believe in baptismal regeneration (a doctrine more favoured by the High Church party), and promised that he would try to bring the truth to them gradually, without startling them.

If the returns to Thomson reflected his theology and those to Hamilton his personal gentleness, the returns to Thirlwall are revealing, in contrast, by their extreme sparseness. Thirlwall conducted his inquiries diligently, and if a clergyman omitted some piece of information a curt notice was sent requesting him to furnish it forthwith, that the bishop's statistics might be complete for his charge. But Thirlwall did not alter the form of his questions between 1848 and 1869, and the form was shorter than those of the other bishops. Significantly, there was no space for the clergy to state their opinions, and their answers had to be confined to a few words. From these returns one can learn that many of the Welsh clergy officiated at two or more churches, that many lived a long distance from the church, that many vicarages were extremely dilapidated, and that, as expected, in the remoter northern archdeaconries the services were in Welsh, in the southern ones in English. There is no clue to the personal opinions of the clergy, for Thirlwall evidently did not wish to know them.[86]

If, then, the bishop learned anything about his clergy, it depended a great deal on his own character. The visitation returns were by no means full, and were in part a result of the goodwill the bishop had managed to create towards himself. A bishop with even the best of intentions could not penetrate into the smaller parishes very often, and his legal jurisdiction, as we have seen, was severely limited by many factors. He had to take the role of an officer in the church militant without any of the officer's advantages of organised intelligence and discipline. He could receive complaints from parishioners or through his officials about the way a clergyman conducted himself, and the mid-century was a particularly troublesome period in matters of heterodoxy and ritualism, but if the clergyman had private difficulties it was hard for the bishop to find out about them unless the man came forward himself in some way.

Party conflicts in the Church were naturally a hindrance to confidences between bishop and clergy. At first the Tractarians were inclined to lay a great deal of emphasis on the authority of the episcopate. They looked back to the primitive Church and the days when bishops really had power to guide the beliefs of the people. Newman began by giving absolute loyalty to his diocesan, Bagot of Oxford, as he wrote in the *Apologia*.

> I loved to act in the sight of my Bishop, as if I was, as it were, in the sight of God. It was one of my special safeguards against myself and of my supports; I could not go very wrong while I had reason to believe that I was in no respect displeasing him. It was not a mere formal obedience to rule that I put before me, but I desired to please him personally, as I considered him set over me by the Divine Hand.[87]

Newman withdrew *Tract XC* at Bagot's request, but his respect for the episcopacy was shaken by the hostility of most of the bishops towards his ideas. Manning and Robert and Henry Wilberforce were further disillusioned in 1847 when the government showed itself capable of appointing Hampden to a bishopric, though he was unwelcome to both High and Low Churchmen because of supposedly dangerous theological opinions. Similarly in the Gorham case, and later over *Essays and Reviews* and Colenso, the bishops showed themselves incapable of defending what the Tractarians considered the unalterable doctrines of the Catholic Church against the legal decisions of the State.

Many followed Newman into a Church where the clerical hierarchy had power indeed over the belief of the faithful, and the ritualists who followed in the wake of the Tractarians in the 1860s and 1870s were in a dilemma over the matter. Theoretically they were bound to champion the rights of the bishops as the officers of the Church, and so it was the ritualists in the Church Union and elsewhere who were interested in an increase of the episcopate, maintaining episcopal dignity, and a court of bishops to replace the Judicial Committee in ecclesiastical appeals. In practice, however, they were always running into difficulties because few bishops were likely to sympathise with the behaviour of ritualist clergy in their parish churches. Most of the bishops were besieged with complaints from parishioners about strange 'popish' practices. Tait had to deal with rioting at the church of St George's-in-the-East because of the Rev Bryan King's ritualistic innovations. He also withdrew the licence of Alfred Poole, a stipendiary curate who had introduced confession.[88] Thomson, Waldegrave, Jeune and Jackson were noted for their anti-ritualism. Wilberforce was often plagued with letters from alarmed parishioners; he usually replied to them stiffly, but also wrote in strong terms to the clergyman concerned, warning him to make no changes of which his congregation might not approve. Although many of his clergy urged him to support legislation against ritualism he refused, and did not live to see the passing of the Public Worship Regulation Act.[89]

Hamilton, though not unsympathetic to ritualists, employed the same tactics. After the passing of the Public Worship Regulation Act, the bishop had much more power to act against ritualist clergy, and some of the unsavoury prosecutions which resulted drove a further wedge between ritualists and unsympathetic bishops.[90] Ritualists, therefore, could not expect much support from the bishops, whose office they were theoretically bound to respect, and they often defied them, though at the same time urging them to use their authority against the Broad Church. This rather contradictory but human attitude was embodied especially in Denison, who was prepared to defy Bishop Bagot and undergo a court case lasting four years because of his ideas about the Real Presence, but a few years afterwards he thought that Hamilton should have tried Williams in his own diocesan court, found him guilty of heresy, and excommunicated him summarily if he did not recant.[91]

After the tremendous opposition to Hampden's appointment, prime ministers were careful to nominate bishops who were as inoffensive as possible. Evangelicals, on the whole, were content with the existing method of appointment, especially as they tended to be a favoured group, but High Churchmen were not satisfied and suspected the State's power. They were not willing to give unquestioned loyalty to bishops who might be the tools of a secular Parliament. They had no real cause to complain between 1847 and 1869 because the appointments of that period were unimpeachably orthodox, but discontent broke out again in 1869 when Temple was nominated to fill the seat of Phillpotts in Exeter. As in Hampden's case, it was demonstrated that the Church had no power to refuse a bishop of whom many of its members might disapprove. The dean and chapter of Exeter had to elect the bishop formally, but if they refused they were still liable to the ancient penalties of Henry VIII, which could mean imprisonment and confiscation of their property. Wilberforce, Sir Stafford Northcote and Browne of Ely all urged Temple to disassociate himself from *Essays and Reviews*, especially as a new edition was promptly printed at the time of his nomination with 'Bishop of Exeter' next to his name; but loyalty to his fellow-essayists made him refuse. The Dean and Chapter did elect him by 13 votes to 6, with 4 abstaining, in spite of protests from clergy in the diocese and petitions from Church societies.[92] Significantly, most of the criticism came from High Churchmen rather than Evangelicals, though Ellicott did protest to Gladstone that Temple might at least have gone through the 'quarantine of a deanery'.[93] But Temple's essay had never been considered quite as bad as the others, and his high reputation as headmaster of Rugby made most people share Gladstone's view of him as a pious Evangelical; therefore the storm did not nearly equal that over Hampden. Gladstone anticipated trouble from a group of opponents in the chapter, who did in fact make it difficult for Temple at the confirmation following the election. They went so far, writes Sandford, 'as to render it necessary to summon Dr. Temple's eldest sister . . . to prove that he had been born in lawful wedlock'.[94] He was consecrated by Jackson of London during Tait's illness, with Thirlwall and Browne assisting. They received a protest from some of the other bishops, led by the High Church Christopher Wordsworth, but decided they had no authority to stop the consecration.[95]

In fact Gladstone had gauged the temper of the Church well, and the opposition soon died away, as Temple proved an able bishop. Most moderate churchmen felt secure in a tradition in which the prime minister was limited in his choice only by Church opinion, which he had to take into account. A few High Churchmen, however, wished for more certainty, and wanted a repeal of the law to enable the dean and chapter to refuse to elect if necessary. There was not enough support for this to push it into Parliament, because the majority considered that State-elected bishops prevented factional strife, which would inevitably appear if the Church controlled the nomination of bishops.[96]

Beset with anxieties about ritualists at one end of the scale and Broad Churchmen at the other, with considerable variations in between, the bishops had to use considerable tact in keeping the Anglican clergy working harmoniously together and in co-operation with their diocesans. Again, the success of this depended on the personality of the bishop and on how accessible he was. In 1864 Wordsworth drew a gloomy picture of overworked bishops, fraternising mainly with the nobility and gentry, and fobbing off their clergy's complaints with letters from a secretary or dealing cursorily with long queues of applicants.[97] But this picture was only partly true.

Hamilton, for example, was striving to follow Wilberforce's pattern, without either the advantage or the disadvantage of Wilberforce's striking personality, which usually had the effect of winning or alienating people completely. The picture of an inaccessible bishop which Wordsworth described certainly did not fit Hamilton, who, though he conscientiously attended Parliament and Convocation, was mostly in his diocese and worked hard to keep in touch with his clergy. He kept records of his meetings with them, which, though not as careful and efficient as Wilberforce's, do give a more personal description of his impressions. Hamilton built up a reputation for gentleness and fairness to his clergy which was appreciated even by his opposites, Tait and Thirlwall. The Rev Bryan King found refuge in his diocese after the scandalous anti-ritual riots at St George's-in-the-East. King, it is true, had much in common with Hamilton theologically, but Hamilton was also willing to prefer men of the Evangelical party. In 1865 he offered the living of Monkton Wyld to the Rev L. Lester, formerly of Swanage. Lester came to see him, doubting whether he would be accepted in a parish which had previously been occupied by a High Churchman. Hamilton dealt kindly with him, telling him that 'differences between honest minded true-hearted Churchmen were often more apparent than real', and left him to make his own choice. Lester went to Monkton Wyld.[98]

Hamilton, like most other bishops, was informed of the opinions of his clergy by their fellows, who would report any suspicious movements amongst themselves to their superior in a way not unknown in other professional bodies. In 1857 Hamilton was warned by the 'Rev L.' that S. Leathes, the curate of St Martin's, Salisbury, had changed his views during his diaconate and was now a follower of Maurice. The curate, 'Rev L.' reported, disregarded ordinances, 'dwelt much on feeling & experience as a test of Spiritual Condition', and was probably not sound on the doctrine of vicarious atonement, which many Broad Churchmen rejected as immoral and unjust to the idea of a perfect God.[99] Hamilton had ordained Leathes deacon with some misgivings, because the man was so violently opposed to the Evangelicals. Leathes was summoned, and explained that his former vehemence against Low Churchmen had been due to private fears which threatened to drive him either to Rome or atheism. Hamilton noted:

> With regard to his present state, he said that Mr. Maurice had enabled him to see that God was Love—that Religion was a matter of the heart & not of Dogmatic Theology such as Pearson and Hooker—that he could not accept the ordinary explanation of the Doctrine of the Atonement—that he accepted the Doctrine—that he could never love a God who was he thought, ready to punish him——.[100]

Hamilton cautioned Leathes on his faults of impetuosity and lack of sound reasoning, but he ordained him priest later, and he left the diocese to take a curacy in Soho.

In another case concerning a curate, Hamilton again acted on information and summoned the offender, T. Gregg, to answer charges of false doctrine made against him by the Rev D. Hogarth, who was Gregg's rector at Portland. Hamilton's journal does not say what the false doctrines were, but he prepared himself carefully for the interview and was primed with all his correspondence with Gregg, his answers to the ordination examination questions, a summary of the charges against him, with portions of the Scriptures and the Prayer Book to test Gregg's ideas. They went through these passages together, and Gregg managed to convince Hamilton that his views had been misrepresented, though he was rebuked for not confessing his difficulties at the time of the ordination examinations. Like Leathes, he was pardoned and went to another curacy in the diocese.[101]

Thirlwall, on the other hand, did not conform to the ideal of the bishop which was coming into being, with efficiency measured mainly in terms of speech and motion. Though he did not neglect his duties, his calm and reserved temperament did not endear him to his clergy, many of whom were not well-educated. Thirlwall had the additional disadvantage of being an Englishman at a time when Welsh nationalists were demanding the appointment of Welsh bishops. He came to a diocese in which there were many hostile elements; his enemies, the Halls, continually reproached Russell with his appointment, which they considered a failure. Lady Augusta wrote to a sympathiser: 'Sir B[enjamin Hall] . . . echoed and re-echoed his entreaties for a *native* Bishop—pointing to St. David's as a sad proof of what he had always said, would be the result of all the most learned Englishman *could* or *would* ever perform.'[102]

Russell appointed Ollivant to Llandaff, hoping that his connection with Lampeter would soften partisan feelings, but this was regarded as mere hypocrisy. Tempers were inflamed further in 1851 with the outburst of rivalry between St David's College and the nationalist school at Llandovery. Thirlwall defended St David's College, and wrote to Archdeacon Williams, who had been one of the founders of Llandovery, that he did not think the headmaster there was sufficiently well-equipped as a classical scholar.[103] Thirlwall thus managed to stir up the hostility of an influential clique, which probably prejudiced his relations with his clergy, some of whom sided with the archdeacon. His own remoteness made the rift even wider. The Rev J. Evans of Crickhowell was one such aggrieved minister; he described Thirlwall's behaviour to another nationalist friend:

> With another Clergyman I called once at his house, and his conduct was more like a Russian Bear than anything else. He hardly would ask us to take our seats. . . . At a Confirmation in this town he since passed a number of us Clergy in the street as if we were unworthy of his notice. . . . He bowed to no one, he shook hands with no one, he said nothing, when I spoke to him as he was going down the street to the Church he did not in the least pause or stop, though there was no hurry. . . . It is notorious that he is one of the most awkward men that walk into society.[104]

This was a prejudiced view, exacerbated because Thirlwall had not promoted Evans to a canonry, but even those who wished to speak well of Thirlwall had some difficulty in explaining his reserved manner. One of them wrote after Thirlwall's death:

> The truth is that the Bishop though severely just was by no means deficient in kindness though he was not remarkable for *showing* the latter quality. His clergy, on this account often used to consult the late Archdeacon Archard Williams rather than their Bishop when they wanted friendly counsel.[105]

The clergy were not invited to visit Thirlwall, and the gap between them was great. Malicious stories were circulated about him. One, arising from his well-known fondness for animals, asserted that he was always accompanied by a dog which had been trained 'to know and bite a curate'.[106]

Gladstone, who had Wilberforce as his ideal bishop, thought that Thirlwall's episcopate had been a failure because he had not been able to awaken men's sense of devotion; Gladstone preferred a bishop like Temple, who showed more signs of fervent religion, even if the theology differed from his own.[107] Thirlwall received honour from politicians and scholars and respect from his colleagues. Stanley lamented his passing, for to many liberal churchmen he symbolised the relationship between Christianity and scholarship and the comprehensiveness of the Anglican Church.

Stanley thought Thirlwall had shown how a bishopric could be saved from purely material preoccupations, 'timid counsels, unequal measures, and narrow thoughts'.[108] Thirwall would have thought that the bishop's role in defending the Church was not to gather the clergy behind him under some doctrinal banner, or even to win them by personal popularity, but to promote their education and prevent them from cutting themselves off from a world which presented them with many new difficulties in matters of faith. But the strange reticence which prevented Thirlwall from being a forceful bishop like Wilberforce, whom he much admired, also prevented him from producing any works which would advance the Church's cause in the intellectual field, and he remains a curiously anomalous and mysterious figure.

Even in the sphere of diocesan government, everything depended on the energy of the individual bishop, and in the hands of men like Wilberforce, Hamilton and Thomson the episcopate was gradually remodelled to make the bishop a force within his diocese. The majority of appointments in the time of Palmerston were, however, so unimaginative as to retard any major activity among the bishops. Nor, in spite of High Church hopes, were the bishops really able to govern the opinions of their clergy; any discipline they were able to impose must come from tenuous personal contacts, for there was great difficulty in resorting to legal action. At every step the bishops' tasks were inextricably entangled with the question of the relationship between Church and State, which made both lay and clerical statesmen proceed with great caution during this period. Until the Church's legal and financial systems were removed from the control of the State the bishops' powers to influence Church affairs were limited. Of course, from the point of view of liberal churchmen, episcopal interference with the private judgment of the clergy was not desirable, and they fought to save the establishment in order to prevent such interference; but to numbers of conservative churchmen with a literal belief in the divine inspiration of the Bible the Church called for more defence against rationalism than Erastian bishops could provide, and the events of the early 1860s showed the weakness of bishops like Wilberforce and Hamilton who hoped to impose the conservative view. So many churchmen turned to defensive organisations which were to be controlled, not by the dignitaries of the Church, but by the rank and file.

Notes to this chapter are on pages 254–7

Chapter 8 CHURCH DEFENCE

Societies to defend the Church's position in the nation had been known since the late eighteenth century, when the 'Church and King' clubs openly allied the Church with Toryism, but during the mid-nineteenth century there was an unprecedented attempt to organise the scattered energies of the Church. Large and well run societies were already flourishing, especially the Society for Promoting Christian Knowledge, founded in 1699, and the Society for the Propagation of the Gospel in Foreign Parts, founded in 1701. The religious census of 1851 listed twenty-one major Church societies for education, missionary work, church-building and relief of poor clergy.[1] They were all concerned with raising funds for specific objects. Although some of them, especially the National Society, involved themselves in Church defence by resisting the encroachments of Dissenters into education, this was not their main object, for most of them had been formed in days when the Church's privileges and doctrines were not as fiercely assailed as in the mid-nineteenth century. In the 1840s, in response to new problems, many small societies sprang up, most of them including both clergymen and laymen, with the intention of defending the Church from attacks of all kinds. After a period of success and failure, the energies of these small groups were combined in the late 1850s and the 1860s into a number of well-supported centralised bodies, the most important of which were the ultra-High Church English Church Union and its Low Church counterpart the Church Association. Apart from these groups, the Church Congresses, which began in 1861, signalised the desire for unity and defence, as did a movement for the revival of diocesan synods, which ran parallel to the revival of Convocation. All these groups intended to defend the Church, although there was some confusion over what the term 'Church defence' implied. Some wished to reaffirm the Church's doctrines; others to prevent disestablishment. The legal successes of the Broad Church in the 1860s, however, affected all of them and drove them to greater efforts, for they all equated the Broad Church with their common enemies: disestablishment, dissent, and unbelief.

In the 1840s small groups of clergy and faithful laymen gathered in large towns to form defensive societies. It is difficult to estimate how widespread these were because they left few records, but it is clear that they were motivated by two threats which occurred almost simultaneously. The first was ominous government action on education. Lord John Russell had tried unsuccessfully in 1839 to establish a 'normal' training school for teachers which would combine both general undenominational religious instruction and specific instruction from the clergy of the pupils' own denominations. Peel's government tried, only four years later, to pass a Factory Bill which provided the same system for factory children in new schools to be supported mainly from the rates.[2] Peel's proposals were not particularly far-reaching, for he still considered that Anglican schoolmasters were necessary, but the High Church was appalled at the suggestion that children should be taught outside the established Church. A number of church unions sprang up to protect education from the encroachments of a secularising State. Peel was unsuccessful because of strong objections from Dissenters as well as from Anglicans.

The other movement which aroused alarm was the Liberation Society, formed by Miall in 1844 to organise Dissenters against the Church's privileges. This society also objected to the government's educational policies as likely to preserve the advantages of the Anglican Church in education. Archdeacon Denison thought the Liberation Society had infiltrated the Liberal party in Parliament, and became therefore more suspicious of the State's intentions towards the Church.[3] Nor were his fears without foundation; the support of organised dissent was extremely helpful to Gladstone in 1868, and the Liberal party was united in its desire to disestablish the Irish Church. One of the major interests of the Liberation Society was to lobby MPs and demand that candidates for Parliament should support the Dissenters' views. These tactics of the Dissenters were to provide a model for the Church defence societies.

The societies which called themselves church unions were at first concerned with education, and those which called themselves church defence associations with attacking the Liberation Society: two complementary aims. The most important of the early church unions began in Bristol in 1848, with Denison as its secretary. Nine clergymen met on 20 January 1848, constituted themselves a society, and invited twenty other churchmen to join them. They asked for 5s 6d as an annual subscription.[4] Over the next twenty years they met, usually at monthly intervals, to express criticism of various aspects of the relations between Church and State. They objected to State interference in education, the Gorham judgment, the appointment of Hampden, legal impediments to proper exercise of 'spiritual discipline' (ie ritual practices), marriage with a deceased wife's sister, the Divorce Bill and the Judicial Committee's decisions on Williams, Wilsons and Colenso. From these objections it will be seen that the society was a focal point for the ritualists in Bristol. During the early 1850s, when feeling against the results of the Hampden and Gorham cases was high, there were as many as sixty members at each monthly meeting, including both clergymen and members of the gentry like Sir Charles Anderson.

Similar unions came into being in Manchester, Exeter, Chester, Lincolnshire, Coventry, Gloucester, Norwich and Yorkshire. In London there were two groups called 'South Church' and the 'Guild of St Alban'. The original educational policy of the first unions was soon superseded after Peel failed to push through the Factory Bill, but the Hampden and Gorham cases revived Church fears of State interference with doctrine. During the scandal created by Hampden's appointment, a small 'Watching Committee on Church Matters' was formed in London, and changed its name in the following year, 1849, to the 'London Union on Church Matters'. It was composed of fairly prominent London churchmen, both clerical and lay, who belonged to either the ritualist or old High Church parties, and the leaders of local unions sometimes attended it. Bishop Blomfield sanctioned it because it was not a particularly aggressive body. It was divided over whether to demand the revival of Convocation or not.[5] A more militant 'Metropolitan Union' was started by those who left the London Union because they thought that Convocation was the Church's best hope and wanted to exert all their efforts to revive it. It was, however, largely replaced by Henry Hoare's more influential Society for the Revival of Convocation, and finally died as its purpose was achieved. The chief success of the London Union, in co-operation with the Metropolitan Union, was a huge public meeting in 1850 to protest against the Gorham judgment. This took place on 23 July, and was very well attended by members of local unions from all over the country, whose ranks had swollen with dissatisfied High Churchmen. They filled two large halls and repudiated the judgment, but this had little effect except to satisfy their own consciences and make the governments of the next twenty years rather more careful in their selection of bishops.[6]

The movement lost popularity during the 1850s because it was associated with the ritualist party, against whom public feeling turned after the 'papal aggression'. Lord Feilding, who had chaired part of the public meeting, seceded to Rome, the Bristol Church Union quarrelled internally over whether to declare itself against Rome or not, and Blomfield antagonised the ritualists by asking the incumbent of St Barnabas's, Pimlico to resign after the anti-ritual riots. Denison also fought with the Bristol Church Union, which disapproved of his mixing religion with politics when he opposed Gladstone's candidature for Oxford in 1853. Sir Charles Anderson was a friend and supporter of Gladstone. Denison was horrified when Gladstone supported the 'conscience clause' allowing Dissenters and unbelievers to withdraw their children from Anglican religious instruction at school.[7] The London Union, however, managed to retain enough life to raise a fund anonymously to aid Denison's defence in the trial over his views on the Eucharist; it opposed the Evangelicals' movement to hold religious services in halls and theatres, and petitioned against the Deceased Wife's Sister Bill.

The church unions had nothing definite to attack in the 1850s, and so their membership dwindled. In 1853 Conybeare described them as the quintessence of the agitating spirit of ritualism. 'These are clerical institutions', he wrote, '(including sometimes a few laymen), which meet together at intervals, usually once a month, to make speeches and pass resolutions concerning things in general, and their own neighbourhoods in particular.'[8]

The ritualist party itself soon revived, and gathered strength among the clergy and a well-to-do section of the lay population. Among the most influential laymen in the movement were the Hon Colin Lindsay, fourth son of a Scottish earl, the founder and president of the Manchester Church Society, and A. J. B. Beresford Hope, a wealthy philanthropist and effective polemical writer. Such men liked to think of the ritualist movement as the 'Church Party' and the chief defender of the Church's doctrines and privileges. They were all interested in the revival of Convocation and, when this had been achieved, they set about organising the ritualists, using for that purpose the added vigour which the alarms of the 1860s gave them.

The beginning of a central organisation was the Church of England Protection Society, formed in London by a small group of churchmen, including Denison, under the chairmanship of Sir Stephen Glynne, Gladstone's brother-in-law.[9] Its activities in 1859, its first year, were to investigate the legality of Tait's suspension of the ritualist curate Alfred Poole, and to offer legal advice to the Rev Bryan King after the riots at St George's-in-the-East. It had sixty members.[10] In December 1859 Lindsay's Manchester Church Society asked eleven similar bodies to send delegates to a central meeting to discuss some form of centralised organisation. The unions of Chester, Exeter and Bristol, the Protection Society and the Guild of St Alban all professed interest, but six others, including the London Union, did not reply. On 11 January 1860 only six people attended, and Bristol and Chester did not manage to send representatives. This group decided that affiliation was necessary, and accepted the Protection Society as their central point, with a committee of management to which each branch should send two lay and two clerical members. Its name was changed to the English Church Union in June, and Lindsay remained its chairman until 1867. In 1860 it had 203 members. Its success continued because the former Protection Society, which had already attracted men like John Keble, grew out of all bounds. In 1861 its numbers increased to

435, in 1862 to 780. It had over 3,000 members by 1866, 7,895 by 1870, and continued to grow throughout the remainder of the century.[11] By 1886, when ritualism was becoming more respectable, the Union had fourteen bishops among its members, together with 2,600 clergy and 17,000 laity.[12] Its membership reached 40,000 in 1900. Many local church unions affiliated with it, so that by 1863 it had twenty branches with their own committees, who were subordinate to the central chairman and council and contributed to its support. It published its own pamphlets, and its affairs were reported in the *Church Review* a monthly paper which became weekly in 1862. It naturally received plenty of encouragement in the ritualist journals: the *Christian Remembrancer*, *Literary Churchman* and *Ecclesiastic*. Its avowed aims were to protect those under any hindrance in spiritual matters—that is, ritualists who were being prosecuted—and to 'defend and maintain, unimpaired, the doctrine and discipline of the Church of England'.[13]

The Church Union, favoured by all the most influential men in the ritualist movement, including Pusey, obviously met a need for ritualist self-defence by means of combination. Membership, which included an associated group of ladies, was entirely of clergy and well-to-do lay people, although by 1866 it also had a following among undergraduates at Oxford and Cambridge. It hoped to bring poorer people into parish organisations, but this idea had no success, possibly because of the continued association in many people's minds between ritualism and popery, a connection which was not discouraged when Colin Lindsay and his wife joined the Church of Rome in 1868. The ritualists were also cut off from the working class because at first they opposed popular forms of worship in places other than churches and did not favour any shortening of the services, though they did encourage more frequent evening services. A more definite attempt to reach the working classes was made in 1876, when a committee the Union set up to defend A. Mackonochie, a prosecuted ritualist, and to campaign against the Public Worship Regulation Act, developed into the Church of England Working Men's Society. The Society aimed to send out lay working-class evangelists as missionaries among their own kind, but the Union first had to quell doubts about the papal tendencies of ritualism.[14] By the end of the century, however, there were many ritualist clergy running mission-type churches in the slums of the large cities.

The Union itself became increasingly militant during the 1860s. It worked through the usual methods of platform lectures, meetings, propaganda publications and petitions, especially to Convocation. Naturally its members did not consider themselves a sectional party, but as defenders of the doctrines of the whole Church, and they anticipated and feared anti-ritualist laws. The increasingly powerful central committee was divided into a number of *ad hoc* committees, the most important of which was the legal expenditure committee, which managed the funds raised to provide legal aid for prosecuted ritualists. There was also a lectures committee. In 1868 it reported that local branches were spending far too much on lecturers, almost to the point of bankruptcy.[15] The central committee remained in close contact with the proliferating local unions, and although the second chairman, Sir Charles Wood (later Lord Halifax), disclaimed any interest in politics, the Union members were not discouraged from trying to influence local politicians to favour their ecclesiastical views. Sir Charles Wood wrote to a local committee in 1868:

> It seems to me that our correct course is to do what we can as individuals to influence the candidates with whom we may be brought into contact: remembering that our support at the present time to whichever side we accord it, will be a reason henceforth for strongly urging our wishes upon our representatives in Parliament, when the necessity with respect to legislation, whether upon Ritual, or any other then important matters should suggest the expediency of so doing.[16]

The central committee also urged their local clergy members to see that Catholic proctors were elected to Convocation, and as many clergy were apathetic towards the elections it is likely that an active group could have achieved considerable influence in this way.[17]

Church Union members were particularly hostile to any form of rationalism in religion, and especially to the Broad Churchmen, who, they thought, were undermining Anglicanism from within. They petitioned Convocation to pronounce synodical judgments against the essayists and Colenso, and were the implacable opponents of the Judicial Committee, whose ecclesiastical function they believed should be given to the Upper House of Convocation, to which should be joined any theologians whom the bishops might summon to help them.[18] In the 1860s they became an important pressure group, but aroused much anger inside and outside the Church and were not on good terms with the episcopate, to whose power they had to pay lip-service. The bench of bishops, to them, was a tool of the State, and they particularly feared Archbishop Tait, scourge of ritualism. They petitioned Convocation against Voysey in 1868, but did not receive a completely friendly reception. Archdeacon Moore of Stafford, who did not like such unofficial organised bodies, said: 'The English Church Union is to us an unknown society. We know no more about it than we do about the Church Association, and I think we ought not to recognise these voluntary associations.'[19] The petitions of the Church Union, however, were weapons for the High Church members of Convocation.

The Union offered Archbishop Thomson £500 in 1869 to help pay for his prosecution of Voysey, but the Evangelical Archbishop refused it. Voysey himself thought it was a bribe to induce Thomson to prosecute him, but G. B. Roberts, later historian and secretary of the Union, claimed that the money was not offered until the prosecution was under way.[20] According to the early minutes of the Church Union, Roberts's claim was the right one.[21] The York branch of the Union asked the central committee to take up the matter, and in 1868 a special committee was set up to consider what must be done. Edward Churton, Archdeacon of Cleveland, wrote to tell this committee that Voysey's words would be heard by few if he were not brought into court, and that tolerance towards him was the best way of silencing him.[22] The committee could not accept this view, and one member relished the idea of forcing Tait and Thomson, the enemies of the ritualist movement, to act against such heresies in court.[23] After Thomson had announced his intention to prosecute, Sir Charles Wood wrote to the president of the Church Association to suggest that they sink their differences and aid Thomson in the common cause against Voysey. He also pressed Lord Shaftesbury to use his influence with the Evangelicals to promote this.[24] Such actions made the Union unpopular with liberal-minded churchmen and were an expression of the litigious spirit of the Church at this time.

During the 1870s the Union's resources were needed to help the legal expenses of the clergy prosecuted under the Public Worship Regulation Act, but when the drawbacks of the Act were realised the temper of the Church became more gentle. The Union is still, however, in conjunction with the Anglo-Catholic Congress, the focal point of the Anglo-Catholic section of the Church. It no longer insists on a literal interpretation of the Bible, but is still critical of State interference. Like most Church groups, it is more interested in social problems than it was in the 1860s, but still aids clergy with legal advice if necessary.

The actions of the Church Union provoked a strong reaction among Evangelical churchmen. The Church Association was founded by Evangelicals in 1865 'to uphold the Principles and Order of the United Church of England and Ireland, and to counteract the efforts now being made to assimilate her services to those of the Church of Rome'.[25] Since this group was mainly concerned with frustrating the work of the Church Union, and did not have much concern with Church defence except in this particular, it is not necessary to describe it in much detail except to show how the Church's efforts to draw itself together to face the armies of apathy and unbelief were continually hindered by party prejudices. In fact the actual beliefs of the two societies coincided on their attitude to the Scriptures; they both interpreted the Bible literally and opposed any attempts to challenge its historical accuracy. On matters of ritual they differed, of course; the Church Association was scandalised by ornate vestments, church decorations, confession and the 'Romish' views of the Eucharist held by the Church Union. Its paper, the *Church Association Monthly Intelligencer*, contained drawings and denunciations of specific churches where these abominations were to be found. It was as successful in recruiting members as the Church Union, with about 100 local organisations by 1867 and 308 clergy among its members. Its revenue that year was £6,802, mainly from subscriptions, and it was particularly popular in Manchester.[26] It had few notable men amongst its members except Lord Shaftesbury, who was president of the local branch in Dorset. It worked by much the same means as the Church

Union, by lectures and distribution of papers and pamphlets, but is also spent money on proceedings against ritualists in the ecclesiastical courts. It offered Archbishop Thomson £500 to aid his prosecution of Voysey, whose views were as abhorrent to them as they were to the ritualists, and this was apparently accepted by the Evangelical Archbishop and collected by subscription,[27] though, as mentioned earlier, he had refused a similar offer from the Church Union. Like the Church Union, it did not appeal to those without means; it had a membership fee of 10s a year. Also like the Church Union, it has continued to the present day, though in 1851 it became known as the Church Society; it is no longer for militant purposes.

It was obvious that groups who desired Church unity were frustrating their own aims by insisting on a rigid body of doctrine, and the money they spent on ecclesiastical prosecutions seems wasted in view of the Church's more pressing problems. They served mainly to exacerbate party hostility within the Church.

The Church Union and the Church Association were militant groups which worked against each other. The Church Institution turned its energies mainly against the State, and hoped to enlist all churchmen behind it by putting forward no special dogmas. It began at almost the same time as the Church Union, in December 1859, and, like the Society for the Revival of Convocation, was brought to life by the activity and finance of Henry Hoare. Hoare, roused by antagonism to the Liberation Society and elated by his success in resuscitating Convocation, wanted an association which should co-operate with Convocation and bring the laity to help in the work of the Church. He intended to use the ruridecanal chapters as a basis, because in some dioceses they included laymen as well as clergy, and to give them a central organisation through which they could make their feelings known to Convocation and Parliament. Most of the bishops were friendly to Hoare, and Tait, Wilberforce, and the two Sumners favoured the idea. Hoare himself was a moderate churchman, tending towards Evangelicalism; his father had been a member of the Clapham Sect and he had personal connections with the Wilberforce family. During the 1850s he wrote pamphlets to show that the clergy and laity must co-operate to save the Church from State interference. The first place to adopt his idea was the deanery of Sutton in the diocese of London, where in 1856 an experimental meeting of clergy and sixteen 'lay consultees' was held to discuss the perennial question of Church rates.[28]

In 1858 Tait and Wilberforce supported the idea of such gatherings, and various other deaneries took up the plan. In 1859 Archbishop Sumner, his brother, and Tait agreed to select lay consultees for a central group in London. Hoare corresponded with the city and suburban clergy to impress his ideas upon them, and held numerous meetings at his house;[29] 320 consultees were elected and these chose the executive committee of seven, whose secretary kept in communication with the rural deans. As a result, the Church Institution, 'an Association of Clergy and Laity for Defensive and General Purposes', was formed, with its own offices in Trafalgar Square and Hoare as its treasurer, though it did not have its own newspaper until the publication of the monthly *National Church* in 1870. It began with 29 rural deaneries participating out of the 585 in England and Wales; all of these were from the South and Midlands except for two in Wales.[30] It put forward no doctrines and concentrated on resisting any secular encroachments on the Church's temporal privileges; it told its members by circulars what was happening in Convocation and Parliament, and petitioned against the abolition of Church rates and similar measures. Most of the bishops blessed it; even Thirlwall, who heartily distrusted any organisations of the kind and at first warned his clergy against joining it, came to consider it harmless.[31] It did not grow as fast as the dogmatic societies, which again is some indication of the active churchman's sense of priorities at that time. It had about 400 members in 1862, mostly of gentry and middle-class people, but by 1870 it had three subordinate county organisations in York, Devon and Cornwall.[32]

Wilberforce hoped that the Institution would bring apathetic middle-class people back into active Church work, and thought it had achieved this result in Oxford.[33] Hoare came to speak at one of Hamilton's meetings of archdeacons and rural deans in 1859, and managed to rouse their enthusiasm for separate ruridecanal chapters of clergy and laymen to discuss other than doctrinal issues, but Hamilton did not encourage his clergy to join the Church Institution lest they should alienate those who did not accept its ideas.[34] Nevertheless four Salisbury groups were among the original twenty-nine which joined. Hoare travelled extensively to promote his plan and went to see Thirlwall in St David's, but the two men had little in common and failed to reach any real agreement. Thirlwall did think the Institution better than church unions or synods, but did not encourage meetings which had no specific purpose, and his diocese had little to do with such affairs. He was also politically opposed to the Institution on such measures as the disestablishment of the Irish Church. Church Unionists like Denison encouraged co-operation with the Institution because it had the same temporal aims as themselves, but thought their own organisation more important because it defended what they believed was the authentic teaching of the Church.[35] So the Church Institution, though its aims could appeal to many churchmen, and though it had support from the bishops, did not win to itself the fierce energies of either the Church Union or the Church Association. It was also hindered by having a 'clerical' flavour which apparently deterred prominent laymen from joining it.

The Church Institution was destined to be unsuccessful in most of its objects, though its enemies the Dissenters were to be equally unsuccessful in their attacks on the establishment and Church property. It may have been consoled by the similar failure of the Liberation Society, for both groups were defeated as the government gradually assumed control of education, though it was a slower process than either society had expected. In 1886 the Institution, which became known as the Church Defence Institution, had a branch in every diocese, and hoped to penetrate each large town and rural deanery. It was distributing 500,000 tracts a year, and had an income of £5,716, mainly from donations.[36] It was never financially stable, and concentrated particularly on the distribution of literature. It had a chequered career in the twentieth century. During the First World War it was practically bankrupt, but in 1923 it was amalgamated with the Press and Publications Board, a committee of the Church Assembly, to take charge of the Church's publications, and it continues in that capacity today as the Church Information Board. Its information services have thus superseded its original defensive purposes to a large extent. Its original eclecticism has probably been responsible for its adoption by official centres in the Church for purposes which the more partisan societies could not have performed.

The Church Congresses were a more publicised and popular method of healing the Church's divisions. They had great success in the 1860s and afterwards. Like the other organisations, they were the work of a few determined individuals, in this case two secretaries of the Cambridge Church Defence Association, William Emery and W. J. Beamont, who were both clergymen and resident Fellows of Cambridge colleges. Emery, a lecturer in mathematics at Christ's College, who seems to have been the most influential, was an organiser by nature and spent much of his career in promoting schemes for bringing churchmen together. He was influenced by Hoare's ideas and founded the Association in 1858; he also found time to be secretary to two missionary societies and to form a volunteer rifle movement.[37] His part in diocesan organisation will be explained later in this chapter, but his main work was to begin the Church Congresses, of which he was honorary secretary until the end of the nineteenth century.

The first Congress met in the hall of King's College in November 1861 and lasted for three days. The Cambridge Church Defence Association had written to the secretaries of all the other Church organisations inviting their members to attend, and prominent people were also individually notified. Subjects proposed for discussion included laws affecting the Church, education, lay co-operation, Church rates, subdivision of dioceses and clerical incomes. All these remained favourite topics in the mid-century. The Archdeacon of Ely presided, and, though not given much space in the press, the Congress had a moderate success. The pattern of Congresses was set by asking certain members to read prepared papers and allowing others to speak on the subject of the paper, each for a certain time. There was no voting or summing up, for the aim of the Congress was to air ideas, promote understanding and suggest possible courses of action without forming specific plans. Questions of doctrine were strictly forbidden. A report of the Congress was published in which the organisers explained that it had been an attempt to bring together the scattered energies of the Church, which had already been aroused by the condition of the times:

> The restless attacks, the systematic organization, and the avowed purposes of the opponents of the Church of England, encouraged by the indifference of the apathetic, and backed by the support of the irreligious, awakened a short time since the minds of Churchmen from their characteristic disregard to the signs of the times, and urged them to use every effort for the preservation of their constitutional rights and privileges.[38]

Oxford took up the idea, and, after corresponding with the secretaries of the Cambridge Congress, several Oxford churchmen decided to hold a second Congress in July 1862. Wilberforce was naturally more interested in such a venture than the aged Bishop Turton of Ely had been, and consented to be president. The Congress committee included local clergy and members of colleges, and the honorary vice-presidents included the Duke of Marlborough, the Earl of Carnarvon and Sir Roundell Palmer, who were university officials. The respectability of the gathering was therefore assured; its refusal to espouse any particular party cause was shown by the appearance on the committee of clergy from the Evangelical stronghold Magdalen Hall, as well as ritualists like Liddon.[39] This meeting received considerable notice in the press and was even more successful than the Cambridge Congress, although it was not term-time and many members of the university were away. Fifteen subjects were discussed, all concerning the Church's practical problems—its finances and its relations with various sections of the population. The *Guardian* gave plenty of space to the Congress, including verbatim reports of some of the speeches, although it criticised the absence of controversial questions like pew rents.[40] *The Times* said it was a harmless waste of time and showed how far the Church had lost touch with ordinary affairs, while the *Nonconformist* considered it a confession that the Church could not achieve its purposes through Convocation.[41]

The number of people at the first two Congresses is not known for certain, but the membership for Oxford was estimated at about 735.[42] In subsequent years attendance swelled enormously as Congresses were held successively in Manchester, Bristol, Norwich, York, Wolverhampton, Dublin and Liverpool.

Naturally most of the members were interested local people, though there were always many clergy from far afield, except at the Dublin Congress. More and more distinguished names were added to the list of honorary vice-presidents. It came to include Lord Derby, Lord Lyttelton, Joseph Napier, Lord Ebury and the foremost names in Church organisation: Colin Lindsay, Beresford Hope, Henry Hoare and Sir Stephen Glynne. At the 1864 Congress at Bristol, Archbishop Longley consented to be patron, and thirteen English bishops (including Thirlwall) were on the list of honorary vice-presidents. The Congresses at Norwich and York had even more episcopal support, and the York Congress was attended by both archbishops, who conducted solemn services in York Minister. In that year (1866) the number of Congress members grew to 3,073; 2,147 bought tickets for the whole Congress and 926 tickets were sold for single days. The numbers declined in Dublin in 1863, understandably, and Wilberforce was the only English bishop to brave the sea crossing, but in Liverpool the following year the attendance increased.[43]

There was no permanent committee to organise the Congresses, but the committee of each Congress set up a board of reference to decide upon the next location from applications sent by local groups of churchmen. The Bristol Congress committee in 1865, after consulting the secretaries of past Congresses, drew up a set of rules to regulate this and other general business of the Congresses. After a town was chosen the interested people formed an *ad hoc* committee which kept in contact with the secretary of the previous Congress and in this way maintained some continuity. The Congresses managed to support themselves by the sale of tickets; in 1869 the Liverpool committee put up a sum of money to guarantee themselves against possible loss, but there was none.[44] The numbers of clergymen and laymen on the committees were equal. Local townspeople became anxious to have the Congress in their midst because it naturally stimulated trade. The Congress organisers hoped that the meetings would have a beneficial effect on local people who were ignorant of Church matters by displaying the power and dignity of the Church assembled for consultation.[45]

Like the Church societies, Congresses were at first attractive only to people of means. Local clergy attended in strength, but there must have been many even among the clergy who could not afford the expense of coming to them. At the York Congress, appropriate to a diocese ruled by one of the most popular of English prelates, a working men's meeting was held, and the men were addressed by several of the Congress speakers. They were told about the Church's work, but some of the High Churchmen complained that the tone of the addresses was not sufficiently Anglican and might have been used by any denomination.[46] Another such meeting was held at Wolverhampton, where 2,000 working men attended. The committee of that Congress was enthusiastic about the meeting's success and exhorted other Congresses to follow its example.

> Let the Church, so far as she is represented by the Congress, come boldly among the masses and fear not. The healthy excitement occasioned by the meeting of the Congress amidst these hundreds of thousands will draw their attention to the Church, and give to them a high estimation of her office, her life, and her desire for their good.[47]

The York Congress also discussed the particular problems of the Church in Staffordshire, but the Congresses do not seem to have been serious in attempts to evangelise the working masses. The population of York at the time, as Kirk Smith has pointed out, contained workers who were skilled and organised; many of them attended church and chapel impartially, and Archbishop Thomson's personality particularly appealed to them.[48] It is impossible to say whether the lowest and most ignorant section of the working people were attracted to the meetings, but it would seem unlikely that they were.

During the 1860's the Congresses tended to dwell on the same type of subject: missions at home and abroad, clerical and lay education, parochial work, the Irish Church, clerical incomes, dilapidations of church property and the functions of the cathedrals were hardy subjects and continued to stimulate. Although the Congresses renounced any discussion of doctrine, they did reflect on the problems of unbelief at all levels of the population, and 'recovery of alienated classes' was brought up from time to time. The larger issues of Church discipline, the ecclesiastical courts and the relationship between science and religion could not avoid leading them into the question of the right of clergymen to free critical inquiry. The speakers were carefully chosen to present the views of different sections of the Church, and political and social differences were also taken into consideration. At first the Congresses tended to sound rather High Church because Evangelical clergy were usually suspicious of organised gatherings, while the ritualists revelled in them; but more and more prominent Evangelicals responded to the invitation to speak, and at Norwich Pusey faced the Evangelicals Thomas Birks and Edward Garbett. They debated the 'spirit in which the researches of learning and science should be applied to the study of the Bible', and, as might be expected, the Tractarian and the Evangelicals were not really at variance on this point. Pusey was rather more disparaging of science than the others, who believed that science should be the handmaid of religion. He was not at his best because of his limited knowledge of the subject; his address denied Darwin's ideas and affirmed the truth of the Book of Genesis. He also adduced as further evidence that, '. . . the Negro race bears marvellously the impress of the levity and sensuality of their forefather Ham.'[49]

The Congresses were often repetitive and the same speakers spoke on the same subjects more than once, though presumably to a different audience. Garbett elaborated his ideas again in 1869 on the topic of 'Phases of unbelief and how to meet them'. Several other speakers also decried the frivolousness and vanity of unbelief, and maintained that it could be met only by an informed clergy possessing a strong moral earnestness.[50] Denison aired his particular views at several Congresses. In fact the Congress in Bristol in 1864 was suspiciously ritualist; it was attended by Pusey, Keble and Denison, who did not read papers but joined in a discussion on diocesan synods and took advantage of the occasion to deplore the Judicial Committee's decision on *Essays and Reviews*. Keble also affirmed his belief in the necessity of the idea of eternal punishment for the wicked, and told a harrowing anecdote to strengthen it.[51] On the whole, however, the Congress did manage to avoid party faction to a surprising degree and, though the meetings were occasionally disorderly, to put forward several points of view without rousing too much rancour among the members.

The noise and publicity of the Congresses attracted plenty of adverse criticism. With the exception of the Rev John MacNaught, who maintained at the 1869 Congress that infidelity should not always be attributed to wickedness but sometimes to an intense desire for the truth, Broad Churchmen did not attend them. Benson, who belonged to a more liberal Cambridge school of theology, was dismayed by them. In 1864, at a fund-raising meeting in Oxford under Wilberforce's auspices, Disraeli had announced himself 'on the side of the angels' and attacked both Darwinism and the Broad Church.[52] Benson felt that the times were moving towards authoritarianism in the Church, and wrote in 1865:

> What bad times these are—our own churchmen are going no one can see where. Disraeli's and S. Oxon's alliance and these congresses seem to me to augur worse than anything since the Reformation . . . if it were not for such men as [Westcott] is, and Temple, and one or two who can both think and believe, I should fear that thought and faith were at last parting because they had found their married life so unhappy.[53]

Voysey took a similar attitude and objected strongly (from hearsay) to the York Congress, where he believed the general tone had been in favour of Church dogma rather than morality.[54] Mark Pattison, on the other hand, saw the Oxford Congress as a triumph for the High Church party and a victory of morality without intellect. In an essay he associated the Congresses with a general decline of learning in the Church. 'There was animation, unanimity, vigour, arranged on behalf of the most meagre poverty of conception, the most disappointing barrenness of moral purpose.' He also noted in his diary:

> . . . though the Congress was weak in intellect, it was strong in character. Its moral weight was great. It exhibited herein, a faithful picture of the general position which the Ch of E. now occupies in the country. It has conquered and possessed itself of the average & respectable Englishman—the good women of the highest rank; the better sort of clergy, of average, but not eminent abilities—and the wealthy laity—it is making rapid progress with the orderly and devout part of the middle class. It only remains that it embrace the artisan, who is, as yet, outside. The literary class will never suffer themselves to be comprehended in a society

founded on the prohibition of free opinion. But in the secure occupation of property, capital, respectability, & average mediocrity, the Church can afford to despise literature.[55]

Pattison's bitter words were not entirely fair. The Congress could only keep itself together by avoiding subjects which called for theological learning and yet roused party animosity. It necessarily concentrated on practical questions. Yet Pattison's general conclusion was correct, as the Congress debates on science and religion make clear. The average Congress speaker, once he strayed from practical problems, was usually ill-informed and given to pious platitudes which did not even begin to come to grips with the problem of the alienation of many educated men from the Church. Nor did many of them betray much understanding of the attitude of the poor towards the Church.

During the 1870s the nature of the discussions changed somewhat. Nearly every year there was a debate over the relationship of science to religion, and more attacks on Darwin's ideas. This reflected the Church's anxiety at the popularity of Darwinism among the younger generation owing to the polemical methods of Huxley. Interest also turned more towards the problems of the working classes, in particular what line the clergy should take towards strikes and strikers. Again, the discussion reflected a division of opinion within the Church, some advocating that the clergy should be strictly impartial, others taking the side of the employers. This was a sign that the Church was beginning to take a belated interest in the problem of labour, but the tone of the addresses to working men was still inevitably patronising. It was not until later in the century that the Anglo-Catholic group began to take a more sympathetic view of working-class problems and even to attack the attitude of employers. Except for the occasional voice of a hard-pressed city clergyman, the Congresses of the mid-century showed a disappointing lack of awareness of social problems.

Broad Churchmen were not the only critics of the Congresses. Many churchmen thought that, far from revealing the strength and dignity of the Church, the Congresses were noisy and frivolous and incapable by their very nature of doing any real work. The Congresses were too bustling and flamboyant, said an article in the moderate *Churchman*, and the ritualist *Ecclesiastic* objected in 1864 that the businesslike tone of the first Congresses had been lost because of lecture-room dilettantism and unrestricted admission of women, who lowered the intellectual standards of discussion by their mere presence and took up too much room with their crinolines.[56] It also reported that too many important subjects were discussed in too short a time, and that sometimes two debates were held in different halls simultaneously. Canon Jebb deplored in Convocation that most people were attracted by the showy publicity of Congresses and were not interested in the deliberation of wise men.[57] Most of these criticisms came from High Churchmen who did not think that Congresses could ever gather much strength of purpose. These men wanted an authoritative body to defend the Church's doctrines and privileges. At the same time as the Congresses, therefore, there was a movement to revive diocesan synods, which men like Denison hoped would replace Congresses and become the solemn deliberative instruments of all Church action.

Diocesan synods, like Convocation, were part of the old structure of the Church in England and therefore particularly favoured by ritualists, who were very conscious of the Church's past. Before the English Reformation the bishops had assembled their clergy regularly in synods, and had possessed wide judicial powers through them. In days of poor communications they helped to bring the Church's officers together, but they had been ended by Henry VIII. In the 1850s the same arguments were produced for their revival as for the revival of Convocation: that they would be legal as long as they did not attempt to frame new canons or pass judgments. The movement for synods revealed the sense of urgency in the Church, especially High Church fears of the secular State, the threat from dissent towards the Church's privileges, and a general anxiety about the status of religion which seemed threatened by doubters inside and outside the Church. Henry Hoare, though more interested in Convocation and the Church Institution, also advocated synods which should include churchwardens and other laymen; in 1853 he lectured to a group of clergy in Chichester on the desirability of synods with Convocation at their head. The meeting was enthusiastic, but the movement did not produce any results until the mid 1860s, several years after the revival of Convocation.

The first synods held in England after the Reformation were not part of this general movement but were intended to provide an arena for a particular bishop to express his views. In 1850 Wilberforce invited his clergy to attend a 'synod' in the cathedral on 20 November to sign a declaration 'against the late usurpation of the Bishop of Rome', who had recently set up Roman Catholic sees in England. Wilberforce kept a careful check on the clergy, and knew who did not come to the meeting and who did not sign. Out of 547 incumbents and 261 curates, 81 were unaccounted for and only 61 refused to sign the declaration. This, however, was hardly a real synod, as it lasted only one day and had one specific purpose. It was less a conference between bishop and clergy than an occasion to pass a resolution on a subject which aroused almost universal alarm.[58] Nevertheless it revealed a High Church tendency which Wilberforce exhibited strongly, and which the Broad Church deplored, to regiment the clergy and subject them to their bishop's wishes.

A synod more worthy of the name took place in the following year, when Phillpotts sent a pastoral letter to the clergy of Exeter asking the rural deans and two clergy from each deanery to attend a meeting. He requested them to send him topics for discussion, but the main purpose of the synod was to defy the 'papal aggression' and to justify Phillpotts's views on baptismal regeneration as the authentic doctrine of the Church of England. High Churchmen were still disturbed about the decision of the Judicial Committee on the Gorham case in 1850. The synod met from 25 to 27 June and began with Communion and with a sermon by one of the prebendaries against the Gorham judgment. Phillpotts first delivered an address on diocesan synods themselves; he did not think it necessary that all the clergy of the diocese should come, but the bishop should consult their representatives, 'for a Diocesan synod is the Bishop consulting his clergy'. The parish clergy were to discuss the set topics in the ruridecanal chapters beforehand, and their opinions were to be reported by their representatives at the synod. Phillpotts then took up the major business of the meeting and proceeded to lecture at length on baptismal regeneration, supported by numerous quotations from the Church Fathers. The clergy discussed the question; Prebendary Oxenham maintained the right of synods to pronounce on doctrine, since neither the bishops as a body nor the universities had power to do it, and because many people had joined the Church of Rome because they despaired of a situation where nobody's pronouncement was considered authoritative. Oxenham regarded church unions as an irregular but praiseworthy attempt to counteract the Hampden and Gorham cases. The others evidently agreed with him, and they unanimously accepted a declaration affirming baptismal regeneration and another against the Church of Rome. They also discussed catechism, lay cooperation and the need for more frequent services.[59] But in spite of Phillpotts's protestations the Exeter synod was hardly a free consultation between bishop and clergy. Phillpotts was not a man to suffer any opposition and his clergy knew it. Apart from the parish clergy, there were all the cathedral officials and higher dignitaries of the diocese whom Phillpotts had appointed—and he was notorious for providing places for his sons and relatives. In any case there was little chance of disagreeing with him, but the synod set an encouraging precedent to which High Churchmen could point, though future synods never had quite such singularity of aim as the redoubtable Bishop of Exeter's.

A strong party of High Churchmen of the more ritualistic type certainly favoured the restoration of diocesan synods as a means of conserving Church power and defending its doctrines. Some thought that disestablishment was inevitable if the State continued to threaten the Church's prerogatives, and they looked to a system of ruridecanal chapters, diocesan synods and Convocation to govern the Church when it was released from State control. Those who were less extreme did not want synods to have extraordinary powers but to work within the existing framework of Church and State and give the Church a stronger voice in it. They argued that synods would make the powers of the bishops and Convocation greater and at the same time more democratic. Certain Evangelicals also favoured revival for the opposite reason that it would give bishops more power to discipline their clergy and help to put down ritualism without resorting to the law courts.[60] Archdeacon Edward Bickersteth, nephew of the great Evangelical leader and brother of the Bishop of Ripon, said at a Church Congress that no bishop need fear synods:

> If he comes down somewhat from the autocratic position of a Church and State Bishop, he is borne upwards again with a new power, and with a more clear recognition of his pastoral and paternal character. . . . Nor let it be deemed presumptuous to think that by [synodical] means the Ritual question might settle itself without State interference; and wild speculation on things divine, and rash and unscrupulous criticism of the Sacred Text, might be so discountenanced by the moral sense of a united Church, as to render comparatively unnecessary the formal condemnations of a Provincial Synod.[61]

In spite of the increasing support among the clergy, the movement for diocesan synods lagged behind that for the revival of Convocation, though they became a favourite topic for discussion both in that body and at the Congresses. Obviously synods needed not only the consent but the active encouragement of the bishop of the diocese, and the bench of the early 1860s received the idea cautiously, as was their custom, fearing that synods might detract from their authority and give opportunities to factions among the clergy. Gradually, however, a few of the more enterprising bishops did hold synods and encouraged their more suspicious colleagues by their example, though a few sees like St David's had to wait for the death of their diocesan before synods could be held.

There was also active opposition to synods, and even their supporters quarrelled amongst themselves over their nature and function. Some objected that synods would divide the Church parties even further by bringing strife into the open, and that the clergy would not be able to agree even on practical matters like the administration of diocesan funds; this was a sad reflection on the divided state of the Church. Massingberd, Chancellor of the Lower House of Convocation, thought that different synods might come to different conclusions and make the Church look foolish, and he doubted whether they could carry out any practical decisions.[62] Far from limiting the power of the bishop, synods might give him the opportunity to become a despot; because the bishop was the source of much honour and patronage in his diocese, it could hardly be expected that the ordinary clergy could remain independent of him in the synods, and they would have to comply with his wishes.

The supporters of synods could not even decide what name to use. Extreme High Churchmen like Pusey, Keble and Denison wanted to use the name 'synod' to show that the ancient gatherings had been restored with all their old powers. They wanted synods to affirm the doctrines of the Church (as they saw them), especially after the *Essays and Reviews* trial, and hoped they would replace the Judicial Committee as courts of appeal. *Essays and Reviews* and Colenso had shown them that the bishops had no power to repress heresy, and the ritualists hoped that synods would restore that power. Pusey was at odds with the Church Union over this idea. The Union naturally supported diocesan synods, but as it was a body for lay and clerical co-operation it wanted laymen to have a voice in them, though not in matters of doctrine. Pusey thought that synods were purely clerical affairs and that laymen should not presume to speak in them. There was some doubt on whether the laity had been allowed to vote at the old synods, either by numbers or by a group vote.[63]

Others thought that 'synod' was a dangerous word, and preferred to use the less forceful 'conference' to show that the Church had no intention of usurping the judicial functions of the State. This remained a difficult question throughout the period. Nor could they decide how the clergy should attend; the numbers of clergy in the larger dioceses seemed to preclude gatherings of all of them at once, yet the idea of electing representatives to a synod, as Phillpotts had required, was not entirely satisfactory because the whole intention of a synod was that every clergyman should have his own vote. Perhaps, too, it was unfair to make the views of the majority binding on the rest. During the 1860s, however, several members of the Lower House of Convocation, aided by pressure from Church Unions in the various dioceses, began to urge synods on the reluctant bishops. One of the most active supporters of synods in Convocation was Richard Seymour, a canon of Worcester, who proposed in 1863 that synods should be held because the bishops' visitations were too formal at the time, and too convival afterwards, to allow any real communication between bishop and clergy. He thought that churchwardens should attend, and also any learned men who might correct the synod's errors. The synod should not ignore contemporary political issues but should be mainly concerned with practical diocesan affairs. He argued that bishops need not fear the synods but should use them as means to arouse the latent power in their dioceses; bishops who tried to act alone only revealed their helplessness to administer discipline to the clergy.[64]

Convocation, as usual, moved slowly and the debate continued in 1864. Christopher Wordsworth supported Seymour, but their opponents still claimed either that laymen had no place in the Church's councils or that synods would only divide churchmen against each other more deeply. Denison urged forcibly the need for synods which could impress the will of the Church on Convocation and Parliament, and the Lower House finally passed a resolution in favour of annual synods and sent it to the Upper House for consideration.[65] But the Upper House moved even more slowly, and by 1866 all that had been achieved was a committee which finally reported in favour of regular conferences, the time and composition of which should be left to the individual bishops. Such conferences should include the laity, who should have an equal vote with the clergy and should discuss practical matters, not doctrine.[66] Bishop Browne of Ely said that his own clergy were not satisfied with meetings between bishops and rural deans alone. The report did not satisfy the suspicious Thirlwall, who thought he was being forced into holding a conference in St David's with his uncongenial clergy, and so it was amended to emphasise that conferences could only be held at the bishop's pleasure. The bishops were nervous of moving too quickly, and, in spite of the protests of Ellicott and Browne, decided to postpone discussion of the report until the following session, so that they could consider it more calmly.

In 1867 Ellicott opened the discussion by agreeing with the form of conference proposed by the committee; naturally, as an Evangelical bishop, he opposed the ritualist idea of a 'synod', and argued that it would interfere with the relationship between Church and State and have no legal power to act. George Selwyn, who had recently replaced Lonsdale in the see of Lichfield, then gave a long and interesting speech; he had been Bishop of New Zealand before his appointment to Lichfield and was a popular missionary hero. He was also the only bishop present with a working experience of synods, for he had held them regularly in New Zealand with considerable success; indeed they were necessary to a scattered and independent missionary clergy. Lonsdale had been interested in synods; Selwyn proposed to take up where he had left off and hold synods annually in the archdeaconries and every three years on a full-scale diocesan basis. Laymen should be represented at all synods, which should discuss only practical questions and accept both a majority vote and the bishop's veto.[67]

Tait did not like the name 'synod' and both he and Wilberforce objected to a regular meeting of clergy which had no specific matter to discuss. 'When we have something to do', Tait said, 'call them together, and that is a more natural and simple course than the organization of a cumbrous machinery for doing nothing.'[68] Wilberforce was content with the existing structure in his diocese, which consisted of regular meetings between bishop and rural deans; he also had an elected diocesan board to deal with practical affairs. The unenterprising Jackson of Lincoln and Pelham of Norwich reported that their clergy favoured synods but that they would wait and see the results of any that might be held in other sees. Ollivant's clergy in Llandaff were either against synods, except for special purposes, or were apathetic. The Welsh bishops generally suffered from the disaffection of both clergy and laity, a result of centuries of episcopal neglect, and they could not change this attitude quickly. They therefore did not want to be committed to any particular course of action which Convocation might lay down. Finally, the bishops adopted the committee's report, which was merely a cautious affirmation in favour of 'conferences' rather than 'synods', and which left all the initiative to the individual bishop. Synods were gradually restored in a haphazard manner.

It is surprising that Wilberforce was not more favourable to synods, because, as he said himself, 'I admit the great advantage of bringing together the Clergy and the Laity, and the Clergy and Laity and the Bishop, and my life has been spent in inventing opportunities for that purpose.'[69] He did think that the clergy and laity already had sufficient opportunity to express their wishes to the bishop in his diocese, but Wilberforce, like Phillpotts, was not a man to brook any opposition in his administration, and the idea of synods which might oppose the bishop's will, even if he could overwhelm them with his veto, cannot have been attractive to him. The closest he came to synods was by calling two conferences in 1866 and 1867. The first was held in Queen's College for three days, and the main function of the meeting was sermons and addresses given by various eminent churchmen on the subject of the inspiration of the Holy Scriptures. The speakers included Payne Smith (Regius Professor of Divinity), Christopher Wordsworth and Joseph Napier, who spoke on the Irish Church, while others spoke on the Church in the colonies and on Church unity. The tone was orthodox throughout; Payne Smith argued that science would ultimately be found to support the Bible and that the dating of fossils to pre-Biblical days had recently been discredited. He rejoiced that the rationalist school of German theology was being overthrown by a new generation, and attacked Ewald and Baur.[70] This was truly a meeting for Church defence, called in response to contemporary doubts about the Church, but it was more like a Church Congress than a synod, and attracted clergy from outside the diocese.

Wilberforce held a similar meeting in the following year, this time to defend the miraculous Incarnation of Christ against rationalists like John Seeley, whose *Ecce Homo*, published in 1865, had stressed the humanity of Christ to the detriment of His divinity in a Strauss-like fashion. This meeting was elevated by a reasoned though difficult speech by W. C. Magee, the future Bishop of Peterborough. Magee's arguments were from an orthodox standpoint, but unlike many of his contemporaries he realised that nineteenth-century rationalism rested on a different basis from eighteenth-century deism, and made some sharp thrusts at the nebulous phrase 'conscience of humanity', so dear to Broad Churchmen like Wilson and Voysey. Wilberforce preached at both conferences and was in his element; he was very persuasive, very rhetorical, and showed his own serene confidence in the truth and accuracy of the Bible which no amount of heterodox questioning or scientific argument could shake.[71]

These two forceful meetings were rapid responses to immediate challenges, not attempts to provide a regular and lasting framework of Church unity on which the Church could rest its defence. Wilberforce was indeed one of the most brilliant defenders of the Church in his day, but his methods were individualistic. He relied on carefully-chosen and trustworthy lieutenants, but his ideas were directed towards government from the top. The real synodical experiment was left to a much less colourful man, Browne of Ely, whose projects, together with Selwyn's, encouraged the rest of the episcopate towards this form of Church gathering.

Edward Harold Browne was a moderate High Churchman of the safely orthodox type favoured by Palmerston, though not of the school Shaftesbury usually persuaded Palmerston to appoint. He was also more scholarly than most of the Palmerston bishops, and became Norrisian Professor of Divinity at Cambridge after leaving St David's College, Lampeter. He was a mild, kindly man, who disliked controversy; he was tolerant to the Broad Church in practice, and was one of the bishops who consecrated Temple, though he had previously attacked *Essays and Reviews*. According to C. K. Kitchin, his biographer, he lacked the vehemence of Phillpotts and the eloquence of Wilberforce, but made up for it by a great energy which restored the diocese to activity after years of feeble administration from the elderly Bishop Turton.[72] He thought that Church defence would be better served by improved organisation from within rather than merely warding off attacks from outside. He therefore encouraged meetings of bishop, clergy and laity.

The kind of synod which Browne organised in Ely became the model for most gatherings in other dioceses, but its preparation took several years. Browne asked his clergy's opinions of synods and found them favourable. In 1865 he held a two-day conference; the first day for the rural deans and higher officials, the second for a more general meeting of clergy and selected laymen. They decided that frequent ruridecanal chapter meetings and diocesan conferences were desirable, though Browne stipulated that the subjects for discussion should be mainly practical. The 1865 conference also performed a practical function by arranging for a diocesan fund and a diocesan society to administer it, for the endowment of curacies, aiding poorer clergy and other such works. They also considered education and missions. At the same time, Archdeacon Emery began holding regular conferences in his archdeaconry at the time of his visitation, to discuss subjects like middle-class education. In 1867 the Cambridge Church Defence Association, still an active body under Beamont, petitioned Browne to restore a regular diocesan synod, including laymen. Browne circulated the idea among his clergy, but he himself rejected the idea of a 'synod' with doctrinal and judicial functions, and favoured a 'congress'. He wrote: 'A Diocesan "Congress" would be very different from a Diocesan "Synod"; and I should much deplore the assembling of such a large body merely to hear speeches from a few popular orators, or to excite one another to strong feelings on great party questions.'[73]

The conference was split into four sections, one for each archdeaconry, to make the meetings of a practicable size: all clergy and churchwardens were invited. Browne particularly desired to prevent the isolation of the country clergy from the affairs of the Church, which he believed to be a great danger to its corporate life. About 400 people attended in each section—about half the number summoned—to talk about the maintenance of the established Church, lay work, Church unity and Church rates.

On the whole the conferences were a success. The Cambridge conferences, so close to the university, attracted many eminent churchmen including, in later years, Westcott, Lightfoot and Maurice. Browne retained control of the meetings and decided the topics for discussion; the bishops did not want such conferences to interfere with their authority.[74]

Some bishops opposed synods unbendingly. Prince Lee of Manchester was one, and Thirlwall apparently found a kind of 'synod' of clergy and laity from several parishes already existing in his diocese but promptly discouraged it.[75] He thought the difficulty of finding suitable laymen was insuperable, for in Wales many of the laity were disaffected. He also thought, with some justification, that synods would inevitably reflect the views of the bishop who convened them; or, if he were a bishop without force of character, they would dominate him, which would be equally undesirable. Thirlwall was immediately challenged by Canon Seymour, who argued that Convocation had never envisaged synods as doctrinal or judicial bodies, but that they were intended to strengthen the hand of the bishops against the State. Thirlwall could only reply that there was a strong party in Oxford and elsewhere which favoured synods 'for the guardianship of the faith', and that all organised activity was dangerous.[76] There were no synods in St David's in his lifetime.

Elsewhere the synodal movement was gaining momentum. Selwyn's plans for a full diocesan synod were realised in 1868. At the beginning of his episcopal work in Lichfield he managed to visit forty rural deaneries between January and July before a brief farewell trip to New Zealand. He found his clergy anxious for conferences, and began by holding a series of meetings like Browne's in the three archdeaconries. He too abandoned the name 'synod' in favour of 'conference', and held his first general diocesan conference in June of the same year. It dealt with the questions he considered most important to the contemporary Church: rescue of alienated classes, help for colonial dioceses, further missionary activity, education, church and school building, lay co-operation and the training of ministers.[77] The conferences had no legislative powers and consisted of lay and clerical representatives from each rural deanery, according to its size. The conference was later held annually, and the conferences in the archdeaconries stopped. Therefore, as in Ely, the conferences did not attract all the clergy, but probably represented the most enthusiast churchmen in the diocese, not the apathetic ones whom the bishops wanted to arouse. Unlike the Congresses and most of the other organisations, however, the conferences had some hope of attracting curates and other poorly-paid clergy who could not afford to travel long distances.

More and more conferences were held in different dioceses. Lincoln, under Wordsworth, had a synod of clergy only, reflecting his High Church views. Norwich and Bath and Wells had conferences which included laymen. Thomson began holding conferences in 1869, as did Jacobson of Chester. By 1881 every diocese except London, Llandaff and Worcester had a conference or synod of some sort, and London was preparing to hold its first. Their constitutions and frequency varied greatly, so several leaders of the conferences gathered to form a Central Council of Diocesan Conferences and Synods to co-ordinate the conferences and enable them to bear on Parliament for practical action. Each diocese had a parliamentary committee to keep an eye on political events and bring them up at the conferences. In 1885 the Council decided that infidelity and the relations of science and religion were fit topics for conferences, which suggests that party hostility over these points had softened somewhat. The conferences also gradually widened their scope of discussion to include more social problems—rather late, it would seem.[78] Conferences thus became an established feature of Church life and have remained so to the present day, held annually in every diocese. The diocesan boards of finance, which were set up by the conferences, became a vital part of diocesan administration and helped to arouse support for clerical education as well as increasing the incomes of the poorer clergy.

It will be noticed that none of these societies or conferences made a really determined attempt to beat the Church's critics on intellectual grounds, except perhaps for the conferences which Wilberforce held in Oxford. The Church Union and Church Association could draw up petitions and put as much pressure as possible on Parliament and Convocation to frustrate the Church's attackers, but doctrines were hard to defend and the enemies were as diffuse and scattered as the Church societies themselves. The Broad Churchmen had little in common with each other except for their rejection of certain parts of the Bible and their claim to freedom of opinion. Far and beyond them stretched the groups of anti-Church and anti-Christians of many kinds, from the Liberation Society to Bradlaugh's secularists.[79] In 1870 a band of churchmen of much prestige, including Tait, Thomson, Lord Salisbury, Lord Shaftesbury and other members of the nobility and clergy, mainly of the Evangelical party, formed the Christian Evidence Society. Its aims were stated imposingly.

> The spirit of the times leads men to sift every question which is presented to them. Every institution, however venerable, is called on to justify its existence. . . . This spirit of critical inquiry extends even to our common Christianity. . . .
>
> Another prevalent temper of the times is that of lawlessness. Multitudes refuse . . . to receive the declaration of God as an authoritative rule for the regulation of their conduct. . . . Attacks upon the Bible and the system of religion which the Bible teaches, vary greatly: taking at one time, the form of inquiry conducted with professed reverence; and, at other times, breaking out into open blasphemy.

> . . . the CHRISTIAN EVIDENCE SOCIETY has therefore been instituted, that a common ground of operation may be offered to all Christian men, who, in various departments, and in various grades of society, are seeking to hold fast 'the faith once delivered to the saints', and to defend it against the assaults of scepticism and unbelief.[80]

The society had no definite course of action, but promoted lectures and publications against the Church's enemies (especially Mill and Spencer), open-air discussions, and classes of children who were taught the evidences of Christianity. The classes included studies of standard works by Mansel, Paley, Butler, Edward Garbett and Archbishop Whately. Prizes were offered as an incentive. The subscription for members was half a guinea a year, so its membership must have been drawn from the more leisured classes, and it made up its annual deficit by a reserve fund. It was, however, the first of the Church societies to use the methods of the secularists in order to attract the working classes. By 1886 it was distributing 98,950 handbills a year and holding public lectures on the Albert Embankment, in Hyde Park and under St Pancras' railway arches.[81] The Society still continues today, though its original aim of preserving belief in the literal accuracy of the Bible did not meet with great success. At the same time as this society was formed, the SPCK also decided to pay more attention to the fight against rationalism. It set up a Christian evidence committee which published tracts affirming the accuracy of Scripture, but this suffered continually from lack of money and material and had great difficulty in providing suitable literature.[82]

It may be seen today that groups which began in division have performed much valuable work for the Church in the twentieth century. The diocesan synods, particularly, formed the basis of much needed Church organisation. Yet in the mid-century, when the need for such organisation was just being realised, too much energy was wasted on party efforts; time and money were spent on litigation to defend or prosecute one Church party or another. This factiousness made sober churchmen unduly suspicious of any organisation, as can be seen in Thirlwall's opposition to diocesan synods. For this reason it was nearly twenty years before synods were generally accepted. Nor did any of the earlier societies make any real efforts to reach the working classes; except for the evangelising work of the Christian Evidence Society, the activities of such groups were the preserve of the gentry and middle classes, for whom they often provided a kind of polite entertainment. This is in strong contrast to the activities of the secularist groups, whose emphasis was always on mass meetings and popular lectures and debates. Bradlaugh, especially, achieved a popularity among working men that no member of a Church party society could hope for. The publicity and excitement which factional societies aroused was perhaps disproportionate to their numbers in the Church as a whole, but it did not augur well for the Church's reputation among the educated and uneducated alike. The diocesan synods, which kept as free as possible from party conflicts, were one beneficial result of the Church's search for the centre of unity in the mid-nineteenth century, though their future usefulness was perhaps impaired because they were so slow in getting under way. Had their progress not been obstructed by party divisions when they were first planned, they might have provided a focal point for the Church reorganisation which was so badly needed.

Notes to this chapter are on pages 257–9

Chapter 9 CLERICAL EDUCATION

THE PARTY disagreements which confused and disrupted the Church extended into that part of its activities which was vital not only for 'defence' but for its preservation: the supply and training of the ministry. This subject has been discussed elsewhere in more detail, notably by F. W. B. Bullock,[1] but it will be dealt with here as one of the most important problems of the nineteenth-century Church, exaggerated, like its other problems, by party conflict. In clerical education, as in Church finance and social work, there was a pressing need for some kind of central organisation. Church finance came within the scope of the State, which managed to carry out widespread reform, but other aspects of the Church's work were still arranged by voluntary effort. The mid-nineteenth century saw a growing awareness of the problem, but the atmosphere of hostility within the Church was not favourable to its solution.

In the first place, no churchman believed that there were enough clergy to carry out the work of the Church. The census of 1851 revealed that there was one clergyman to approximately every 1,035 people in England and Wales;[2] twenty years later the gap had widened slightly so that there was one clergyman to every 1,097 people, even though the number of clergy had increased by 3,374.[3] Of course these figures express the relation of the clergy to the people only ideally. The religious census of 1851, although it was highly inaccurate in detail, did reveal the general state of affairs. Of a population of nearly eighteen million in England and Wales, over five-and-a-quarter million did not attend any form of religious worship, although theoretically capable of doing so, and of the remaining worshippers the number of Dissenters almost equalled that of Anglicans. Within the Church, too, there were enormous disparities. In 1861, in the diocese of London alone, three parishes were nominally assigned more than 30,000 people each, with only three or four clergymen to minister to them; eleven more parishes were assigned over 20,000. Yet four parishes in the surrounding countryside had under 400 people each, and some of the wealthier city parishes were almost as small.[4] Churchmen naturally thought in terms of a parochial system in which the minister was intimately connected with every member of his flock, and to them the numbers of clergy did not seem sufficient.

Other reforms were suggested too; the Evangelicals in particular favoured popular preaching campaigns, the revival of cathedrals for popular worship instead of rather exclusive ceremonies, and more efforts on the part of the clergy to speak to the people in a language they could understand. Many High Churchmen tended to resent any vulgarisation of the Church's teaching and were opposed to religious services being held in halls and theatres, but many of them also supported the breaking down of class barriers in the congregation, especially by the abolition of pew rents. But in spite of these ideas the parochial system was always kept in view during the mid-nineteenth century, and to preserve this more clergy were necessary, even though the clerical body still included men whose salaries were less than £100 a year. It can be argued from hindsight that this clinging to the parochial system was outworn and that the Church might have done better to attempt a closer understanding of the problem of popular disaffection, but, given that most churchmen were agreed in their support for the parochial system, their failure to improve it must be considered.

The second problem was closely related to the first. While the Church was barely maintaining its numbers in relation to the population, the character of the clergy themselves seemed to be changing, because the two ancient universities which had formerly supplied most of the recruits to the clergy were no longer the main source. While the numbers of clergy increased, the numbers of university graduates among them declined. In 1800 more than half the graduates from Oxford and Cambridge entered the ministry, but by 1874 this figure had dropped to 35 per cent.[5] From 1840 to 1870 the decline was quite sharp and aroused alarm. In 1841 Oxford and Cambridge provided 86 per cent of the candidates for holy orders, the Universities of Dublin and Durham 7 per cent between them, and candidates from all other sources were only 7 per cent. During the 1860s the proportion of Oxford and Cambridge graduates dropped to 65 per cent, Dublin and Durham provided 9 per cent, and candidates from other sources were now 26 per cent of the whole. The early 1860s, in particular, showed a marked decline in the number of ordinands; the 1862 figure of 489 was the lowest for the whole period from 1850 to 1868, with Oxford providing only 120 men instead of its usual yearly average of 180.[6] Bishop Sumner of Winchester thought that this was due to the violent controversies of the time, which, he imagined, discouraged young men from entering the Church.

This, of course, was not the only reason for the decline in graduates. Professions outside the Church were opening for young men from middle-class families. Forty years earlier, the young Connop Thirlwall had complained that men of education had very little choice of career, but by 1860 the civil service, the law and the colonies were providing richer occupations than the the Church, whose revenues could not expand enough to pay all its members well, even when the most glaring inequalities were being slowly levelled out. Promotion in the Church was too often dependent on the whims of private patrons, and men without connections, however zealous, could not always hope for a reward for their services. Voluntary societies like the Poor Clergy Relief Society and the Curates' Aid Society were necessary to provide (insufficient) relief for the lowest ranks of the clergy. Perhaps the Church should not offer temptations towards worldly ambition, but on the other hand it was hardly possible for a priest to perform his duties adequately if his life were a constant struggle to provide for himself and his family. Some clergy had no houses attached to their parish and were forced to pay rent out of their meagre stipends. In addition, to join the Anglican clergy young men had to provide their own education, and had to be supported until they were twenty-three years of age because they could not be ordained deacon any younger. Not everyone could afford to wait while others of the same age were already supporting themselves by other means.

Social attitudes also demanded very high standards from the clergy. The Evangelicals, whose ideas tended to dominate middle-class society in the mid-nineteenth century, laid many restraints on the lives of the clergy, sometimes resulting in the gloomy puritanism which Samuel Butler described with such horror in *The Way of All Flesh*. A member of the Liverpool clerical society—which had expelled the Broad Churchman MacNaught—complained that society prevented the clergy from indulging in normal recreations, even from growing beards, and then despised them for being 'bloodless'. This, he thought, was bound to deter recruits from the ministry.[7] The stereotyped parson in eighteenth-century literature had too often been a gross, florid, hard-drinking Tory. By the mid-nineteenth century the image of the parson in popular literature, especially of the ritualist clergyman, tended to be anaemic and effeminate; a tendency which the 'muscular Christianity' school of Hughes and Kingsley did its best to counteract.

Although churchmen recognised that clerical poverty had much to do with deterring young men from the Church, Bishop Sumner was not alone in finding doctrinal reasons. Ritualist clergy, who believed their view of doctrines and ceremony was correct, thought that young men, especially graduates, who had accepted ritualist ideas were deterred by ritual prosecutions and disfavour in high places.[8] Most Broad Churchmen, also, believed firmly that the Church's inflexibility was losing it candidates. Their arguments centred on the nature of clerical subscription to the Articles and Prayer Book. Coleridge and Arnold had led the way in the desire for a Church from which no Christian should be excluded, and Stanley argued that subscription was the greatest barrier to intelligent graduates. Articles which had been drawn up three hundred years before were not applicable to nineteenth-century conditions. The existence of parties within the Church showed that the clergy could subscribe to the Articles while interpreting them in a variety of ways, and they were not successful in preventing heresy. Only public opinion could stop ministers from teaching strange doctrines. Stanley hinted that he knew at least nineteen students who were unwilling to subscribe to all the complicated and disputed clauses in the Articles and had therefore given up the idea of joining the ministry.[9]

Tait also was concerned at the decline of likely candidates, and supported a mild relaxation of the terms of subscription, though, unlike Stanley, he did not want to abolish subscription altogether. He thought that only the sincerely religious would be worried by subscription, which could have no power to keep out hypocritical or cynical men.[10] Orthodox clergy, on the other hand, believed that any relaxation would open the Church to what the Rev James Fendall called 'the popedom of private judgment installed in the seventeen thousand pulpits of England . . . whether in the form of Roman apostasy or of German neology'.[11] Constant criticism from men like Lord Ebury resulted finally in the slight relaxation implied in the Clerical Subscription Act of 1865, after several years of debating in Convocation and a Royal Commission. The Act, however, made very little difference to the number of ordinands.

Although Bishop Baring of Gloucester was grateful that the bishops no longer had the burden of half-literate clergy, not many churchmen were satisfied with the kind of education the clergy received, inside or outside the universities. Bickersteth of Ripon, like Tait and Wilberforce, believed that in such an unquiet age the clergy needed to be of vigorous intellect to deal with the problems of a more educated congregation. Bickersteth said of his own diocese:

> I believe . . . that the intellectual tone of the population over a large portion of this diocese peculiarly demands that the clergy should be men of intellectual vigour, of deep and earnest piety, of strong common sense, willing to abridge their own liberty in things lawful but not expedient when self-denial is called for. . . . Here, if anywhere, the minds of men are active, vigorous and keen, quick to apprehend the point of the argument, and to detect the absence of mental and even spiritual attainment. It will not do to confide the ministry of our Church to half-educated men, to persons who, in point of intellectual standing, are inferior to those by whom they claim to be recognized as authorized instructors.[12]

The point was reinforced because it came from Bickersteth, representative of the Evangelical party, which was not traditionally interested in learning as a quality of the priesthood.

Many leading clergymen complained that most young clergy

came to their work completely unprepared for the demands it would make upon them. The universities were still nominally religious bodies, but there was little attempt to foster religious life. Undergraduates had to attend compulsory chapel services, usually once a day and twice on Sundays, but these services rarely aroused reverence in either the students or the Fellows, although there were exceptional cases like Charles Simeon at Cambridge early in the century, and later Newman at Oxford, who managed to instil a deep sense of piety in their students. F. J. Foxton, a rather querulous Broad Churchman, said in 1862:

> The country curate is commonly, at the outset of his career, a raw and inexperienced youth, transplanted from the corrupt atmosphere of our universities . . . without any previous education that can with propriety be called religious, unless we are to consider such the attendance on a few 'Divinity Lectures', being 'crammed' with Greek Testament, 'Tomlyn's Theology', and 'Paley's Evidences', and attending the Matins and Vespers of his College Chapel—an indecent mockery of public worship.[13]

While Foxton, like Thirlwall before him, denounced the immorality of university life, Mark Pattison believed that learning was now considered a quality inferior to zeal among the clergy. His strictures against the zealousness which he thought was replacing learning at all levels of the clerical hierarchy were misplaced, for zeal was undoubtedly needed, but he did object with some justice to clergy who engaged in continual controversy without much knowledge behind their arguments. 'When the organ is hushed', he wrote, 'and the congregation silent, and the preacher ascends the pulpit, then the weak side of Anglicanism reveals itself.'[14] Even the most orthodox churchman would hardly have argued with Pattison over this. Most of the bishops, themselves not famed for learning, believed that zeal was not enough, and that even the poorest congregation could tell whether a priest was well acquainted with his subject or not. At a time like the mid-nineteenth century, when the truth of Christianity was being questioned openly in many parts of society, the clergy needed, as Bishop Ellicott said, to display a level of high Christian culture which would be able to confront even the most educated of critics.[15]

The defects in clerical education lay at the door of the universities, where attempts at reform were delayed by party hostilities for over twenty years. As Foxton said, most of the young clergy had received little education that was specifically theological. Students at Oxford and Cambridge, whatever their future career was to be, were given a classical education; at Cambridge they had mathematics as well. In Oxford theological teaching was in the hands of six professors; at Cambridge in 1850 there were only four divinity chairs. The Royal Commissions appointed to investigate the state of the two universities reported in 1852, and included a description of theological education in their reports. The findings were similar for both universities. The Cambridge Commission thought four chairs inadequate to provide a theological education, and suggested that the large endowment for the Lady Margaret chair, which amounted to about £1,854 a year, should be divided to pay for another chair.[16] This advice was not acted upon until 1860, when the Hulsean Professorship began on money from an obsolete foundation. Not only was the number of chairs inadequate, but the existing ones were not being used to the best advantage. Nothing forced the professors to teach, and it depended largely upon the individual whether any lectures were given. The Norrisian Professor was obliged to give fifty lectures a year, but these were to include substantial readings from the works of Bishop Pearson, according to the founder's request, and so their scope was necessarily limited. The Lady Margaret Professor at the time of the Commission was John James Blunt, who delivered good and conscientious lectures, but this was of his own volition.

In Oxford the position was almost the same. The Regius Professor lectured thirty-five times in the year for the benefit of any graduate students who cared to attend. The Bampton Lectures had begun in 1780 and had often provided stimulating and controversial matter, but the amount of actual teaching still depended on the energies of the professors and of individual college tutors. At Oxford the divinity professors were often inactive because their lectures were not compulsory for students and were therefore badly attended. This applied equally to most of the science professors and all those whose work was outside the examination curriculum.

All undergraduates had to study some elementary theology,

whatever course they took and whether they intended to take orders or not. By a statute of 1850, Oxford students had to answer questions on the four Gospels in Greek in their first public examination; in the second, the compulsory *Literae Humaniores* school included more Greek Testament, some sacred history, the subjects of the books of the Old and New Testaments, the evidences of Christianity and the Thirty-Nine Articles and their scriptural proofs. For honours in this school more ecclesiastical history was added. The Cambridge requirements did not differ much, and relied heavily on Paley's *Evidences*. Candidates in the final examinations had to show that they had attended a term of lectures by the professors in their subjects, but the divinity lectures did not count in this system.

This theological knowledge was all that was required for a university degree, but both Oxford and Cambridge provided extra education through a voluntary examination in theology. The Oxford examination began in 1842, and in 1844 the Hebdomadal Board proposed to make it compulsory, but many junior members of the university were against all examinations in divinity in case the examiners tried to use them as tests of orthodoxy, and the proposed statute was withdrawn.[17] Neither the university nor the bishops attached much importance to the voluntary examination, and it was generally not a success. It required further residence in Oxford after the BA degree was taken, and so involved further expense, which was discouraging to candidates. Only seven men passed it between 1844 and 1863.[18]

The Cambridge voluntary examination, which also began in 1842, had more beneficial effects. It succeeded where the Oxford one failed because in 1843 Whewell, the Vice-Chancellor, suggested that the bishops demand it as a necessary prerequisite for all Cambridge candidates for orders. Most of the bishops agreed, and it was thought that the examination had helped to raise the standards of Cambridge graduates. The examination was open to all bachelors of arts and was based on a term of divinity lectures. There was also a voluntary examination in Hebrew, which was not popular. In 1865 Browne of Ely said that the examination, though not ideal, had been extremely helpful in weeding out unsuitable candidates before he examined them himself.[19] In fact the voluntary examination had become compulsory. It also created a demand for the lectures of the divinity professors, which were well attended, though the Norrisian lectures were still formally weighted with readings from Pearson and the students came from compulsion rather than inclination.

The Oxford and Cambridge Commissions were not satisfied with this state of affairs, and rejected the idea that one kind of education was suitable for both lay and prospective clerical students. Significantly, they treated divinity as though it were a specialised branch of study, not something that could be picked up in the course of a general classical education. The Oxford Commissioners urged that a separate faculty of theology be formed, with an equal status to the other honours schools, but they did consider that the clergy should be trained at the universities, where they might mingle freely with lay students and gain a truly liberal education. They thought it reasonable that clergymen should stay longer at the university, so that they might acquire both a general and a specialised education.[20] The Cambridge Commission also recommended an honours examination in theology, and suggested that men who were not Cambridge graduates should be allowed to take the voluntary examination.

The universities were dilatory in taking up these recommendations. In the university reforms of 1854, the Hebdomadal Board at Oxford, which had consisted of heads of colleges, was replaced by a new Council, elected by all resident Fellows. The High Church conservative element was very strong at first and much opposed to the creation of a theological faculty.[21] Their view was that divine studies would be degraded if they were made the subject of competition in examinations. Pusey, looking back to Newman, believed that ideally the whole life of the university should provide a devotional training, which would make artificial promptings like examinations unnecessary. Jowett aroused their suspicion because he wanted a separate theological school which should include a great deal of modern Biblical criticism. E. A. Freeman told the Oxford Commission that a divinity school was not feasible because of Church controversies; it would be impossible to find a scheme to satisfy all parties, and furthermore, divinity examinations would encourage intellectual display rather than sincere opinions.[22]

At Cambridge, where there was less party tension and a board of theological studies already existed, theology was made an alternative special subject in 1865. The voluntary examination continued until 1873, and the theology tripos was begun in 1874, to be taken both by undergraduates and by honours graduates from other fields. There was no theology school in Oxford until 1869, when it was established on lines suggested by Pusey, with a board consisting of the divinity professors, vice-chancellor and proctors. By this time there had been a complete change in attitude, and it was the High Churchmen who favoured the new school and the Broad Churchmen who opposed it. This was because it had become apparent to the High Church that the universities were no longer Anglican preserves. Dissenters were allowed to take the lower degrees at Oxford in 1854 and at Cambridge in 1856, and they began to agitate also for the MA degree, which would give them a voice in elections of university officials. This power was finally conferred in 1871, but, before that, Pusey and the conservative clergy began to see that a theology school might be one way of preserving Anglicanism. Pusey wanted a faculty in which the choice of examiners would be subject to the veto of the divinity professors, who were necessarily members of the Church of England. Liberal clergy like Jowett, who had previously desired a theological faculty, were not willing to accept it on these terms. Henry Smith, the professor of geometry, believed that the examiners would use theological examinations to determine a candidate's doctrinal opinions.[23] Pusey certainly did regret that candidates for orders were not tested more thoroughly on the soundness of their opinions, but Burgon declared that it was unlikely that any candidates would use the examination to declare themselves heretics. If, he said, a candidate denied the Messianic nature of prophecy, which many Broad Churchmen queried, he would be failed because he was a fool, not because of his views.[24] This was hardly reassuring to the liberal group, though the faculty was finally founded more or less on Pusey's lines, with the proctors presumably tempering the judgments of the divinity professors. The new faculty was not a success for many years because the colleges did not support it with tutorial teaching.[25]

It would not be fair, however, to equate the amount of theological knowledge required for examinations with what might actually be learned at the great universities. The colleges all provided extra teaching, but it is difficult to know how much theology was included in this. Many of the Oxford colleges refused to give information about their activities to the Commission; some of the Cambridge ones described their teaching as based upon the examination requirements. Yet the main responsibility for theological training rested with individual tutors. The influence of men like Newman and Pusey is well-known, and other teachers also took it upon themselves to provide a more thorough theological training than the university required. Blunt at Cambridge lectured frequently, and his lectures, later published as the *Obligations and Duties of a Parish Priest*, became a popular work on the subject, going into six editions between 1856 and 1872, and influencing the ideas of young men like Benson, Lightfoot and Westcott.[26] Blunt told his students that a priest needed to combine knowledge with practical zeal to succeed in his vocation, and advised them to avoid pretentiousness and latinate words. But not all students were fortunate enough to find a devoted teacher.

The knowledge the examiners required was also rather limited and old fashioned. They depended on 'standard' works, and rarely took into account the discoveries of recent times. For 'evidences' the syllabus centred on divines of the previous century like Butler and Paley. German literature, as previously mentioned, was ignored. The examination questions did not call for any great originality or considered thought from the student; he was asked to produce the traditional proofs of a doctrinal point, and was not expected to investigate them or be aware of contemporary controversy surrounding them. Much depended on memory alone. From the kind of set work and the quality of the examination questions, it must have been an unavoidable temptation for the ordinary student to cram his theology much as he did his Euclid, as the Dean of Durham remarked. 'I used to think they crammed Pearson, and Bishop Ball, and Butler, and a little of Hooker; and just as candidates for the civil service examinations are crammed, so candidates for the Holy Orders get up their Butler and their Pearson by a very much shorter process.'[27] He added that the practice had 'gone out', but during most of the nineteenth century it was possible for many clergymen to pass at the universities on a minimum of theological knowledge.

Another defect in the clergyman's education, when it came to fighting rationalism, was not only that he tried to defend himself from the standpoint of Paley, which was not applicable to contemporary criticism, but that he usually knew very little Hebrew. All Hebrew study was optional, and there were not many clergy who could defend the Old Testament from foreign philologists. Significantly, the foremost scholars in Hebrew, like Pusey and M'Caul, had not learned it in England but had made an effort to study it abroad. Jowett, after 1850, was able to begin a course on the history of philosophy, and he stressed the work of Bacon, Locke, and Mill.[28] After 1850, too, the Greats course was opened to include some modern criticism, and this may have helped to bring students into contact with contemporary research through authors like Niebuhr.

Of the remaining places where a theological education was offered, the Universities of Dublin and Durham and King's College, London, were the most respected. Both Durham and Trinity College, Dublin, had separate theology schools long before Oxford and Cambridge. In 1833, a year after its foundation, Durham began to issue a licence in theology for students with a Durham BA or its equivalent, while Dublin provided a two-year course in theology, to be taken after the BA, and which the Irish bishops demanded of their ordinands. The theological department of King's College began in 1846 and provided a theological education much more thorough, but almost as old-fashioned as Oxford. King's College itself had been specifically founded in 1828 to combat the irreligious tendencies of University College, and under its Principal, W. Jelf, it sought to inculcate doctrinal orthodoxy. Bishops received candidates from King's without misgivings after Maurice had been dismissed. Perhaps it is significant that the edition of Gibbon's history recommended for study at King's was an expurgated one.

In 1854 the Royal Commission which was appointed to investigate the functions of the cathedrals in society reported that very little was being done by those bodies to promote clerical education.[29] The chapter of Durham had hastily invested in the foundation of the university to prevent its large revenues falling into the hands of the Ecclesiastical Commission, but of the rest, only Chichester (1839) and Wells (1840) had founded theological colleges to provide extra training for university graduates, and these had sprung from the efforts of two individuals, the Bishop of Chichester and the Archdeacon of Bath. In Lichfield and Exeter, where Lonsdale and Phillpotts both favoured the foundation of theological colleges, the clergy were in a state of turmoil on the subject. Phillpotts had offered his chapter £300 towards the expenses of a college if they would give up a house for it. The chapter replied that they had no unencumbered property, and in any case discouraged the whole idea, partly because they thought the temptations of the city of Exeter, so much larger than Wells, would prove too much for the theological students, but mainly because, '. . . the discordant, not to say extreme opinions on religious matters, which unhappily exist in Exeter, would interfere with the calm and serious study of theology, and the acquisition of sound and sober views of pastoral duty and ecclesiastical discipline.'[30]

Although the Exeter clergy may have held reasonable suspicions of Phillpotts's intention to set up a college where his own form of High Churchmanship would be taught, there was much less reason to suspect the mild and moderate Lonsdale. Yet three of his rural deaneries prevented him from realising his idea for four years, by unrelenting opposition. They echoed the sentiments of the chapter of Exeter—that theological colleges, shut off from the liberal education of the universities, would encourage narrow sectarianism and party conflicts.[31] They obviously feared that ritualism would become dominant in the college unless it were carefully supervised, not by the bishop alone, but by a committee of all those who had subscribed to it. Lonsdale, however, persevered until a college was founded in 1857 to train both graduates and non-graduates, with special emphasis on pastoral work. It succeeded because of Lonsdale's tact and compromise with his clergy, but Phillpotts did not have equal success. He managed to found a small non-residential college in 1861, which had an unpaid warden, but the college was poorly financed, had little support and lasted only six years.

St David's College, Lampeter, has already been mentioned. It was in difficulties until late into the century because its course lasted three years, while other theological colleges demanded only two, thus attracting penurious candidates. Queen's College in Birmingham, originally a medical school, also opened a successful theological department in 1848.

Because of growing dissatisfaction with university education and the belief that more clergy were needed, other colleges associated with cathedrals were founded: in Salisbury in 1861 and Gloucester in 1868, both small, and accepting both graduates and non-graduates. Wilberforce founded the college at Cuddesdon in 1854, after experiencing the same opposition as Lonsdale and Phillpotts.[32] Most of these diocesan colleges did have High Church tendencies, as the Evangelicals who opposed them had feared. Wilberforce wanted Cuddesdon to provide a devotional life, parochial training and theological studies to supplement the work of the universities, and appointed Alfred Pott as principal and Liddon as vice-principal. Cuddesdon was under a cloud when the witch-hunting Golightly accused it of ritualism and forced Liddon's resignation.

Cuddesdon and the other diocesan colleges were also intended to fill the vacant year after a student had taken his BA and before he was ordained, but there was no compulsion for graduates to enter these colleges, nor did they have to stay to complete their courses, and so the system of education could not always be as thorough as the founders wished. Like the universities, they gave formal training in doctrine, but Bible teaching again urged moral rather than critical study. The test papers at Cuddesdon begged orthodox answers, as Professor Chadwick shows.

> What did Adam lose at the Fall, and how far was that which he lost unrestored in or exceeded by the Grace of the Redeemer?
>
> Show the extreme importance of determining the exact conditions of the Paradisiac man and the thoughtless levity of treating this and kindred questions as 'speculative'.[33]

Like Wilberforce, Hamilton had a definite doctrinal objective in founding a theological college. He was becoming increasingly distressed by the prevalence of rationalism in the universities, and the college at Salisbury, he told his clergy, was introduced to counteract tendencies which were becoming common among clergymen. His desire was to train men, 'not only to discredit the prevailing error, that religion is either a matter of opinion or of sentiment, but also receive with a strong intellectual grasp the authoritative teaching of the Church—to appreciate the scientific exposition of this authoritative teaching.'[34]

The Evangelicals also had their own theological colleges, which were all for men who could not afford a university education. St Bees in Cumberland and St Aidan's at Birkenhead were founded in 1816 and 1846 respectively and provided two years' training. Students were expected to know some Latin and Greek before entering them, and were given practical work on the composition of sermons as well as in doctrinal and pastoral theology.[35] St Bees had been founded by an Evangelical bishop of Chester and was one of the most successful colleges for non-graduates. By 1851 it had provided the ministry with over a thousand men.[36] St Aidan's was founded by Joseph Baylee, a well-known Evangelical writer and opponent of the Liberation Society, with the encouragement of J. B. Sumner. These two colleges gained most as the supply of university graduates decreased, because bishops were more willing to accept their men when they did not have much choice.

Yet for most of the century theological colleges were accepted as a necessary evil. Churchmen believed that their use was to provide graduates with some extra theological education and a period of 'holy rest, of sacred study, and calm meditation' before they took orders.[37] They could not hope to compete with the universities; indeed, as many of them were poorly endowed, they sometimes lacked facilities such as good libraries which were essential to a proper clerical education. But this was a minor argument. The main objection was that if the clergy were educated separately from the laity they would be alienated from society as a whole, and this would also foster schism within the Church itself. This view explains the long-delayed development of theological colleges. As one pamphlet writer said, the universities, with all their defects, guarded against heresy, because of 'the residence of a large body of learned clergymen, men of independent minds and habituated to patient investigation, who would be little likely to concur in the support of error.'[38] This was a somewhat idealistic view of the universities, where party strife flourished as well as in any other part of the Church, but at least there was a large cross-section of ecclesiastical opinion which an intelligent student might value. The Evangelicals were particularly suspicious of theological colleges, which might become semi-Jesuit seminaries under ritualist influence, while Broad Churchmen were equally afraid that they would inculcate extremes of opinion, whether High or Low. This emerged especially in the evidence given to the Oxford Commission, for the liberal section of the Oxford Fellows welcomed the Commission and were willing to express their opinions fully. These may be best summarised in the words of Bonamy Price.

> The intellectual culture of the [clergy] would become narrower and more cramped if carried on solely under clerical influence: their view of Theological doctrine would be less comprehensive, less catholic in the true sense of the word, less accurate, and less fitted to obtain its just influence over the literature and thought of the country. A strong sense of separation from the rest of the people would be likely to arise in the minds of the Theological Students; and the jealousy with which the clergy have so often regarded the progress of knowledge, and to the mischievous effects of which history bears such lamentable testimony, would be perpetuated and strengthened. The sympathy of the clergy with the rest of their fellow-citizens, and consequently that of the nation with them, would be weakened, and the influence of the Church and perhaps even its existence, brought into peril.[39]

Evangelicals took much less interest in the founding of colleges than High Churchmen. Between the founding of St Aidan's, which continued to struggle against inadequate finance, and the founding, seventeen years later, of the London College of Divinity at Highbury in 1863, no Evangelical undertook such work. Colleges like St Bees and some missionary training schools had been founded much earlier in the century, during the early revival of Evangelicalism in the Church, but after this no Evangelical bishop except J. B. Sumner encouraged the founding of colleges. This is surprising when it is remembered that in their early days the Evangelicals insisted that a university education was not as important to a minister as zeal and humility and the ability to speak directly to the congregation; yet by the middle of the century they were asserting that only the universities were capable of providing the right education for the ministry, such was their fear of the power of ritualism to penetrate any closed group. The London College of Divinity was founded, not by a bishop, but by a wealthy Gloucestershire vicar.[40] It had strictly Evangelical rules, and the date of its foundation was also a period when Evangelical concern at the growth of ritualism was increasing, culminating in the formation of the Church Association in 1865.

Conversely, the High Church party, which had always placed more emphasis on learning than had the Evangelicals, was the first to move away from the idea that the universities must monopolise clerical education, though they did this regretfully. It was, therefore, High Church bishops like Phillpotts, Wilberforce and Hamilton, in a minority on the bench, who took the initiative in founding colleges, and their intention was the preservation of sound doctrine from the attacks of the Broad Church and the secular State, both of which seemed to have too much power in the universities. Hamilton's intentions in founding his theological college have already been quoted; he also maintained a rather Evangelical view that unlearned men could be good ministers if their doctrines were sound.[41]

In view of the conflicts within the Church in the mid-nineteenth century, it was perhaps inevitable that clerical education, both inside and outside the universities, should become a battlefield. Convocation debated long and fruitlessly on the subject, and a committee of the Lower House presented a report in 1865 enumerating the acquirements which they considered desirable in a theological education. The ideal was a combination of solid scholarship and training for parochial duties, especially speaking and preaching, but there was no suggestion of how to implement it. Convocation considered that the universities were the proper places for such teaching, and thought it desirable that graduates should stay an extra year to study divinity.[42] Convocation, however, had no means to direct any centralised effort towards reforming clerical education.

Theological colleges were gradually accepted as essential to the Church. Edward White Benson, who began like many others with the assumption that education was the prerogative of the universities, decided by 1871 that they were out of touch with Church life. When he was appointed to a canonry in Lincoln cathedral in 1869 and found that the position had no duties, he decided that it was time the cathedrals applied themselves to the problem of education, both clerical and lay:

for I think at this time the Church of England is in such danger of losing her hold—if it is not lost—on higher education for her clergy—her university tenure being most precarious—we are bound to supplement it and the Cathedral system offers an ancient recognized calm and safe mode of education if only a few more people will give themselves to its development. To revive or extend such organization is my most earnest desire—greatly stimulated by what I have seen of candidates for orders as Chaplain to the Bishop of Lincoln.[43]

Benson began a voluntary theological school for such candidates in Lincoln, and these in turn began a night school for foundry workers.[44] Diocesan effort was encouraged when diocesan synods became an accepted part of the Church machinery, but the Church moved slowly, and it was nearly half a century after the founding of the first colleges at Chichester and Wells that colleges were fully accepted into the Church.

The final responsibility for clerical education belonged, however, to the bishops, because the standards they required in their ordination examinations determined the whole tone of the clergy. It was no secret that, because of the shortage of suitable candidates and the difficulty of finding curates for poorly-endowed benefices, bishops were forced to pass men of a low standard, even though the examinations themselves might be demanding. In Wales, particularly, where only the poorest candidates would be satisfied with a curacy in one of the remote mountain parishes, the bishops had to accept men of little education. As William Conybeare pointed out as late as 1853, '. . . even now, within sight of those cathedrals which we associate with Copleston and Thirlwall, indigenous pastors are to be found who cannot speak English grammatically, and who frequent the rural tavern in company with the neighbouring farmers.'[45] Although a Welsh-speaking minister who associated closely with his flock was not necessarily a disadvantage, at their worst the Welsh clergy could be illiterate and drunken. Slow improvement came with resident bishops, better grammar schools and the founding of St David's College, but there was still many a bishop in England, as well as Wales, who accepted a Welsh candidate with misgivings but had no other choice.

Standards in the theological colleges were often determined by what the bishop required. Rowland Williams, who thought a three-year course was necessary for St David's students, was discouraged when Campbell of Bangor accepted into his diocese candidates from St Aidan's who had been previously rejected at Lampeter. St Aidan's had only a two-year course, and so poor students would go there rather than Lampeter, knowing that it would make no difference to their chances.[46] Campbell probably feared that Williams had infected his students with his own religious opinions, but other bishops behaved irresponsibly towards the colleges. The college at Chichester declined because Ashurst Turner Gilbert, who succeeded Otter as bishop, took no interest in it and disapproval of theological colleges generally. As C. R. Sumner said in his charge of 1862:

> Unless the Bishops insist on requiring something of that devout spirit, and power of mind, and aptitude to teach, which are essential for usefulness in the ministry, a decent inoffensiveness of character and a perfunctory performance of duty will be often the best offerings brought as qualifications for the service of the sanctuary.[47]

By the middle of the nineteenth century the bishops were much more aware of their duties in ordination than many of their predecessors had been. In the eighteenth century it had not been unusual for a bishop to demand that an ordination candidate travel the length of England for a perfunctory examination and ordination in London, because the bishops of the poorer dioceses were almost always non-resident. By the 1860s most bishops were conscientious in their examinations, but Wilberforce led the way, as in many other fields of episcopal activity. He invited ordination candidates to stay at Cuddesdon during the period of examination, which usually lasted two or three days, and he led them in prayers and discussion as well as criticising their examination. papers. He also demanded a specimen of original work and asked them to write sermons for him to see.[48] Wilberforce believed that ordination was one of the bishop's gravest responsibilities, and feared lest he should ordain any unworthy man, but the practice of holding the examination in the days immediately preceding ordination made it difficult to fail a candidate, and the bishop and his examining chaplains were usually lenient.

Wilberforce was confident that the standard of his candidates was improving, but his views were not shared by Ellicott of Gloucester or Bickersteth of Ripon. Ellicott deplored the lack of sound scholastic attainments in his candidates and their ignorance of both Hebrew and Greek and of doctrinal theology.[49] Bickersteth had difficulty in attracting university graduates to his diocese and took men from theological colleges without enthusiasm. He tried to weed out the worst by interviewing them all some months before ordination, asking them to construe some parts of the Greek Testament and to give their views on fundamental doctrines, but he could not afford to be too particular.[50] Hamilton also interviewed candidates six weeks before the examinations and warned them of their weaknesses. At his first ordination examination he was so shocked by the standard of some of the candidates that he decided to hold an oral examination as well in future; the first attempt was not very successful, but as Hamilton settled down in his diocese he found it useful to discuss the examination papers with the candidates. A group of candidates in 1855 seemed particularly unpromising, as Hamilton described them in his journal.

> Mr Butt—feeble in manner & not much prepared.
>
> Mr Falkner—a very strange man once near Rome—then nearly a sceptic & now doubtful about himself.
>
> Mr Leathes a good orientalist—an odd man—seems to choose orders because he must have some definite duty. On leaving he asked for my Blessing—& wept on receiving it—I have recommended him for Westbury.
>
> Mr Monkhouse—very bad health—feels unequal to duty—too much exertion to collect thoughts—had had difficulties about Baptism & is ignorant of Doctrine now though he thinks he admits it. I advised his withdrawal.
>
> Mr Peppin: Pleasing manners, quite unsound about III John. Cannot believe *all* children regenerate—because many many baptised children have evil tempers. . . . I dismissed him.
>
> Mr Trubbeck [?] a nice young man. fairly prepared.
>
> Mr Whitehead—well prepared at King's College.[51]

It was generally recognised that standards differed from diocese to diocese. Hamilton was willing to give preference to zeal without much learning, but Tait wished to attract learned clergy.

In 1864 an anonymous tutor, who presumably crammed ordination candidates before their examinations, published a pamphlet to warn them what kind of questions to expect in the various dioceses. He said that Sumner of Winchester concentrated on doctrinal questions; Tait, Browne and Wilberforce asked for competence in Greek grammar; Lonsdale, Graham of Chester, Waldegrave of Carlisle and most of the Welsh bishops asked simpler questions on fundamental doctrines and their scriptural roots. His examples of the kinds of question the bishops asked show that most were like those at Cuddesdon and depended a great deal on sheer memory of Biblical events. Candidates in Ripon, for example, were asked to 'give an account of the division of the kingdom which took place after the death of Solomon'. In Lichfield some questions dealt with the problems of ordinary parish work, and others required a somewhat jejune knowledge of contemporary controversy, such as, 'State and answer objections to the reception of the Pentateuch as a divine revelation.'[52] Both Lichfield and Chester examination papers had a strong bias towards the 'evidences' of Christianity, and obviously demanded an orthodox answer.

Once a man was ordained he often had little time to further the theological education which might have been neglected at the university. Parish clergy were expected to perform many activities in addition to their purely religious duties. Teaching of both adults and children, charitable causes and missionary committees took up most of their time, and zeal and energy were qualities much admired by society. Most of them also seem to have considered it their duty to plunge into the religious controversies of the day, in spite of lack of knowledge of learned subjects. One examining chaplain reported that many candidates for ordination could give a superficial account of contemporary controversies, but their actual knowledge of the Scriptures was tenuous.[53] The more learned members of the clergy feared the harm that ignorant criticism could cause in lowering the clergy in the eyes of educated people, and they had good reason, as the great number of ill-informed pamphlets written by clergymen shows. As the Warden of Queen's College, Birmingham, said:

> We do not want men who know no better than to denounce and anathematize the Spirit and pursuits of their own times. We want

> men who have studied the credentials and documents of the faith so as to have a firm grasp of its reasons—who have good sound arguments at hand, and so are not short of temper, nor afraid of argument, nor obliged to silence because they cannot convince. We want men who are not merely *in* the age, like fossils, but *of* the age, in the best and highest sense; and who, because they are so, can influence the age. . . .[54]

Yet while there were learned and tolerant men like Thirlwall and devout and tolerant men like Lonsdale, and they were to be found in all sections of the Church, the many priests who devoted much energy to partisan clamours did cause great damage to the vital development of clerical education. A Church divided against itself was not able to combine to effect reforms, as this chapter has tried to show. The comparatively quiet development of diocesan synods, which embraced churchmen of all opinions, did, however, lay the foundations for a more rational approach to the subject. In 1912, when party hostility had weakened and diocesan organisation was much improved, a Central Advisory Council for the Training of the Ministry was set up by Convocation. In 1924 it passed under the control of the Church Assembly, and included members of theological college staffs and members of theological faculties at the universities. University graduates were then required to have eighteen months' extra training, and non-graduates were required to have three years' training. A general ordination examination was begun, to prevent variations in the standard from diocese to diocese. The diocesan boards of finance, which were one result of the synodical movement of the 1860s, also help to pay for the training of clergy. But, like reforms in most aspects of Church organisation, improvements in clerical education were delayed for a period which proved dangerously long for the Church.

Notes to this chapter are on pages 259–61

Conclusion

In his book on the thought and influence of T. H. Green,* M. Richter argues that the Evangelical movement lost its force partly because of its lack of intellectual content. It began with a popular appeal, speaking a simple language which uneducated men could understand, but its strength diminished as its converts became increasingly respectable and the nineteenth century gradually became too sophisticated for it. The Broad Church seems to have suffered from the opposite failing; it tried to give religion an intellectual basis but never managed to achieve a direct popular appeal. Maurice's Christian Socialism was the chief attempt to reach the working class through undogmatic Christianity, but its limited resources and conservative self-help attitude soon killed it.

Yet all sections of the Church were directly or indirectly concerned at the obvious irreligion of much of the working class. At all times there were devoted Anglicans, clerical and lay, at work in the slums of the great cities in an attempt to make the Church a reality to the indifferent masses through charity organisations, the National Society's schools, working-class churches and missions. True, there were still many clergy living in rural ease on comfortable salaries, and forming, with the squire, the nucleus of village administration, but since the ecclesiastical reform in the first half of the century the Church had become decidedly more energetic, and the hardworking priest received the praises of society and the approbation of middle-class novelists. Nevertheless, the mid-Victorian period gives the historian an impression of energy directed to little purpose. The Church seemed to be

* M. Richter, *The Politics of Conscience. T. H. Green and His Age.* 1964.

going through a similar phase to the secular administration, torn between individualist ideals and the obvious need for centralisation in order to remedy social abuses efficiently. In bodies like Convocation and diocesan synods the Church was providing itself with the machinery for central direction equivalent to the creation of new departments in government like the Board of Health. The Church's organisations were even slower to move than the government bodies, and Victoria's reign had ended before it really gathered its forces together; nor had it succeeded in winning over the 'alienated classes'.

Church energy was obviously dissipated in its long battles with dissent, which took up a great deal of parliamentary time between the 1820s and the 1870s, until pressure of business became so great that governments became reluctant to take up time with Church affairs. Hostility to dissent helped to draw churchmen into a superficial unity over subjects like the disestablishment of the Irish Church. It also produced some social results which appeared beneficial; during the first three-quarters of the century churchmen and Dissenters scrambled to provide schools for the poor lest the other side gain an advantage in education. It is notorious that this competition failed to provide England with enough elementary schools, while it long delayed any decisive State action on the matter.

One social idea which churchmen of all parties agreed on to some extent was that the religious belief of the working class would be conditioned by the 'tone' of belief among the educated. This was the basic assumption which lay behind all the theological quarrels of the mid-Victorian Church. I have tried to show how the reaction to educated doubt led to a split in the Church over the Broad Church compromise, which tended to confirm High Churchmen and Evangelicals in some of their more extreme literalist views. It was the Broad Church's misfortune to bring more conflict where they had first hoped to bring peace, and close the ranks of the orthodox even more uncompromisingly against free inquiry for a time. The tragedy of this period was that so many good men failed to understand each other because they believed that only their own opinions could be true. Their mutual bitterness was harmful to the Church, for the sight of eminent churchmen engaged in violent doctrinal conflict, attended with much publicity and personal recrimination, did not enhance the Church's popularity.

Few churchmen realised that the ideas of educated men had little influence on the working class. The growth of secular societies, the popularisation of Darwin, and, later, the secularism of working-class socialists seemed to show that the working class might be responsive to educated doubt; but in most cases religious doubt was part of an active opposition to the whole social system, and was confined in any case to a small section of the more literate workers. The Church had for too long been identified with the governing classes, and it was natural that working-class agitation, whether Chartist or socialist, should take a secular and anti-clerical attitude. The roots of working class doubt lay in the social conditions generated by the industrial revolution, when thousands left the relatively compact village life to live in sordid and anarchic urban slums. Most churchmen, whatever church party they favoured, still regarded poverty as inevitable, even if not actually caused by sin, and believed that individual effort was better than State intervention. It was not until the end of the century that the Church's attitude began to change from paternalism towards 'collectivism', and the impetus came, not from the Broad Church but from the descendants of the Tractarians, led by Bishop Gore and the Christian Social Union.

In the mid-century many able churchmen spent their time in rarefied arguments over obscure points of theology, and the leading Broad Churchmen, with the exception of Maurice and Kingsley, were more withdrawn from social problems than most, although they insisted that their ideas were of vital importance to the whole of society. They seemed to adopt the same policy of 'downward filtration' which Macaulay had applied to education in India, in the hope that once the upper ranks of society were educated they would educate the rest. This took no account of the great chasm which divided the educated middle class from the illiterate slum-dwellers of those times. Nevertheless the 'downward filtration' idea led many to believe that the faith of the nation might hinge on the precise definition of the atonement or the literal accuracy of the Book of Genesis. In a Church certain of its position in society, such doctrinal dissension may be a sign of spiritual vigour, but in a Church threatened by so many external dangers as the Church of England was at this time the excessive preoccupation of many churchmen in such matters could only detach them further from the mass of the population.

It remains to be asked whether, if any one attitude towards religious inquiry had been generally accepted, the Church of the mid-Victorian period might have been able to gather its resources for a successful combat with religious apathy among both educated and uneducated. Lately the Broad Church has been praised because many of its ideas about the Scriptures have become commonplace; yet the ideas of Williams and most of the other controversialists, couched in language which they knew must upset many orthodox churchmen, were hardly conducive to the peace and tolerance which were to be the cornerstones of the national Church they desired. The answer was to be found more with men like Thirlwall and Stanley, who believed that free inquiry must satisfy each individual seeker but who objected to free inquiry itself being turned into an object of dogma. But in this period of loud intolerance the tolerant were overwhelmed and enervated. It was opinionated men like Wilberforce who were the men of action, and as all their doings were surrounded with dogmatic pronouncements, their usefulness was often obscured by party hostilities. It is impossible to say with certainty that, if the Church had not been so concerned with conflicts over religious inquiry, it might have been a more powerful force today; but perhaps with more central direction, common purpose and agreement among the clergy, the active energies which were so plentiful in the Church at that time might have been harnessed for its good and not its division.

Abbreviations

Addit MSS	Additional Manuscripts of the British Museum.
Borthwick	The Borthwick Institute of Historical Research, York.
Charges	As episcopal charges have very long formal titles, the diocese and date of delivery are given in notes thus: W. K. Hamilton, *Charge, Salisbury*, 1858.
DNB	*The Dictionary of National Biography.*
Hansard	*Hansard's Parliamentary Debates*, third series.
Lambeth	Lambeth Palace Library.
NLW	The National Library of Wales.
Parl Papers	*Parliamentary Papers.*
RCC	*The Report of the Church Congress*, followed by the location and date of the Congress.

Notes

Except where otherwise stated, the place of publication is London.

Chapter 1 CHURCH PROBLEMS AND CHURCH PARTIES

(pages 13–39)

1 Tait, A. C. *Charge, London.* 1862, p 5.
2 *Parl Papers,* 1852–3, Vol lxxxix (33), p cliii ff.
3 Ibid, p xli.
4 For a discussion of changes in the nature of scientific thought before Darwin, see Gillispie, C. C. *Genesis and Geology*. Harvard, 1951.
5 For a fuller discussion of intellectual doubt see Willey, B. *Nineteenth Century Studies*. Penguin, 1964, and *More Nineteenth Century Studies*. Chatto and Windus, 1956.
6 Harrison, F. 'Neo Christianity', *Westminster Review*, No 18. 1860, p 331.
7 See Sylvester Smith, W. *The London Heretics*. Constable, 1967, Ch 2.
8 Cockshut, A. O. J. *Anglican Attitudes*. Collins, 1959, pp 20–24.
9 Lambeth, Tait MSS 75f, 154. Reflections at Llanfairfechan, 12 Sept 1863.
10 *Spectator*, 25 May 1861, p 555.
11 Kemp, E. W. *An Introduction to Canon Law in the Church of England.* Hodder & Stoughton, 1957, p 74.
12 For Hampden and Gorham see Chadwick, O. *The Victorian Church*. A. & C. Black, 1966, pp 237ff, 250ff.
13 *Hansard*, 1860, Vol clviii, p 846.
14 For a full discussion see Hinchliff, P. *John William Colenso.* Nelson, 1964.
15 Walsh, J. D. 'The Origins of the Evangelical Revival', *Essays in Modern Church History in Memory of Norman Sykes*. Black, 1966.
16 These were: the Sumner brothers, Baring, Bickersteth, Campbell, Davys, Graham, Hampden (who became an orthodox Low Church bishop), Jackson, Lee, Ollivant, Pelham, Phillpott, Turton, Villiers and Wigram.

17 Kitchin, G. W. *Edward Harold Browne*. 1895, p 243.
18 Newman, J. H. *Apologia pro Vita Sua*. First published 1864; 3rd Fontana ed 1965, p 101. See also Burgon, J. W. *Lives of Twelve Good Men*. 1888, Vol 1, Ch 4.
19 Addit MSS 44, 183. (Gladstone Papers) f 369. Hamilton to Gladstone, 25 Aug 1868.
20 *Literary Churchman*, 16 June 1860, p 221.
21 Pattison, M. 'Learning in the Church of England', *Essays*, ed H. Nettleship. Oxford, 1889, Vol 2, p 278.
22 Denison, G. A. *Notes of My Life*. Oxford, 1878, p 134ff.
23 For full studies see Ashwell, A. R. and Wilberforce, R. G. *Life of Samuel Wilberforce*. 1880–2 and Newsome, D. *The Parting of Friends*. John Murray, 1966.
24 For a full survey of Tait and ritualism see Marsh, P. T. *The Victorian Church in Decline*. Routledge, 1969, especially Ch 7.
25 Notably by Forbes, D. *The Liberal Anglican Idea of History*. Cambridge University Press, 1952.
26 For the origins of this term see Sanders, C. R. *Coleridge and the Broad Church Movement*. North Carolina, 1942, pp 8–9.
27 Chadwick, O. *The Victorian Church*. Black, 1966, p 116.
28 Williams, E. *Life and Letters of Rowland Williams*. 1874, Vol 2, p 36n.
29 Stanley, A. P. '*Essays and Reviews*', *Edinburgh Review*, No 113, 1861, pp 472, 497.
30 Abbott, E. and Campbell, L. *Life and Letters of Benjamin Jowett*. 1897, Vol 1, p 362. See also *Essays and Reviews*, 12th ed 1869, p 452.
31 Wilberforce, S. *The Revelation of God the Probation of Man*. Oxford, 1861. Sermon 2, pp 32–3.
32 A Layman (G. Smith). *The Suppression of Doubt is not Faith*. Oxford, 1861, p 2.
33 Garbett, E. *The Bible and its Critics*. 1861, pp 347–8.
34 Tait MSS 80, f 37. Temple to Tait, 21 Feb 1861.
35 Eighteenth-century ideas are developed fully in Cragg, G. R. *Reason and Authority in the Eighteenth Century*. Cambridge, 1964, Creed, J. M. and Boys Smith, J. S. *Religious Thought in the Eighteenth Century*. Cambridge, 1934; and Stromberg, R. N. *Religious Liberalism in Eighteenth Cenutry England*. Oxford, 1954.
36 *Essays and Reviews*, pp 166–7.
37 Jackson, J. *Charge, Lincoln*. 1861, p 46.
38 Pattison, M. *Memoirs*. 1885, pp 302, 314.
39 Wilberforce MSS dep c 201. Burgon to Wilberforce, 11 Feb ?1870.
40 MacNaught's ideas are set out in *Free Discussion versus Intolerance*. 1856; *The Doctrine of Inspiration*. 1856; and *Christianity and its Evidences*. 1863.
41 Abbott and Campbell. *Life and Letters of Benjamin Jowett*. Vol 1, p 275.
42 Pattison, M. *Essays*, Vol 2, p 296.

43 Pattison, M. 'Philosophy at Oxford', *Mind*, No 1. 1876, p 86.
44 Prothero, R. E. and Bradley, G. *Life and Correspondence of Arthur Penrhyn Stanley*. 1893, Vol 2, p 239. See also Abbott and Campbell. Vol 1, p 160.

Chapter 2 THE THREAT FROM GERMANY (pages 40–65)

1 Ward, W. R. *Victorian Oxford*. Cass, 1965, pp 149–50.
2 Trans in Bernard, H. H. *Cambridge Free Thoughts*. 1862, pp 23–47. See also Epstein, K. *The Genesis of German Conservatism*. Princeton, 1966, pp 128–37.
3 Pfleiderer, O. *Development of Theology in Germany since Kant*. 1890, pp 5–26. Kant's ideas about the origins of morality were most clearly developed in the *Grundlegung zur Metaphysik der Sitten*. 1785, trans White Beck, L. Indianapolis, 1959.
4 Storr, V. F. *Development of English Theology in the Nineteenth Century*. 1915, pp 171–3.
5 Schleiermacher's ideas were most fully expressed in *Die Christliche Glaube*. 1821–2. See also Reardon, B. M. G. *Religious Thought in the Nineteenth Century*. Cambridge, 1966, p 44ff.
6 See also Schweitzer, A. *The Quest of the Historical Jesus*. tr W. Montgomery, 1910, p 72ff.
7 eg *Foreign Quarterly Review*, No 25. 1845, p 520.
8 Pattison in *Westminster Review*, No 11. April 1857, pp 354–9. Schweitzer *Historical Jesus* p 107ff.
9 Jaeck, E. G. *Madame de Stael and the Spread of German Literature*. New York, 1915, pp 177, 188, 195–206.
10 Nitsch, F. A. *A General Introductory View of Professor Kant's Principles Concerning Man, the World and the Deity, etc.* 1796. Willich, A. F. M. *Elements of the Critical Philosophy*. 1798. See also Welleck, R. *Immanuel Kant in England*. Princeton, 1931, pp 7–10 and throughout.
11 *Life and Letters of Barthold George Niebuhr*. trans S. Winkworth, 2nd ed 1852, Vol 1, p 138.
12 *Cambridge Free Thoughts*. trans Bernard, H. H. and ed Bernard, I. 1862.
13 Strauss, D. F. *The Life of Jesus*. Birmingham, 1842–4, Vol 1, p. vi.
14 See Beard, J. R. ed. *Voices of the Church, in Reply to Dr. D. F. Strauss*. 1845, p xiii. I have not been able to find any number of Hetherington's publication, but see no reason to doubt Beard, who was a sober Unitarian.
15 Mackay, R. W. *The Tübingen School and its Antecedents*. 1863, p 12.
16 See Murphy, H. R. 'The Ethical Revolt against Christian Orthodoxy in Early Victorian England', *American Historical Review*, No 60, July 1955, pp 800–1. Also Willey, B. *Nineteenth Century Studies*. Penguin, 1964, p 230.

17 Shaen, M. J. ed. *Memorials of Two Sisters*. 1908, pp 189, 239, 223 etc.
18 Ibid, pp 137–8.
19 Harrold, C. F. *Carlyle and German Thought*. Yale, 1963, pp 7–8.
20 Carlyle, T. *Sartor Resartus*. 1831, Book 1, Ch 11.
21 Cordesco, F. *The Bohn Libraries*. New York, 1951, full list.
22 Ibid, p 15ff.
23 *Quarterly Review*, No 145. 1843, pp 99ff, 186.
24 Stanley, A. P. '*Essays and Reviews*', *Edinburgh Review*, No 113. 1861, p 466.
25 *Westminster Review*, No 47, 1847, p 136ff; and No 14, 1858, pp 188–9.
26 Cureton, W. '*Hippolytus and His Age*', *Edinburgh Review*, No 97. 1853, p 12.
27 Rose, H. J. *The State of the Protestant Religion in Germany*. Cambridge, 1825, p 4.
28 Pusey, E. B. *An Historical Enquiry into the Probable Causes of the Rationalist Character lately predominant in the Theology of Germany*. 1828.
29 Pattison, M. *Memoirs*. 1885, p 210.
30 Beard, J. R. *Voices of the Church*. p v.
31 Dewar, E. H. *German Protestantism and the Right of Private Judgment*. Oxford, 1844, p 206 etc.
32 Perry, W. C. *German University Education*. 1845.
33 Palmer, W. 'On Tendencies towards the Subversion of Faith', *English Review*, No 10. 1848, pp 428, 438, 441.
34 Hare, J. C. 'Thou Shalt not bear false witness against thy Neighbour', 1849; in *Miscellaneous Pamphlets*, Cambridge, 1855, p 47.
35 Introduction to Saintes. *Rationalism in Germany*.
36 Bierer, D. 'Renan and his Interpreters', *Journal of Modern History*, No 25. 1953, p 385. See also Schweitzer. *Historical Jesus*, p 180ff.
37 *Edinburgh Review*, No 90. 1849, pp 338–9n.
38 Machin, G. I. T. 'The Maynooth Grant, the Dissenters and Disestablishment', *English Historical Review*. 1967, pp 70, 75.
39 Massie, J. W. *The Evangelical Alliance: its Origin and Development*. 1847, p 114ff.
40 *Evangelical Alliance*. Report of the Proceedings of the Conference held at Freemasons' Hall. London, 1847, Appendix C.
41 *Evangelical Christendom*, 1 Feb 1861, p 61; 1 March 1861, p 111.
42 Pattison, M. *Memoirs*, p 166. Kant's philosophy did not, however, receive favourable treatment in Oxford until later in the century.
43 Mansel, H. L. *The Limits of Religious Thought*. Oxford, 1858, pp 121, 131, 146.
44 '*Essays and Reviews*', *Quarterly Review*, No 109. 1861, p 295.
45 *Edinburgh Review*, No 113. 1861, p 474.

Chapter 3 GERMANY AND THE BROAD CHURCH (pages 66–81)

1 Coleridge, S. T. *Confessions of an Enquiring Spirit*. Black ed, 1963, p 64.
2 Coleridge, S. T. *Aids to Reflection*. Bohn ed, 1893, pp 135, 143–7.
3 Ibid., p 114.
4 For a full study see Sanders, C. R. *Coleridge and the Broad Church Movement*. North Carolina, 1942.
5 Carlyle, T. *The Life of John Sterling*. 1851, p 69.
6 *Hippolytus and His Age* was written in English and published in 1852, while *The Constitution of the Church of the Future*, 1846, *Egypt's Place in Universal History*, 1844–57, and *Signs of the Times*, 1855–6, were translated in 1847, 1848–60 and 1856 respectively.
7 Bunsen, F. *A Memoir of Baron Bunsen*. 1868, Vol 2, p 255.
8 Williams, E. *Life and Letters of Rowland Williams*. 1874, Vol 1, p 310.
9 Preface to Bunsen's *God in History*. trans Winkworth, S. 1868, pp vii–viii. Exeter Hall was a popular meeting place of the Evangelical party.
10 Rose, H. J. 'Bunsen, the Critical School, and Dr. Williams', *Replies to Essays and Reviews*. Oxford, 1864, p 66.
11 *Evangelical Christendom*, 1 March 1861, p 144.
12 Hare, A. J. C. *Memorials of a Quiet Life*. 1872, Vol 1, p 195.
13 Powell, Baden. 'The Study of the Christian Evidences', *Edinburgh Review*, No 86. 1847, p 415.
14 Stewart Perowne, J. J. and Stokes, L. ed. *Letters Literary and Theological of Connop Thirlwall*. 1881, p 195.
15 Thirlwall, C. *A Letter to the Rev. Rowland Williams*. 1860, p 68.
16 Kant, S. *The Metaphysics of Morals*. trans White Beck, L. Indianapolis, 1959, p 23. Temple, F. *And ye shall know the truth. . . .* Marlborough, 1858, p 7.
17 Maurice, F. ed. *The Life of Frederick Denison Maurice*. 2nd ed 1884, Vol 1, p 468; Vol 2, p 253.
18 Prothero, R. E. and Bradley, G. *The Life and Correspondence of Arthur Penrhyn Stanley*. Vol 1, pp 373, 380.
19 *Evangelical Christendom*, 2 Feb 1863, p 61.
20 Abbott and Campbell. *Jowett*. Vol 1, p 175. See also *Essays and Reviews*, pp 411, 496, 522.
21 Stephen, L. *Studies of a Biographer*. 1898. Vol 2, p 136.
22 Hare, J. C. *Guesses at Truth*. 4th ed 1866, Vol 2, p 337.
23 eg Hare, J. C. *Miscellaneous Pamphlets*, p 53. *Essays and Reviews*, p 180. Williams, E. *Life of Rowland Williams*, Vol 1, p 242.
24 *Essays and Reviews*, pp 127–32ff.
25 Williams, E. *Life of Rowland Williams*. Vol 1, p 242.
26 Mill, J. S. *Autobiography*. 1873, Bantam ed, 1965, pp 133–4.

27 Willey, B. *More Nineteenth Century Studies.* Chatto & Windus, 1956, p 162.
28 Kegan Paul, C. *Memoirs.* 1899, pp 215, 36.
29 Stephen, L. 'The Broad Church', *Fraser's Magazine.* March 1870, p 313.

Chapter 4 ROWLAND WILLIAMS
(pages 82–106)

1 Owen, J. 'The Rev. Dr. Rowland Williams', *Contemporary Review,* No 14. 1870, p 58.
2 His early ideas are noted in his Commonplace Book, N.L.W. MS 4603c. This has no page numbers. See also *Life of Rowland Williams.* Vol 1, Ch 2.
3 Hawkins, E. *The Duty of Private Judgment.* Oxford, 1838, p 6ff.
4 Williams, E. *Life of Rowland Williams.* Vol 1, pp 348–9.
5 Williams, E. ed. *Stray Thoughts from the Notebooks of Rowland Williams.* 1878, p 60.
6 Williams, E. *Life of Rowland Williams.* Vol 1, p 242.
7 Conybeare, W. J. 'The Church in the Mountains', *Essays Ecclesiastical and Social.* 1855, pp 10, 15 etc.
8 NLW Letters from Llanbadarnfawr Parish Chest 1842–55 (typescript), pp 11, 81–2.
9 Ibid. A. Hall to James, 2 June 1850, p 62.
10 Williams, R. *Lampeter Theology.* 1856, pp 35–50.
11 Kegan Paul, C. *Memoirs,* p 262.
12 Williams, R. *Lampeter Theology,* pp xii, 30.
13 Stewart Perowne, J. J. and Stokes, L. *Letters Literary and Theological of Connop Thirlwall.* 1881, p 54.
14 NLW. Miscellaneous material relating to Connop Thirlwall. C. Thirlwall to J. Thirlwall, 6 Oct 1827.
15 Thirlwall, J. C. *Connop Thirlwall.* SPCK, 1936, pp 18, 23.
16 Thirlwall, C. *A Letter to the Rev. Thomas Turton.* Cambridge, 1834, p 20.
17 Morgan, J. *Four Biographical Sketches.* 1892, pp 72, 89.
18 *Parl Papers.* 1870, Vol xix (8), p 470. See also Marsh, P. T. *The Victorian Church in Decline.* Routledge, 1969, pp 40–51.
19 Hare, A. J. C. *Life and Letters of Frances, Baroness Bunsen.* 1879, Vol 1, p 140.
20 Williams's view of the position is given in *An Earnestly Respectful Letter to the Lord Bishop of St. David's.* Cambridge, 1860, pp 1–9. Thirlwall's in *A Letter to the Rev. Rowland Williams.* 1860, pp 5–15.
21 Williams, R. *Christian Freedom in the Council of Jerusalem.* Cambridge, 1857, p 8.
22 Ibid, p 101.
23 Thirlwall, C. *Charge, St. David's.* 1857, p 72.

24 *Essays and Reviews*, p 92. This was one of the places where it was hard to separate Williams from Bunsen. He was legally given the benefit of the doubt; in fact he held such a notion of the Old Testament, but not of the New.
25 Williams, R. *Earnestly Respectful Letter*, p 14.
26 Ibid, p 17.
27 Ibid, p 51.
28 Perowne and Stokes, *Connop Thirlwall*, pp 248, 328.
29 Thirlwall, C. *Letters to a Friend*. ed A. P. Stanley, 1881, p 54.
30 Thirlwall, C. *Letter to Williams*, pp 59, 20, 83.
31 Perowne and Stokes, *Connop Thirlwall*, p 236.
32 Williams, E. *Life of Rowland Williams*. Vol 2, p 99.
33 *Spectator*, 20 April 1861, p 417.
34 Tait MSS 75 f 149. 12 Sept 1863.
35 Pusey House, Hamilton MSS narrative of reflections on his appointment as Bishop of Salisbury, 25 March 1854.
36 Ibid. Journal 1858, 22 Nov 1858, p 81.
37 Ibid. 21 Dec 1858, p 83.
38 Williams, R. *Persecution for the Word*. 1862, p 237.
39 Hamilton MSS, Journal, 4 July 1862, p 210.
40 Hamilton, W. K. *Charge Salisbury*. 1864, pp 55, 58.
41 NLW MSS 7942D (A. O. Evans papers), No 65. Williams to his sister, 30 Dec 1869.
42 Dr Williams' Library, London. Free Christian Union Papers 24. 133 (116). Rowland Williams to E. Enfield, 13 June 1868.
43 Wren Hall, Salisbury. Visitation Return 1864 for Broad Chalke, q 52.
44 Williams, E. *Life of Rowland Williams*. Vol 2, pp 270–1.

Chapter 5 H. B. WILSON AND THE NATIONAL CHURCH (pages 107–26)

1 Coleridge, S. T. *On the Constitution of the Church and State according to the Idea of Each*. 2nd ed 1830, p 50.
2 Arnold, T. *Principles of Church Reform*. 1833, pp 28–9.
3 Ibid, p 37.
4 Meyrick, F. *The Bible? The Church? Conscience? Which is Supreme?* 1867, p 2.
5 Wilson, Harry B. *Contention for the Faith*. 1849, pp 13–15.
6 Faber, G. *Oxford Apostles*. 2nd ed Faber, 1936, p 424.
7 Davidson, R. T. and Benham, W. *Life of Archibald Campbell Tait*. 1891, Vol 1, p 279. Also Church, R. W. *The Oxford Movement*. 1922 ed, p 290.
8 Reprinted in Kennard, R. B. *In Memory of the Rev. Henry Bristow Wilson*. 1888, p 39.
9 Wilson, H. B. *Letter to the Rev. T. T. Churton*. Oxford, 1841, pp 9, 29.

10 Wilson, H. B. *The Communion of Saints: an attempt to illustrate the true principles of Christian Union*. Oxford, 1851, p 52.
11 Ibid, pp 126–7.
12 Coleridge, S. T. *Aids to Reflection*, pp 108–9.
13 Wilson, H. B. *Communion of Saints*, p 186.
14 Ibid, pp 228–30.
15 *Rationalism in the Pulpit of the University of Oxford*. ?1854, p 22.
16 Wilson, H. B. *A Letter . . . on University and College Reform*. 1854, passim.
17 Wilson, H. B. 'Schemes of Christian Comprehension', *Oxford Essays, contributed by Members of the University*. 1857, pp 113–14, 121–3.
18 Kennard, R. B. *In Memory of the Rev. Henry Bristow Wilson*. 1888, pp 127–8.
19 Prothero and Bradley. *Stanley*. Vol 2, p 34.
20 *Essays and Reviews*, p 183. Cf also Coleridge, S. T. *Aids to Reflection*, pp 111, 114.
21 *Essays and Reviews*, pp 212–3.
22 Coleridge, S. T. *Church and State*, pp 94–6.
23 *Essays and Reviews*, p 248.
24 Muir, J. *A Brief Examination of Prevalent Opinions on the Inspiration of the Scriptures . . . by a lay member of the Church of England*. 1861.
25 Ibid, p 24.
26 Wilson, H. B. *Three Sermons composed for delivery at the opening of a New Organ*. 1861, pp 26–30.
27 Williams, E. *Life of Rowland Williams*. Vol 2, p 83.
28 Atlay, J. *The Victorian Chancellors*. 1906–8, Vol 2, p 264.
29 *Declaration of the Clergy*. Oxford, 1864.
30 Pattison MSS 112, Wilson to Pattison, 7 Feb 1870.
31 Jowett MSS Box E, J 6. Miscellaneous Notes.
32 Pattison, M. *Memoirs*, p 317.
33 Benson MSS 1853–78. Benson to Lightfoot, 9 Jan 1865.
34 Vidler, A. R. *The Church in an Age of Revolution*. 2nd ed Pelican, 1965, pp 130–3.
35 Ibid, Ch 17.
36 Kennard. *Wilson*, p 19.

Chapter 6 CHARLES VOYSEY
(pages 127–37)

1 Prothero and Bradley. *Stanley*. Vol 2, p 4.
2 Voysey Papers. Voysey to Allsop, 22 Jan 1870.
3 Voysey, C. *An Episode in the History of Religious Liberty in the Nineteenth Century*. Ramsgate, ?1871, pp 5–7.
4 *DNB*.

5 Voysey, C. *An Episode*, p 22.
6 Williams, R. *Broadchalke Sermon Essays*, pp 94–8.
7 Thomson, E. H. *Life and Letters of William Thomson*. 1919, p 216.
8 Ibid, p 153ff.
9 Thomson, W. *A Pastoral Letter to the Clergy and Laity of the Province of York*. 1864, pp 11, 20.
10 Tait MSS 80, Pusey to Tait, 25 Dec 1863.
11 Chadwick, O. *The Victorian Church*, p 545ff. Storr, V. F. *English Theology*, p 341.
12 Voysey, C. *The Sling and the Stone*. 1866, Vol 2, p 12.
13 Ibid, 1869, p 141.
14 Ibid, 1868, Vol 1, p 7.
15 Voysey, C. *Defence . . . in the Chancery Court of York*, p 35.
16 Prothero and Bradley. *Stanley*. Vol 2, p 376.
17 Voysey MSS, Voysey to Allsop, 28 Feb 1870 and 5 March 1870.
18 Ibid. Voysey to Allsop, 2 Jan 1869.
19 Ibid. Voysey to Allsop, 7 April 1871.
20 Sylvester Smith, W. *The London Heretics*, p 129.

Chapter 7 THE AUTHORITY OF THE BISHOPS
(pages 138–85)

1 *Hansard*, 1861, No 164, p 183.
2 Chadwick, O. *The Victorian Church*, pp 468–76.
3 *Hansard*, 1864, No 176, p 1191.
4 Ibid, 1831, No 8, p 342.
5 *Political Correspondence of Mr Gladstone and Lord Granville, 1876–1886* (ed A. Ramm). Oxford, 1962, Vol 2, p 209.
6 *Hansard*, 1884, No 210, pp 441, 477.
7 Addit MSS 44,537 (Gladstone Papers) f 191. Gladstone to Kinnaird, 13 Oct 1869.
8 Baring-Gould, S. *The Church Revival*. 1914, p 201.
9 *Hansard*, 1863, No 171, pp 509–14.
10 Ibid, 1862, No 167, pp 4–29.
11 Ibid, 1863, No 170, pp 1925–45.
12 Ewald, A. C. *Life of Sir Joseph Napier*. 1887, p 256.
13 *Parl Papers*, 1865, xv (3), pp 42–3.
14 Napier, J. *Clerical Subscription Commission*. ?1865.
15 *Parl Papers*, 1867, xx (6), p 721. 1867–8, xxxviii (23), p 7. 1870, xix (8), p 437. See also Marsh, P. T. *The Victorian Church in Decline*, p 102ff.
16 Bligh, E. V. *Lord Ebury as a Church Reformer*. 1891, p 2.
17 *Hansard*, 1868, No 193, p 1099.
18 Ibid, 1868, No 193, p 299. See also Marsh, *The Victorian Church in Decline* Ch 1.
19 *Hansard*, 1869, No 196, pp 1822–28.
20 Ibid, 1869, No 197, p 307.

21 Woodward, L. *The Age of Reform*. 2nd ed Oxford, 1962, p 190.
22 Addit MSS 44, 183 (Gladstone Papers) f 370. Hamilton to Gladstone, 25 Aug 1868.
23 Marsh, P. T. *The Victorian Church in Decline*. Routledge, 1969, p 270ff.
24 Notably by Newsome, D. *The Parting of Friends*. John Murray, 1966.
25 For a fuller account see Chadwick, O. *The Victorian Church*, p 309.
26 Sykes, N. *From Sheldon to Secker*. Cambridge, 1959, pp 47–8.
27 Kirk Smith, H. *William Thomson*. SPCK, 1958, p 76.
28 Wilberforce MSS dep c 186, 1 Feb 1861, p 103, and 13 March 1861, p 112.
29 *Chronicle of Convocation*, 21 April 1864, p 1537.
30 Ibid, 1864, p 1574.
31 Ibid, 21 June 1864, p 1683.
32 Ibid, 22 June 1864, pp 1774–6.
33 *Hansard*, 1864, No 176, p 1543.
34 Ibid, p 1546.
35 Ibid, pp 1560–1551.
36 *Chronicle of Convocation*, 13 Aug 1863, p 1436.
37 *Hansard*, 1867, No 188, p 1173.
38 Ibid, p 1180.
39 Marsh, P. T. *The Victorian Church in Decline*, pp 105–6.
40 Wilberforce MSS, dep c 186, pp 103–5, 110–122.
41 Hamilton MSS, Record of bishops' meetings, p 100.
42 Ibid, pp 112–13.
43 Stephenson, A. M. G. *The First Lambeth Conference*. SPCK, 1967, pp 275–8.
44 Thirlwall, C. *Remains*. Vol 3, p 435ff.
45 *Conference of Bishops of the Anglican Communion*. 1867.
46 Hamilton MSS. Journal 1854–57, 3 Feb 1856.
47 Ibid. Diocesan Journal 1863–8. 19 Jan 1865, pp 29–32.
48 Kitchin, G. W. *Edward Harold Browne*, pp 282–3.
49 Pattison, M. *Essays*. Vol 2, p 299.
50 Arnold, T. *Principles of Church Reform*, pp 48–50.
51 *The Times*, 23 Sept 1869, p 6.
52 *Hansard*, 1861, No 162, p 710.
53 Ibid, 1861, No 164, p 183.
54 Ibid, 1867, No 187, pp 383, 385.
55 Ibid, 1867, No 189, pp 1070–77.
56 Ibid, 1869, No 195, p 1351.
57 *Church Congress Report*. Norwich, 1865, p 177.
58 York Visitation Returns, R VI A 49. 1865, Vol 2, return for Market Weighton.
59 *Hansard*, 1869, No 196, p 9.
60 Ibid, 1869, No 195, p 1344.
61 Wilberforce MSS dep c 186, pp 112, 119–20, and also Addit MSS 44183, (Gladstone Papers), f 343.

62 Brodrick, G. C. and Fremantle, W. H. (ed). *A Collection of the Judgments of the Judicial Committee of the Privy Council.* 1865.
63 *The Times*, 23 Sept 1869, p 6.
64 Pugh, R. K. 'The Episcopate of Samuel Wilberforce', Oxford D Phil thesis. 1957, pp 187–8, 197ff.
65 Abbott and Campbell. *Jowett.* Vol 1, p 122.
66 Kirk Smith, H. *William Thomson*, p 41.
66a Wilberforce MSS, Dep c 197, Wilberforce to Longley 25 Feb 1884.
67 Hamilton MSS Journal 1854–57, 15 July 1855.
68 Ibid. Record of meetings with archdeacons and rural deans etc at Sarum, July 1856, p 52.
69 Ibid. Record of meetings . . . July 1860, p 153.
70 Wilberforce, S. *Charge, Oxford.* 1860, p 9.
71 Thomson, W. *Charge, York.* 1865, pp 5, 19.
72 *Hansard*, 1867, No 186, p 1329.
73 Ellicott, C. J. *Diocesan Progress.* Gloucester, 1868, pp 3–5.
74 Hamilton, W. K. *Charge, Salisbury.* 1858, p 7.
75 Thirlwall, C. *Diocesan Synods.* 1867, p 3.
76 Ollivant, A. *Charge, Llandaff.* 1863, pp 4–5.
77 *RCC.* 1865, Norwich, pp 163–4.
78 Baring, C. *Charge, Gloucester.* 1860, p 32. Bickersteth, R. *Charge, Ripon.* 1861, p 44.
79 Jackson, J. *Charge, Lincoln.* 1861, p 47.
80 Wilberforce, S. *Charge, Oxford.* 1863, p 58.
81 Hamilton, W. K. *Charge, Salisbury.* 1861, p 11, and also Visitation Returns 1864, return from Corscombe.
82 York Visitation returns, 1865, R VI A 49. Return for Adwick.
83 Ibid. Return for Adwick.
84 Salisbury Visitation Returns, 1864, return from Durweston.
85 Ibid. Return from East Lulworth.
86 NLW. Visitation Returns St. David's, 1860 (etc).
87 Newman, J. H. *Apologia Pro Vita Sua.* 1864. Fontana, 1965, p 133.
88 Davidson, R. T. and Benham, W. *Life of Archibald Campbell Tait.* 1891, Vol 1, p 223.
89 Wilberforce MSS dept c 197. Wilberforce to Ashurst, no date.
90 Marsh, P. T. *The Victorian Church in Decline.* Ch 9.
91 Denison, G. A. *Notes of My Life*, p 296.
92 Sandford, E. G. *Frederick Temple—an Appreciation.* 1907, p xxxiii.
93 Add MSS 44,423 (Gladstone Papers), f 328. Ellicott to Gladstone, 17 Dec 1869.
94 Sandford, E. G. *Frederick Temple—An Appreciation.* p. xxxiii.
95 Sandford, E. G. *Memories of Archbishop Temple.* 1906, Vol 1, pp 295–6.
96 eg Goulburn, E. M. *The Existing Mode of Electing Bishops*, 1906, pp 22–3; *RCC*, 1862, Oxford, pp 47–8, and *Hansard*, 1869, No 195, p 1334.

97 *Chronicle of Convocation*, 20 April 1864, p 1505.
98 Hamilton MSS, Diocesan Journal 1863–8, 19 Sept 1865, p 44.
99 Ibid, 1854–8, 5 May 1857, p 295.
100 Ibid, 6 May 1857, p 299.
101 Ibid, 1863–8, 29 Feb 1865, pp 33–4.
102 NLW. Letters from Llanbardanfawr parish chest, p 38.
103 Ibid, pp 81–3.
104 Ibid, pp 105–110.
105 NLW. Miscellaneous correspondence relating to C. Thirlwall. W. Spurrell(?) to B. Johnes, 19 April 1886.
106 Conybeare, W. J. *Essays Ecclesiastical and Social*, p 47n.
107 *Gladstone's Correspondence*. 1868–76, Vol 1, p 44.
108 Thirlwall, C. *Letters to a Friend*, p xii.

Chapter 8 CHURCH DEFENCE
(pages 186–218)

1 *Parl Papers*, 1852–3, Vol lxxxix (33), pp xliii–iv.
2 Chadwick, O. *The Victorian Church*, pp 339–42.
3 Denison, G. A. *Notes of My Life*, pp 135, 182. Also Roberts, G. B. *History of the English Church Union*. 1895, p 6.
4 Church Union: General Minute Book of the Bristol Church Union, 20 Jan 1848–2 April 1867, pp 1–3.
5 For particulars about these groups see Beresford Hope, A. J. B. 'The Church Cause and the Church Party', *Christian Remembrancer*, No 39, 1860, pp 92–7.
6 Ibid, p 97, and also Chadwick, O. *The Victorian Church*, pp 267–9.
7 Denison, G. A. *Notes of My Life*, p 182.
8 Conybeare, W. J. 'Church Parties', *Essays Ecclesiastical and Social*, p 124.
9 The names of the nine clergymen and seven laymen who began it are given in Roberts, G. B. *The History of the English Church Union*, p 10.
10 *The English Church Union: its Rise and Progress*. ?1863, p 4.
11 Ibid, p 5, and Lindsay, C. *More United Action*. 1860, pp 3–4.
12 *Church of England Year Book*. 1886, p 441 and Dant, C. H. (ed). *Distinguished Churchmen and Phases of Church Work*. 1902, p 131.
13 *First Report of the Church of England Protection Society, now called the English Church Union*. 1860, p 30.
14 Inglis, K. S. *Churches and the Working Classes in Victorian England*. 2nd ed Routledge, 1964, p 46.
15 Church Union, Committee Minute Book, 21 July 1868, p 39.
16 Ibid. Sustentation Committee Minute Book. C. L. Wood to A. Chapman, 9 Nov 1868, p 10.
17 Ibid. Committee Minute Book, 21 July 1868, p 43.
18 Roberts, G. B. *History of the English Church Union*, p 37.
19 *Chronicle of Convocation*. 19 Feb 1868, p 1158.

20 Voysey, C. *An Episode in the History of Religious Liberty*, pp 23–4. Dant, C. H. *Distinguished Churchmen and Phases of Church Work.* 1902, pp 137–8.
21 Church Union: Sustentation Committee Minute Book, p 33. Wood to Colquhoun, 15 April 1869.
22 Ibid. Committee Minute Book, p 13, 27 Jan 1868.
23 Idem.
24 Ibid. Sustentation Committee Minute Book, pp 36–7. Wood to Shaftesbury, 19 April 1869.
25 Always on the title page of the *Church Association Monthly Intelligencer*.
26 *Annual Report of the Church Association*. 1867, pp 4–7ff. See also *Annual Report*, 1865, p 24.
27 Voysey, C. *An Episode in the History of Religious Liberty*, p 24.
28 Sweet, J. B. *A Memoir of the Late Henry Hoare*. 1869, p 439.
29 Ibid, p 446.
30 *Church Institution Circular*, 9 Feb 1860, passim.
31 Thirlwall, C. *Charge, St. David's*. 1860, pp 80–4. *Charge, St. David's*. 1866, p 52.
32 *National Church*, Jan 1870, p 4.
33 *Chronicle of Convocation*, 22 May 1863, pp 1298–9.
34 Hamilton MSS. Record of meetings of archdeacons, etc, 21 Sept 1859. Also *Chronicle of Convocation*, 22 May 1863, p 1299.
35 *First Report of the . . . English Church Union*, p 18.
36 *Church of England Year Book*. 1883, p 720. See also 1920, p 181.
37 Lambeth MSS 1782 f 1, relating to Church Congresses.
38 *RCC*, Cambridge, 1861, p iii.
39 *RCC*, Oxford, 1862, p iii.
40 *Guardian*, 30 July 1862.
41 *The Times*, 15 July 1862. *Nonconformist*, 16 July 1862.
42 *RCC*, Liverpool, 1869, p vi.
43 *RCC*, York, 1866, p ix. Ibid, Liverpool, 1869, p vi.
44 Ibid. Liverpool, 1869, p iii.
45 Beresford Hope, A. J. B. *The Place and Influence in the Church Movement of Church Congresses*. 1874, pp 13–14.
46 *Christian Remembrancer*, No 53, 1867, p 236.
47 *RCC*, Wolverhampton, 1867, pp vi.
48 Kirk Smith, H. *William Thomson*, pp 26–7.
49 *RCC*, Norwich, 1865, p 187.
50 *RCC*, Liverpool, 1869, pp 91–116.
51 *RCC*, Bristol, 1864, p 58.
52 Disraeli, B. *Church Policy*. 1864.
53 Benson MSS, 1853–68. Benson to Lightfoot, 9 Jan 1865.
54 Voysey, C. *Dogma Versus Morality, a Reply to Church Congress*. 1866.
55 Pattison, M. *Essays*. Vol 2, p 278, and Pattison MSS 130, p 43, Oct 1862.

56 *The Churchman*, 20 Sept 1866. *The Ecclesiastic*, No 26, 1864, pp 531–3.
57 *Chronicle of Convocation*, 25 Feb 1869, p 150.
58 Wilberforce MSS dep c 197, 25 Jan 1851.
59 *Acts of the Diocesan Synod, held in the Cathedral Church of Exeter, by Henry, Lord Bishop of Exeter*. 1861, passim.
60 See eg the debates in *RCC*, York, 1866, pp 223–36; Bristol, 1864, pp 56–8. *Chronicle of Convocation*, 20 April 1864, pp 1449–1525.
61 *RCC*, York, 1866, p 227.
62 *Chronicle of Convocation*, 20 April 1864, pp 1510, 1512.
63 *RCC*, York, 1866, p 225. *Chronicle of Convocation*, 20 April 1864, p 1506.
64 *Chronicle of Convocation*, 3 July 1863, pp 1403–13.
65 Ibid, 20 April 1864, p 1525.
66 Ibid, 4 June 1866, p 858.
67 Ibid, 20 Feb 1867, pp 1218–23.
68 Ibid, 20 Feb 1867, p 1225.
69 Ibid, p 1227.
70 *Sermons and Addresses delivered at a Conference of the Clergy of the Diocese of Oxford*. Oxford, 1866.
71 Ibid. Oxford, 1867, pp 95–7.
72 Kitchin, G. W. *Edward Harold Browne*, p 255.
73 Untitled published circular from Browne to his rural deans, 25 Jan 1867, pp 5ff.
74 Kitchin, G. W. *Edward Harold Browne*, p 274. *RCC*, Liverpool, 1869, p 32.
75 Morgan, J. *Four Biographical Sketches*, p 105.
76 Thirlwall, C. *Letter to the Rev. Canon Seymour*. 1867.
77 Evans, J. H. *Churchman Militant*. SPCK, 1964, p 167.
78 *Church of England Year Book*. 1886, p 340. See also *Proceedings at the first meeting of the Central Council of Diocesan Conferences and Synods*. 1881.
79 For a full discussion of the various groups, see Sylvester Smith, W. *The London Heretics*.
80 *Fourth Report of the Committee of the Christian Evidence Society*. June 1875, pp 7–8.
81 *Church of England Year Book*. 1886, p 120.
82 Marsh, P. T. *The Victorian Church in Decline*, p 53ff.

Chapter 9 CLERICAL EDUCATION

(pages 219–40)

1 Bullock, F. W. B. *A History of Training for the Ministry . . . from 1800 to 1874*. St Leonards-on-Sea, 1955.
2 *Parl Papers*, 1852–3, Vol lxxxviii (32, part 1), p 222.
3 Ibid, 1873, Vol lxxi (33), p 37.
4 Tait, A. C. *Charge, London*. 1862, pp 115–19.

5 Bullock, F. W. B., *A History of Training*. p 143.
6 *RCC*, Liverpool, 1869, p 63.
7 *The Deficient Supply of Well-Qualified Clergymen . . . a paper read before the Liverpool Clerical Society*. Birkenhead, 1863, pp 13–14.
8 Ibid, pp 21–5.
9 Stanley, A. P. *Letter to the Bishop of London*, pp 15, 20, 22, 31n.
10 *Hansard*, 1863, No 170, p 1936.
11 *Chronicle of Convocation*. 1 July 1863, p 1369.
12 Bickersteth, R. *Charge, Ripon*. 1861, pp 19–20.
13 Foxton, F. J. *The Priesthood and the People*. 1862, p 19.
14 Pattison, M. *Essays*. Vol 2, p 293.
15 Ellicott, C. J. *Diocesan Progress*. Gloucester 1868, p 14.
16 *Parl Papers*, 1952–3, Vol xliv (5), pp 79, 95.
17 Ibid, 1852, Vol xxii (5), pp 101, 639.
18 Ince, W. *Past History and Present Duties of the Faculty of Theology*. 1878, p 39.
19 *Chronicle of Convocation*. 28 June 1865, p 2363.
20 *Parl Papers*, 1852, Vol xxii (5), p 102.
21 Ward, W. R. *Victorian Oxford*. Cass, 1965, p 201.
22 *Parl Papers*, 1852, Vol xxii, (5), p 323.
23 Smith, H. J. S. *The Proposed School of Theology*. Oxford, 1869, p 3.
24 Burgon, J. W. *Letter to Professor Henry Smith*. Oxford, 1869, p 2.
25 Ince, W. *Past History and Present Duties of the Faculty of Theology*, p 40.
26 Bullock, F. W. B., *A History of Training*. p 64.
27 *RCC*. Liverpool, 1869, p 76.
28 Ward, W. R. *Victorian Oxford*, p 131.
29 *Parl Papers*, 1854, Vol xxv (7), pp 311ff.
30 Idem, p 435.
31 *Statement of Facts connected with the movement in opposition to the establishment of a Diocesan Theological College at Lichfield*. ?1856, p 28.
32 Chadwick, O. *The Founding of Cuddesdon*. Oxford, 1954.
33 Ibid, p 32.
34 Hamilton, W. K. *Charge, Salisbury*. 1864, p 58.
35 Bullock, *A History of Training*. p 31.
36 Ibid, p 84.
37 Eden, R. J. *Charge, Bath and Wells*. 1861, p 22.
38 Perry, C. *Clerical Education considered*. 1841, p 13.
39 *Parl Papers*, 1852, Vol xxii (5), p 581.
40 Bullock, F. W. B. *A History of Training*
41 Hamilton MSS. Record of meetings with archdeacons etc 1854–68. July 1860, p 163.
42 *Chronicle of Convocation*. 14 Feb 1865, p 1870ff.
43 Benson MSS, 1853–68. Benson to George Cubitt, 18 April 1870.
44 Ibid, 1873–77. Benson to Purnell, 26 Nov 1875.
45 Conybeare, W. J. *Essays Ecclesiastical and Social*, p 10.

46 Bullock, *A History of Training* p 30. Ellicott, C. J. *Charge, Gloucester.* 1868, p 13.
47 Sumner, C. R. *Charge, Winchester.* 1862, p 28.
48 Pugh, R. K. *Samuel Wilberforce.* Ch 7.
49 Ellicott, C. J. *Diocesan Progress,* p 13ff.
50 Bickersteth, M. C. *Life . . . of Robert Bickersteth.* 1887, pp 162–5.
51 Hamilton MSS. Journal 1854–57. 3 June 1855.
52 *Copies of Bishops' Examination Papers for Holy Orders.* 1864, pp 2–4.
53 *RCC,* Liverpool, 1869, p 53.
54 Ibid, p 67.

Select Bibliography

Manuscript Sources

Balliol College, Oxford	Jowett papers
Bodleian Library	Pattison papers
	Wilberforce papers
Borthwick Institute of Historical Research, York	York Visitation Returns
British Museum	Gladstone papers
Church Union, London	Church Union Records
Keble College, Oxford	Liddon papers
Lambeth Palace Library	Longley papers
	Tait papers
Manchester College, Oxford	Voysey letters
National Library of Wales	Material relating to Thirlwall and Williams
	St David's Visitation Returns
Pusey House, Oxford	Hamilton papers
Salisbury Diocesan Archives	Salisbury Visitation Returns
Trinity College, Cambridge	Benson papers

Unpublished thesis: Pugh, R. K. 'The Episcopate of Samuel Wilberforce, with special reference to the administration of the diocese of Oxford'. Oxford DPhil, 1957.

Printed Sources

Most use has been made of *Hansard*, 3rd series, especially 1860–70, episcopal charges, and Church Congress Reports.

Unless otherwise stated, the place of publication is London.

Abbott, E. and Campbell, L. *Life and Letters of Benjamin Jowett*. 1897.

Best, G. F. A. *Temporal Pillars*. Cambridge, 1964.

Bullock, F. W. B. *A History of Training for the Ministry of the Church of England and Wales from 1800 to 1874*. St. Leonards-on-Sea, 1955.

Bunsen, F. *A Memoir of Baron Bunsen*. 1868.

Burgon, J. W. *Lives of Twelve Good Men*. 1888.

Chadwick, O. *The Victorian Church*, part 1. A. & C. Black, 1966.

Cockshut, A. O. J. *Anglican Attitudes*. Collins, 1959.

Cowherd, R. G. *The Politics of English Dissent*. Epworth Press, 1959.

Davidson, R. T. and Benham, W. *Life of Archibald Campbell Tait*. 1891.

Estlin Carpenter, J. *The Bible in the Nineteenth Century*. 1903.

Forbes, D. *The Liberal Anglican Idea of History*. Cambridge, 1952.

Green, V. H. H. *Oxford Common Room*. 1957.

Inglis, K. S. *Churches and the Working Classes in Victorian England*. 2nd ed Routledge, 1964.

Liddon, H. P. *Life of Edward Bouverie Pusey*. 1893.

Marsh, P. T. *The Victorian Church in Decline*. 1969.

Morgan, B. Q. *A Critical Bibliography of German Literature in English Translation 1481–1927*. New York, 1965.

Morgan, B. Q. and Hohlfeld, A. R. *German Literature in British Magazines 1750–1860*. Wisconsin, 1949.

Owen, R. A. D. *Christian Bunsen and Liberal English Theology*. Wisconsin, 1924.

Pfleiderer, O. *The Development of Theology in Germany since Kant*. Tr J. Frederick Smith, 1890.

Prothero, R. E. and Bradley, G. *Life and Correspondence of Arthur Penrhyn Stanley*, 1893.

Sanders, C. R. *Coleridge and the Broad Church Movement*. North Carolina, 1942.

Sandford, E. G. *Frederick Temple—an Appreciation*. 1907.

Shaen, M. J. *Memorials of Two Sisters*. 1908.

Storr, V. F. *The Development of English Theology in the Nineteenth Century*. 1913.

Thomson, E. H. *The Life and Letters of William Thomson*. 1919.

Ward, W. R. *Victorian Oxford*. Cass, 1965.

Warre Cornish, F. *The English Church in the Nineteenth Century*. 1910.

Willey, B. *More Nineteenth Century Studies.* Chatto & Windus, 1956.
Williams, E. (ed). *Life and Letters of Rowland Williams.* 1874.

Acknowledgements

THE RESEARCH for this book was undertaken on funds given by the George Murray foundation of the University of Adelaide, for which I should like to express my gratitude.

Many people have helped me, but I wish in particular to thank the librarians and staff of the departments of Western Manuscripts in the Bodleian Library and the National Library of Wales, the librarians of Lambeth Palace Library and of Balliol College, Oxford and Trinity College, Cambridge. Dr D. M. Barratt of the Bodleian and Miss P. Stewart of the Salisbury Diocesan Archives gave me much personal assistance. The Rev F. P. Coleman, then secretary of the Church Union, allowed me access to the Union's early records, and the Rev H. L. Short, Principal of Manchester College, very kindly allowed me to see some letters of Charles Voysey which he had just obtained for the college.

I have received valuable advice from Mrs J. Hart and Dr D. Whiteman, also Mr D. H. Newsome and Dr John Walsh. Professor P. T. Marsh generously lent me part of the manuscript of the book later published as *The Victorian Church in Decline*. I am also indebted to Miss Gill Kay for useful criticism.

I should like to acknowledge a debt to the work of Professor Owen Chadwick, whose first volume of *The Victorian Church* has been a constant inspiration to me.

For permission to quote from private papers I should like to thank the Church Union for extracts from the English Church Union's records, the Librarian of Manchester College for the Voysey papers, and His Grace the Archbishop of Canterbury and the trustees of Lambeth Palace Library for the Tait and Longley papers.

This book would not have been written without the criticism and encouragement of Miss Agatha Ramm, the best of teachers.

Index